A Story of South Africa

A Story of South Africa

J. M. Coetzee's Fiction in Context

◆ ◆ ◆ ◆

SUSAN VANZANTEN GALLAGHER

HARVARD UNIVERSITY PRESS

Cambridge, Massachusetts
London, England
1991

Pages 249–251 constitute an extension of the copyright page.

This book is printed on acid-free paper, and its binding materials have been chosen for strength and durability.

Library of Congress Cataloging-in-Publication Data

Gallagher, Susan V.
    A story of South Africa: J.M. Coetzee's fiction in context / Susan VanZanten Gallagher.
      p.   cm
    Includes bibliographical references and index.
    ISBN 0-674-83972-2 (alk. paper)
     1. Coetzee, J.M., 1940– —Criticism and interpretation.
  2. South Africa in literature. I. Title.
PR9369.3.C58Z66   1991   91-10667
823—dc20   CIP

For John
who believes in justice and peace

Contents

Preface

History never embraces more than a small part of reality
—*La Rochefoucauld*

The study of literature in recent years, as J. Hillis Miller almost lamented in his MLA Presidential Address of 1986, has shifted from a focus on language to a focus on history. Numerous critics, from very different perspectives, have recently urged us to acknowledge that literature is situated within a web of historical conditions, relationships, and influences. But while many agree that we need to think historically, there are frequent disagreements over what it means to practice historical criticism. First, critics have different conceptions of what is meant by *context,* that is, the set of conditions, relationships, and influences that surround a work. Some critics emphasize biographical and bibliographic contexts; some critics focus exclusively on the economic and political contexts of a work; others examine a wide variety of discursive practices from the social history of the period. Second, historicist critics disagree about *historical understanding.* To what degree are we imprisoned in our own cultural situation, unable to enter fully into an understanding of the past, conditioned by our own historical moment? How fully can we understand history and, consequently, historical texts? Is the hermeneutic experience most accurately defined by Foucault or by Gadamer? Differing definitions of context and historical understanding lead to a third difference in opinion: the *significance* of the critical project, the ethics it implies, the critical agenda it establishes. In practice, historicist criticism can take many different forms and lead to radically different conclusions.

This study of the fiction of South African novelist J. M. Coetzee participates in the current critical conversation about historicist criticism. Neo-Marxist historicist criticism, concentrating on material and economic history, has rendered harsh judgments about some of Coetzee's novels, accusing him of an irresponsible, or impotent, metaphysical escapism. My project is to resituate Coetzee's fictions in their discursive moments, to examine a variety of social, cultural, and rhetorical contexts from which his novels emerge and in which they participate. Viewing his works within these contexts, we discover how the novels respond to the oppressive practices that have pervaded South African life for hundreds of years. South Africa is a country in which discourse itself has contributed to oppression, a country whose history has been deliberately constructed to maintain white supremacy. Coetzee's response has been to expose and subvert national myths of history, as well as to create alternative narratives, stories to hold up against the nightmare of South African history. The stories he tells emerge from South African realities, but they suggest in their very form and technique that an alternative to those realities exists. Avoiding the authoritative voice of history, Coetzee presents us with a storyteller's elusive, ambiguous, yet melodious account of South Africa..

While I examine a variety of elements in Coetzee's work, I am particularly interested in how his novels respond to the discursive practices of South Africa. Those practices in turn are influenced by a complex mix of material realities, psychological states, and metaphysical beliefs. Although I am well aware of the limits imposed upon us by our historical situation, I believe, with Gadamer, that an approximate and tentative historical understanding is possible. One's own horizon can be broadened and changed because of the influence of another horizon. Coetzee's novels themselves insist on the possibility of exposing a false history and exploring an alternative story. Coetzee's novels also suggest that a more accurate human history would encompass more than just the material world and the will to power; it would include outcast voices and the ineffable transcendent.

The ethics of historicist criticism arises from its emphasis on practice. Louis Montrose says, "In its anti-reflectionism, its shift of emphasis from the formal analysis of verbal *artifacts* to the ideological analysis of discursive *practices,* its refusal to observe strict and fixed boundaries between 'literary' and other texts (including the critic's own), this emergent social/political/historical orientation in literary studies is pervasively concerned with writing as a mode of *action*" (11). Rather than studying historically isolated, timeless objects, historicist critics examine how a work of literature exists in relationship to a past, present, and future. In considering these various dimensions of a work, we look at the various ways that human actions have informed and been informed by it. The distinction between artifact and practice drawn by Montrose illuminates the ethical dimension of historicist criticism, for human practices are more obviously subject to ethical judgments than artifacts are. Social practices, those involving interaction between people, always involve issues of human responsibility. Understood as a product and instrument of human action, a literary work becomes open in a new way to assessment in ethical terms, despite the fact that many historicist critics do not explicitly provide such an assessment.

Unfortunately, ethical critics have often failed to examine a text within its various historical contexts, and have judged it only in terms of one narrow practice. Rather than making complex ethical judgments, too many critics are moralistic—merely establishing moral rules or ethical axioms and summarily judging the work on the basis of these rules, failing to consider the particular practices that produced the work and the variety of practices to which it contributes. Even the recent more thoughtful discussion of Wayne C. Booth in *The Company We Keep* considers only one aspect of the social practice of literature, focusing on "the encounters of a story-teller's ethos with that of the reader" (8), although Booth does take into account that readers come to a text with different histories and so have different reactions. But ethical considerations can and should be directed toward all of the text's historical dimensions, all of the different ways that it is formed by and enters into human history.

Contemporary South African literature provides us with good reason to explore some of the issues of historical and ethical criticism, for it has been produced within historical practices that most would agree are obviously unjust and oppressive, publicly immoral. Just how fully and in what manner those historical conditions enter into the production and consumption of South African literature (if at all) involves us in ethical considerations. If we agree that the various practices embodied in the word *apartheid* are immoral, what difference does that make in our analysis of the practice of literature in South Africa? Operating from the premise that a literary text is both a product of human action and also a means whereby we as readers and critics perform certain other kinds of action, I aim to examine the ethical implications of Coetzee's novel writing.

My own critical ethics grow out of a personal and cultural commitment to work for justice in South Africa. As a third-generation Dutch-American who is a member of the Christian Reformed Church (CRC), a denomination formed by Dutch emigrants, I have familial and community ties of responsibility and guilt to South Africa. My great-aunt was one of the European pilots who opened up the southern tip of Africa after the second World War to greater economic expansion; my church spent thirty years agonizing over its relationship to its sister churches in South Africa before repudiating apartheid as a sin and its theological justification as a heresy in 1984; in 1989 the CRC broke fellowship with the white segments of the Reformed Churches in South Africa; the student and faculty of Calvin College passed a resolution in 1986 that the college disinvest its stock in companies having employees in South Africa, but the board of trustees decided to disinvest only from those companies not operating under the Sullivan principles or not "making progress" under the Sullivan rating system; Calvin College has also hosted Allan Boesak for a year as a visiting multi-cultural lecturer. The Dutch-American Reformed community for years has lived in uneasy concern for South Africa. It was natural for me as a professor of English to begin to explore the paradoxes and dilemmas of this country by reading its literature and criticism. I then began teaching South African literature as a means of allowing more people to hear the stories of the South African people.

In 1991 South Africa faces an uncertain future. For the first time in many years, there are signs that a true political restructuring might take place. Yet the divisions that characterize the country continue, and the resolution of differences is far from certain. South African history may finally be taking a new path, may finally repudiate its historical myths and admit a new story of justice to its narrative. Its struggles to compose this discourse will no doubt continue to be informed by the writing of J. M. Coetzee, who has not only been concerned to testify to oppressive situations and to speak prophetically of the need for change, but has also continually probed the way that South Africa has written its own history. The developing story of South Africa will continue to need such exploration.

Note on Diction

The fact that language is involved in oppression in South Africa makes it necessary for me to preface this book with a disclaimer about the diction I use for the various groups of South African people. The South African system itself is built around supposedly important differences in skin color, blood content, and ethnic heritage that are rigidly defined by means of certain racial labels. Official South African discourse distinguishes between *Europeans* and *non-Europeans,* among *white, coloured, Asian,* and *black* people. In my study, I will use the terms *black* or *African* to designate all people of color who have not been admitted into full citizenship in South Africa. Occasionally I will use the term *coloured* to designate that particular part of South African society so labeled by their identity papers. My use of *coloured* will occur when the particular social and political situation of those people is of interest; it in no way implies my acceptance of such a classification.

History and the South African Writer

South Africa: a land of striking natural beauty and abundant physical resources, a land of unjust social conditions and oppressive political structures. In South Africa today, existence is governed by skin color. Five million whites lead a life of privilege, owning most of the land, receiving the best education, managing the nation's industries, and dictating the country's political and social policies. In contrast, twenty-eight million people—who have varying proportions of African, Indian, and white ancestry—do not have full voting privileges, must live in specified areas, receive a vastly inferior education, possess only 13 percent of the land, and are denied the rights of free speech, assembly, and lawful trial.

South Africa is the land that has deeded to the world the social reality designated by the term *apartheid*. A Dutch word that roughly translates as "apartness" or "separateness," *apartheid* has taken on a new significance in Afrikaans and now is seldom used by the European Dutch in its original sense. *Apartheid* has also been incorporated into English political terminology. Jacques Derrida notes about this borrowed word, "no tongue has ever translated this name—as if all the languages of the world were defending themselves, shutting their mouths against a sinister incorporation of the thing by means of the word, as if all tongues were refusing to give an equivalent, refusing to let themselves be contaminated through the contagious hospitality of the word-for-word" ("Racism's Last Word" 292). The history of the word *apartheid* suggests the difficulties faced by those employing language in a society where such terms as "coloured," "resettlement," and "separate development" can be tools of oppression.

Apartheid has given South Africa a peculiar modern history characterized by waves of protest and ebbs of governmental suppression. In 1960 the South African police opened fire on a crowd peacefully protesting the pass laws and killed sixty-nine people in what became known as the Sharpeville Massacre. Subsequently the government proclaimed a state of emergency and declared the African National Congress and the Pan-Africanist Congress unlawful organizations. In 1961, South Africa broke from the British Commonwealth over the issue of apartheid and declared itself the Republic of South Africa on May 31. As legislation prohibiting opposition increased, the majority of black leaders went underground to conduct a protest campaign of strikes and sabotage. African National Congress leader Nelson Mandela's capture and sentence of life imprisonment in 1964 are the most visible historical markers of the new internal security practices of banning, censoring, and detaining that stifled protest and sent hundreds of blacks into exile in the sixties.

A second wave of protest occurred in 1976 when the black township of Soweto exploded in rebellion against the enforced use of Afrikaans in the schools. Originating among the children of Soweto, the unrest spread across South Africa to other schools and universities. For more than a year, students boycotted classes, marched in protest, and rioted in the townships. The government responded again with violence and oppression. Refusing to meet with recognized black leaders, the government instead detained, without charges or trial, hundreds of people, including children as young as ten. Official figures list 575 dead and 2,389 wounded in riots during sixteen months of protest; most of the victims were schoolchildren (Lodge 330).

A similar pattern occurs again in the 1980s. Despite the massive protests and insurrections that dominated the black townships from 1984 to 1986 and the ensuing world attention and economic sanctions, South Africa remained firmly under the control of the white minority throughout the decade. Apartheid laws and practices continued. From August 1985 until 1990 South Africa was again under a state of emergency, during which the white authorities were able if not to silence at least to muffle all significant protest. The tough security measures allowing detentions without trial, the bans on anti-apartheid political organizations and rallies, and the severe censorship of the press effectively silenced the cries of the oppressed and significantly weakened all attempts at reform. The measure of hope provided by the ouster of President P. W. Botha and the new rule of F. W. de Klerk in 1989 was nonetheless accompanied by the increasing strength of the right-wing Conservative Party, which gained enough parliamentary seats under the charismatic leadership of Andries Treurnicht to become the official opposition party. As the nineties begin, observers of South Africa have begun to hope that the destructive patterns of the previous decades might be overcome. Our sense of guarded optimism is prompted by the changes already announced by the ruling National Party. Speaking at the opening of Parliament on February 2, 1990, President de Klerk announced that bans on the African National Congress, the Pan-Africanist Congress, and many other anti-apartheid groups were being lifted, and on February 11 Nelson Mandela was released after twenty-seven years of imprisonment. Once again, South Africa faces a time of uncertain change.

The Writer's Responsibility

Given this turbulent history, the South African writer faces a unique and difficult situation. Is the primary responsibility of a writer living under apartheid to write or to fight, to produce works of art or to struggle to eliminate injustice and oppression? Or are these false dichotomies? Can poems and plays and stories be actions in opposition to apartheid? Both black and white South African writers have struggled with these issues.

In the maelstrom of events in the 1960s, many wondered along with Lewis Nkosi "whether it might not be more prudent to 'renounce literature temporarily', as some have advised, and solve the political problem first" (*Home and Exile* 132). Outside of South Africa, the Nigerian novelist Chinua Achebe did just that, leaving a career as a writer for twenty years of public service before returning to fiction with the publication of *Anthills of the Savannah* in 1988. Similarly, the South African writer Alan Paton renounced fiction writing to devote himself to the political work of the Liberal Party in the 1960s. He writes in his autobiography, "I was beginning to realise that, deep though my love of literature was and deep as was my love of writing, my love of country was unfortunately greater" (*Journey* 60). *The two possible roles are defined well by Arthur Nortje, a young black South African poet who died in exile in 1970: "for some of us must storm the castles / some define the happening"* ("Native's Letter" 35–36).

Although not all of those who gave up writing necessarily believe that defining and storming are distinct activities, the romantic belief that art and action, literature and life, are separate realms is still common. Paton manifests such an understanding when he explains his decision to give up novel writing: "Circumstances compelled me to take a leading part in the Liberal Party. This is not a good thing for a writer. He may be 'committed,' as they say, but not that far." Given the actions of the South

African government in establishing apartheid, Paton "did not feel able to retire to the ivory tower" ("Paton" 500).

The ivory-tower view of literature can result in the extreme position that literature should have a purely aesthetic or "universal" quality, unsullied by political content. A few literary critics lament that the particular issues of South African society so often appear in its literature and think that the frequent themes of racism, violence, and oppression impoverish and narrow that literature. Randolph Vigne, for one, complains that in Nadine Gordimer's work, "much that happens does so because this is South Africa, not because this is life" (96). Speaking more generally, Martin Tucker claims, "The history of South African literature by white South Africans shows an obsessive concern with the color question. Its exponents sooner or later become propagandists of one view or another." However, in a somewhat circular path of reasoning, Tucker attributes this flaw not to the particular historical situation of South Africa but rather to "the moral, puritanical attitude of South African writers to their work" (227). He fails to see the connection between that moral attitude and the historical circumstances that prompt such an attitude.

Yet many South African writers reject this romantic dichotomy between art and reality to view their work as inescapably tied to their historical situation. As Mafika Gwala explains, "In a society where politics determine most aspects of our social consciousness through separate toilets, segregated transport, pass and curfew laws, the Immorality Act, unequal education—in short unequal rights based on skin colour— our speech and written language forms cannot but be highly politicized" (47). When the Johannesburg literary magazine *The Classic* began publication in 1963, it proclaimed in its first editorial that it was as "non-political as the life of a domestic servant, the life of a Dutch Reformed Church predikant or that of an opulent Johannesburg business man. If the daily lives of these people are not regulated by political decisions, that will be reflected in *The Classic*. If however, the work they do, if their sexual lives and their search for God are governed by political decrees, then that will also be reflected in the material published in *The Classic*. After all, these stories and poems and drawings and sculpture will be about the lives of these people" (qtd. Parker 9). If literature is to depict the lives of the people of South Africa accurately, it cannot escape the political.

The emphasis on literature as a political expression appears repeatedly in those black writers who struggle to survive in South Africa, for their entire lives are governed by the politics of South Africa. As the novelist Richard Rive explains, "The writer who cannot vote, who carries a pass and who lives in a ghetto, must necessarily write qualitatively differently from the writer who can vote, does not carry a pass and lives wherever he pleases" ("Black Writer" 92). Similarly, Gwala claims, "We cannot write outside of our experience in a society where social deprivation is taken for granted. Though 'all literature is propaganda but not all propaganda is literature', we find ourselves having to speak about our experience if we have to change it. Our critical attitudes towards racism, exploitation and inequality will inevitably dominate" (47). This is why Gwala terms writing "a cultural weapon." Similarly, in his foreword to a novel by Alex La Guma, Brian Bunting writes, "It is difficult to propound the cult of 'art for art's sake' in South Africa. Life presents problems with an insistence which cannot be ignored, and there can be few countries in the world where the people, of all races and classes, are more deeply preoccupied with matters falling generally under the heading of 'political'. . . . If art is to have any significance at all, it must reflect something of this national obsession, this passion which consumes and sometimes corrodes the soul of the South African people" (9).

While black authors tend to see the political dimension of literature as inescapable, white writers more often view themselves as having an ethical obligation to respond to the rampant injustice that characterizes their society. Perhaps the most outspoken in this regard is the Afrikaner novelist André Brink. After an early career as a member of the avant-garde Sestigers (writers of the sixties), Brink turned in his fiction to overt political topics and in his criticism to a Sartrean insistence on the ethical responsibility of the South African writer. Given "the state of siege" that epitomizes South African society, the writer must respond: "This, it seems to me, indicates a function of writers in our terrifying and sordid world: to keep the voice of humanity alive; to ensure the survival of human values" (*Writing* 48). Brink enumerates ways the writer might accomplish this goal, including the exposure of truth in an authoritarian world of the lie, the exploration of the roots of the human condition, and the affirmation of human values through the exploration of meaning. "The revolution I am involved in as a writer, is a revolution in the conscience of my people," he concludes (53).

For those authors who see their work as necessarily political or as involving an ethical imperative, there is nonetheless the constant question of the precarious relationship between their art and their commitment. When does a work of literature lose its aesthetic value and become merely propagandistic? One reader's art can easily be another reader's propaganda, as Kenneth Parker points out in noting that as long as South African writers explored liberal humanistic solutions to racism they were applauded, but when they began depicting more radical assessments of the historical situation they were admonished that "politics and literature should not mix" (9). On the other hand, is it possible for a work of literature to have aesthetic value if it fails to fulfill the moral imperative or recognize the political demands of the South African situation? The South African playwright Athol Fugard struggled with these questions in the personal notebooks he kept between 1960 and 1977. In a review of the published notebooks called "Art and Apartheid," J. M. Coetzee points to Fugard's "doubts about the value of his art, which seems to be founded on material privilege, to be personal in its nature, to be only ambivalently committed to tangible political goals. The question of how to commit himself without losing his identity as an artist becomes a central preoccupation of the notebook entries of the mid-1960s" (26). In a manner similar to Brink's, Fugard resolves to follow Sartre and take upon himself the task of bearing witness.

Nadine Gordimer, perhaps the most internationally respected South African writer today, has also thought deeply about these issues. Since the 1950s, Gordimer's stories and novels have demonstrated a growing awareness and treatment of political issues. *The Essential Gesture* (1988), a collection of her essays and lectures over four decades, reveals her ongoing struggle between the responsibility to oppose racism imposed by her historical situation and the responsibility to write well imposed by her vocation as a writer. Is the greater responsibility to society or to art? In several essays Gordimer identifies the tension between what she terms "relevance," a demand imposed from the outside, and "commitment," an existential inner demand. She believes in both "society's right to make demands on the writer" and "the writer's commitment to his artistic vision" (*Essential* 289).

In the South African context, however, the demands of society on black writers differ from the demands on white writers, and several of Gordimer's essays explore those differences. She notes the development of a new kind of black literature in the 1970s, produced in conjunction with the Black Consciousness movement and emerging from the events of the Soweto uprising. Seeing the inescapable relationship of art and action, writers in the seventies began to understand that the act of writing, in itself, can be a revolutionary activity. Black writers have a social responsibility to educate their readers about the reality of black life under apartheid: "Black writers arrived, out of their own situation, at Brecht's discovery: their audience needed to be educated *to be astonished at the circumstances under which they functioned.* They began to show blacks that their living conditions are their story" (*Essential* 274). Writers thus become cultural workers in the social struggle.

Gordimer's understanding of the role of the black writer stems from her agreement with Philip Toynbee's idea that "the writer's gift to the reader is not social zest or moral improvement or love of country, but an enlargement of the reader's apprehension" (*Essential* 107). White writers enlarge readers' apprehensions in different ways. Unable to speak authoritatively of the black experience of exploitation and oppression, the white South African writer's task is "to raise the consciousness of white people, who, unlike himself, have not woken up" (*Essential* 293). Gordimer is skeptical that white writers are of much use in encouraging blacks, since the privileged writer lacks the qualification of sharing the life of the black townships. But she does admit that the writer "brings some influence to bear on whites, though not on the white-dominated government; he may influence those individuals who are already coming to bewilderedly out of the trip of power, and those who gain courage from reading the open expression of their own suppressed rebellion" (*Essential* 294).

These outward demands for relevance are held in tension with the inner demands of artistic commitment. Too much attention to outward demands can result in "agitprop," an art whose forms and content are formulaic and ideologically mandated. In "The Novel and the Nation in South Africa," Gordimer explains how such propagandizing occurs: "The novelist writes about what sense he makes of life; his own commitment to one group or another enters his novel as part of, sometimes the deepest part of, the sense he makes of life. If, on the other hand, the commitment enters the novel not as part of the writer's own conception of the grand design, but as an attempt to persuade other people—then the book is not a novel but propaganda with a story" ("The Novel" 38). In one interview she states: "My writing does not deal with my personal convictions; it deals with the society I live and write in. . . . My novels are anti-apartheid, not because of my personal abhorrence of apartheid, but because the society that is the very stuff of my work *reveals itself.*" She concludes, "If you write honestly about life in South Africa, apartheid damns itself" ("Interview" 81). Rather than propagandizing, she implies, the writer must employ social realism.

Gordimer's statements explain the critical and ironic distance so many critics have found in her work, which can make readers wonder where she stands on certain issues. In rejecting an overtly expressed authorial perspective for writing "honestly," however, Gordimer presupposes a certain definition of honesty. To comprehend the limitations of such a presupposition, one has only to imagine P. W. Botha's or B. J. Vorster's conception of an honest account of life in South Africa. Gordimer's personal abhorrence of apartheid causes her to view life in South Africa in a particular way. Stephen Clingman characterizes her approach as "naive realism," and protests, "Social conclusions are not what simply emerge through the unmediating agency of the writer and her type-writer" (12). His study of Gordimer's novels belies her notion of the writer's objectivity by tracing the forms of ideology that appear in her work. But Clingman concludes that Gordimer's "position of naive re-alism and the morality that infuses it are . . . of significance" because they demonstrate her consciousness of and engagement with history (12).

Gordimer, along with many of her compatriots, has been critical of those South African writers who have failed to engage history in a like manner. The Sestigers have come under particular attack. These Afrikaner writers are best known for their narrative experimentation and their shocking challenges to the accepted sexual and religious mores of the mainstream Afrikaner society. Gordimer asserts, "the evidence that not one of them published anything that was banned shows how they turned away, astonishingly, from the deepest realities of the life going on around them." She continues her critique by damning a particular au-thor: "The Sestigers' outstanding prose writer, and indeed the most sweeping imaginative power in South African literature as a whole, Etienne le Roux, makes the lofty claim that his trilogy, *Towards a Dubious Salvation,* is a 'metaphysical' novel; but if a writer is part of the creative consciousness of the society in which he lives, is it not a form of betrayal, of creative as well as human integrity, to choose to turn away from the messy confrontation of man with man, and address oneself to God?" ("English-Language" 112). Gordimer is not alone in her judgment. Lewis Nkosi claims:

> Despite a massive propaganda campaign which proclaims them to be new leaders of the South African *avant garde,* the group of Afrikaans writers known as the 'Sestigers' have remained on the whole curiously irrelevant, even faintly comic. These vast stretches of mannered, surrealistic descrip-tions, the formidable limitations of the *nouveau roman* in which racial conflict is absent and murder is a metaphysical game, strike us as im-

plausible, unreal, even deliberately fraudulent. Where, one wishes to know, is the sjambok and the gun and the stolen sexual confidences on a private beach at night, the whole ghastly comedy of the laboured heart transplants and the accelerating rate of malnutrition and infant mortality? (*Tasks and Masks* 77–78)

Both Gordimer and Nkosi condemn the Sestigers for irresponsibly turning to metaphysics rather than history.

While not focusing exclusively on the Sestigers, T. T. Moyana has similar criticisms to make about both Afrikaner and English writers who "display strange aberrations of vision" in works that escape into fantasy, explore mystic primitivism, lyrically render the natural beauty of the countryside, or flee to "the safe haven of historical themes." Moyana, like Gordimer, concludes, "So successful has escapist literature been among the Afrikaners that up to 1972 no Afrikaner book had been banned" (86). In fact, no book by an Afrikaner was banned until 1974, when André Brink's *Kennis van die aand (Knowledge of the Night),* a realistic and detailed rejection of apartheid, was banned after selling out its first edition.

I have given these condemnations of so-called escapist literature at length because I think they include some crucial presuppositions about the way that writing in South Africa can be and should be politically engaged and relevant. The first presupposition concerns reception: both Gordimer and Moyana seem to assume that if a work has not been banned, it must not be critically engaged with the issue of apartheid. This line of reasoning not only begs the question but also assumes the infallible perception of the Publications Appeal Board, an assumption that Gordimer was quick to deny when it came to the unbanning of her *Burger's Daughter* in 1980.[1] Understanding a work's political or historical relevance in the light of its reception can be done only by examining the historical circumstances of its particular audience. Surely we do not want to assume that the Publications Appeal Board is the primary audience for South African writing.

Second, these criticisms have a definite bias toward realism. They begin with the assumption that literature must treat certain topics if it is to be relevant and so, in a normative sense, good. Similarly, they privilege the narrative technique of realism as the best means to engage history. Jack Cope's recommendation that future Afrikaner writers use a "real story" and a "realist technique" is fairly typical (196). In insisting that an author write about contemporary events in a realistic fashion or, as Gordimer describes it, writing honestly what you see, such critics prescribe Georg Lukács's "critical realism." These critics' dislike of the metaphysical, the surreal, and the mystic suggests Lukács's own antagonism toward modernism's asocial and ahistorical ideology and form. Such critics might insist with Lukács, "In any protest against particular social conditions, those conditions themselves must have the central place."[2]

Third, and most paradoxically, such criticism assumes that it is possible for an author to escape history. The argument in its entirety is circular: the writer cannot escape the politics of the historical moment in South Africa, yet if the writer does not write about certain contemporary topics in a realistic way, the writer is immorally (or at least irresponsibly) escaping history. Gordimer herself in "English-Language Literature and Politics" admits, "All that is and has been written by South Africans is profoundly influenced, at the deepest and least controllable level of consciousness, by the politics of race. All writers everywhere—even those like Joyce who can't bear to live in their own countries, or those like Genet who live outside the pale of their country's laws—are shaped by their own particular society reflecting a particular political situation" (100). The Sestigers' surreal, sexual fictional worlds have been shaped by the politics of South Africa, just as has Gordimer's fictional account of the South African Communist movement in *Burger's Daughter.* The more pertinent question may be *how* a work has been shaped and in what ways it is enlarging the apprehensions of its readers.[3]

J. M. Coetzee and History

After Gordimer, J. M. Coetzee may be the best known contemporary South African writer. Like Brink, Coetzee is an Afrikaner whose novels and criticism have been widely distributed and well received outside of South Africa. Born in Cape Town on February 9, 1940, Coetzee is descended from Dutch settlers who came to Africa in the seventeenth century. His grandparents on both sides were farmers, and he was raised in a number of small towns primarily in the Karoo, a vast desert plateau that covers most of the Cape Province. His mother was English, so Coetzee grew up speaking English at home but Afrikaans to his relatives and friends. After attending a Roman Catholic boys' college, he received degrees in literature and mathematics from the University of Cape Town in the 1960s. He later earned a Ph.D. in linguistics in the United States in 1968 and since 1972 has taught linguistics and literature at the University of Cape Town.[4] The author of six novels and numerous critical works, he has won Britain's Booker-McConnell Prize (1983), France's Prix Femina Étranger (1985), and the Jerusalem Prize for writing that contributes to "the freedom of the individual in society" (1987). The citation for the latter describes Coetzee as "a great artist" who "stands out in his novel[s] and essays as a fighter for human freedom and dignity" (Mitgang 24). Yet Coetzee's unusual narratives continue to defy critical appropriation and do not fit into the accepted categories of social realism expected of many South African writers.

While many reviewers praise his work for its universal themes, Coetzee's academic critics often manifest an underlying uneasiness about his work's political implications that usually can be traced to their presuppositions about the relationship of literature and life. Coetzee himself divides his critical public into two camps that resemble the distinctions that I have drawn between romantics and realists. In one interview he notes that Americans read his books "in the general terms in which books are read by intelligent, mainly academic type critics" while the South African critics read under the influence of Marxism. "The primary question" asked by his compatriots is, "Where does this book fit into the political struggle?" (Penner 75). In another interview Coetzee identifies the same two readerships but without limiting their nationalities. Speaking of the favorable response his works have received, he explains, "It has come first of all from people whose thinking is politically and historically fairly radical and, secondly, it has come from a fairly middle-of-the-road literary establishment" ("Interview" 9).

Coetzee's categories seem apt when we examine the critical literature. Middle-of-the-road readers look at his novels in terms of their universal qualities, as aesthetic objects that contain transcendent truths. While these critics acknowledge that since Coetzee is from South Africa his work must be politically significant, the majority of their comments focus on the work's universal themes of oppression and colonization. Robert Post, for example, admits "it is only natural that, when considering a South African author writing about victimization, we think specifically of the persecution implicit in the system of apartheid in South Africa," but primarily sees Coetzee's novels as general "statements of opposition to oppression" ("Oppression" 67). Similarly, while granting that Coetzee's "general politicized allegorizing" allows him to avoid being censored by the Directorate of Publications, Kelly Hewson suggests that his work reminds us "that oppression and injustice are not limited to South Africa, that, in some sense, they are eternal" (69, 70). In the first book-length study of Coetzee published in the United States, Dick Penner claims, "Coetzee's fictions maintain their significance apart from a South African context, because of their artistry and because they transform urgent societal concerns into more enduring questions regarding colonialism and the relationships of mastery and servitude between cultures and individuals" (xiii). Penner draws a distinction between Coetzee "the ethical individual, the Afrikaner concerned with injustice," and Coetzee "the teller of tales," who "creates countries of the mind, where the imagination reigns and refuses to be subservient to history's incessant voices" (20, 21).

The historically conscious critics, who are primarily from South Africa, more frequently employ a neo-Marxist perspective to analyze the ideology of Coetzee's work and to deplore his political naivete. Some South African writers, as we have seen, insist that the political should be manifested in literature in very particular ways, and Coetzee's work does not easily fit into these traditions. Some suspect him of acquiescing to the oppressive system. The SASPU *National* review of *Waiting for the Barbarians* declares, "As the CNA award shows, this is a book which will be enthusiastically assimilated into the very system it (vaguely) condemns. In the end it is not a disturbing book, and ultimately it challenges nothing. Coetzee is a fine writer. It's a pity he isn't a bolder one" (qtd. Menàn Du Plessis 77). And, as Stephen Watson points out, Coetzee's treatment of colonialism focuses on its metaphysical base more than its material base: "It is for this reason that, perhaps predictably, Coetzee has aroused the suspicions and then the complaints of many people on the Left in South Africa, people for whom the most important philosophical and political distinction would still be some line of division between an 'idealism,' on the one hand, and a 'materialism,' on the other."[5]

While Coetzee is applauded for his imaginative genius and innovative style, one senses in many critics an underlying wish that he would become a bit more overtly political, that is, realistic. The South African uneasiness with Coetzee's writing emerges clearly in Nadine Gordimer's review of his *Life & Times of Michael K*, published in the *New York Review of Books* in 1984. Coetzee chose an allegorical method for his first few books, Gordimer states sympathetically, "out of a kind of opposing desire to hold himself clear of events and their daily, grubby, tragic consequences in which, like everybody else living in South Africa, he is up to the neck, and about which he had an inner compulsion to write. . . . He seemed able to deal with the horror . . . only—if brilliantly—if this were to be projected into another time and plane" ("Idea" 3). While Gordimer sees *Waiting for the Barbarians* as the North Pole to the South Pole of "the agitprop of agonized black writers," she insists that "a world to be dealt with lies in between" (3). She is apparently much happier that Coetzee has finally taken up that world in *Life & Times of Michael K.* So concerned is she to see the novel as reflecting current events in South Africa that she brushes off the apparent reference to Kafka in the protagonist's name and concludes that the K probably stands for Kotze or Koekemoer, common surnames among Cape Town coloured people.

But writers can be responsibly engaged with history without necessarily being realists. Beginning with the premise that works of literature can never escape historical reality, we can analyze the relationship of a work to its context in ways other than the aesthetic dichotomy or the realistic mandate. The romantic consideration of a work's aesthetics and universal themes often ignores the social and historical situation that both engenders and is engendered by the work. Similarly, the tunnel vision of realism that zeroes in on a particular kind of content may overlook the historical implications of the formal choices of the author. Both the formalist and the neo-Marxist approach have a tendency to fail to consider a literary work as a part of a cultural conversation or as a strand in a complex social network of many different kinds of discourse.

In *Culture and the Radical Conscience,* Eugene Goodheart notes that analyzing the content of a work of literature is not enough to assess its political thrust. Besides "what is said," we must also consider "the way it is said." Goodheart explains, "The political implication of a work is bound up with the imaginative disposition of the artist. His development as an artist, which includes matters of language, characterization, narrative method, may also be a matter of politics." Even literature that claims to be apolitical may contain political implications implicit in its technique. "Modern literature makes a kind of propaganda through its aestheticism . . . in diverting the reader from the claims of the political will or in attacking these claims" (82). André Brink understands the political import of the Sestigers from this perspective, asserting that even if their work "had no overt political slant, its implications were political" (*Writing* 26). Brink believes that in the Sestiger revolt from traditional Afrikaner norms of sexuality and religious belief, their work "has come to signify a revolt against an entire oppressive system" (45). This kind of approach goes beyond the content of the work to examine what an entire movement implies in its historical context. When Brink and Afrikaans poet Breyten Breytenbach began their more overtly political writing in the 1970s, some of their fellow Sestigers reacted by championing "the cause of *l'art pur*"; Breytenbach and Brink responded that all art is political: "even silence and non-commitment . . . implied a political stance" (Brink, *Writing* 27). Examined within historical, social, and political contexts, the formal qualities of a work of literature have new significance.

In recent years, many critics have called for a re-evaluation of and new emphasis on the historical nature and social function of literature. Edward Said argues that in its focus on textuality, contemporary literary theory has ignored the materiality of a text: "texts are worldly, to some degree they are events, and, even when they appear to deny it, they are nevertheless a part of the social world, human life, and of course the historical moments in which they are located and interpreted" (*World* 4). The problem with most contemporary criticism, he concludes, is that it is "worldless" (151). A similar analysis from a Marxist perspective is given by Frank Lentricchia in *After the New Criticism,* in which he condemns the antihistorical, hermetic impulses of formalist theory.

The call to contextualize has been sounded increasingly by the so-called New Historicists. Although this critical movement is still in its early stages of definition and evaluation, some of its common practices can be identified.[6] Moving beyond literary and philosophical sources for literature, New Historicists explore the relationships between non-textual events, different modes of cultural discourse, and the work of literature. One of New Historicism's key assumptions, according to H. Aram Veeser, is that "every expressive act is embedded in a network of material practices" (xi). Louis Montrose says, "its collective project is to resituate canonical literary texts among the multiple forms of writing, and in relation to the non-discursive practices and institutions, of the social formation in which those texts have been produced" (6). In that process of resituation, critics acknowledge both their own historical limitations and the complexity of the text's situation. Brook Thomas explains, "literature is seen in constant relation to the world around it, not so much reflecting its historical situation as responding to it. Because that historical situation is so complex—because there is an overdetermination of defining forces—we will never be able to have a total understanding of literature" ("Historical Necessity" 514).

Although New Historicism has been instigated and practiced primarily by scholars of the English Renaissance, some of its practices will prove useful in analyzing contemporary South African literature. As they struggle to place literary works in social and historical contexts, "to make visible, to give materiality back to, the strands holding the text to society, author, and culture" (Said, *World* 175), Anglo-Americans will find their difficulties to be caused by geographical and cultural distance more than historical distance. For most of us, the world of South Africa is as foreign as the world of Shakespeare. In beginning our analysis of the social and cultural strands of J. M. Coetzee's work, we must first acknowledge the very different cultural ground on which we stand and admit that we can never fully grasp the complexities of the situation of the contemporary South African novelist. Also, as inhabitants of the so-called First World, we are colonizers in both the material and the literary economy. As critics of South African texts, we colonize them, earning our academic living by means of their very existence. Thus, we participate in the very process we seek to uncover and which Coetzee exposes in his fiction.

While Brink and Gordimer have been outspoken on the role of the author in South Africa, Coetzee has said little on the subject. His own historical situation is significant: he is an Afrikaner who speaks Afrikaans, has forebears involved in instituting apartheid, and is now critical of his own tradition and heritage. He sees the South African situation as a manifestation of "colonialism, late colonialism, neo-colonialism" (Coetzee, "Speaking" 23). Coetzee describes South Africa as "a situation of naked exploitation" in which "a group of affluent and virtually post-industrial exploiters" rule over "an enormous number of people who live in a world which is effectively nineteenth century" (Interview 8). Apartheid, he declares in a *New York Times Magazine* article, is "a doctrine and a set of social practices that scars the moral being of whites as it degrades and demeans blacks" ("Tales" 21). Coetzee's most scathing condemnation of the effects of his country's power structures appears in the speech he gave when accepting the Jerusalem Prize in 1987: "The deformed and mutilated relations between human beings, which have been created under the colonial regime and which have been exacerbated under what one summarily calls *apartheid,* find their psychic reflection in an internal life that is deformed and mutilated. All the expressions of this internal life, regardless of the intensity, regardless of what flashes of cheerfulness or despair run through them, suffer from the same deformity, the same mutilation."[7] Coetzee has commented several times sympathetically on the problems facing black writers in his country, yet he has said little about his own role as a writer.[8] The few comments he has made in interviews and essays, as in his fiction, are full of gaps and elusions.

In an interview in 1985, Jean Sévry asked Coetzee about his reaction to Brink's declarations in *Writing in a State of Siege* on the role of the author in South Africa. Coetzee's response neatly sidesteps the question. After stating that he has not read the book, he continues, "As to the question of the role of the writer, there seems to be a model behind the question, a model of a social structure in which people are assigned roles to play, and I am not sure that I would agree with the model underlying the question. I would have to be convinced that such roles are assigned, and by whom." Sévry presses, "Do you mean that you'd rather keep it for your own consciousness rather than giving a pre-definition of your role?" Coetzee replies, "No, I don't want to talk about retaining things for my own consciousness; it is simply that I have my disagreements with that model of social structure. It seems to be a very simplistic model of social structure and it's a model that collapses when one poses the same question regarding tennis-players or sculptors. It's a question that seems always to be asked regarding writers. It seems to me clear it is a question based on unacknowledged premises" (Coetzee, "Interview" 1).

Coetzee's evasion is provocative. Does he actually believe that there is no difference between writing fiction and playing tennis? Is he denying the ethical or political responsibility of the author? Is Coetzee aligning himself on the side of the aestheticists? And does the failure of his work directly to address the social, economic, political, and ethical issues of contemporary South Africa indicate an attempt on his part to divorce his art from history, as some critics have claimed?

Looking at Coetzee's responses in this interview, we should first note his refusal to be categorized. Coetzee does not want to be "placed," to be "labeled," to be "assigned" a role. This refusal stems not so much from a desire to be private ("keeping it for your own consciousness") as from a refusal to accept the implication of the passive agentless construction that does not identify the entity that does the placing, labeling, and assigning. In other words, Coetzee refuses an authoritarian determination of the role of the writer. In so refusing, Coetzee does not deny that a writer performs a function in society; rather, he denies that there is a *particular* function that all writers must fulfill. By refusing the model of social reality implied by the question, Coetzee never directly responds to the issue of how the writer might function in his or her society.

Coetzee's essay "Alex La Guma and the Responsibilities of the South African Writer" demonstrates a similar impatience with those who would prescribe the role of the author. Beginning with Lewis Nkosi's criticism of the technical naivete of black South African writing, Coetzee notes that such an argument "reveals a fairly specific, and *ipso facto* debatable, conception of the role of the writer" (5). Nkosi, according to Coetzee, believes that all South African writers must fulfill a certain role by producing certain kinds of literature. The alternative which he would have us consider is "whether there might not be a whole spectrum of valid literature open to Africa" (6). Once again, Coetzee opts for many possible roles (and forms) rather than one particular role.

Despite his evasions and his refusal to define the role of the author narrowly, Coetzee has acknowledged the overwhelming impact of his historical situation on his work. When he was asked in a 1982 interview how being a South African influenced his writing, Coetzee responded that, in a sense, he faced an easier task than a European writer since his dominating concern (that "situation of naked exploitation") requires a "much less massive effort of the imagination" than European concerns about nuclear annihilation or the meaningfulness of labor (Interview 8). These comments on what he terms the "obscene" benefits of being a South African writer reveal Coetzee's basic assumption that he speaks both from and to his historical situation. However, the context of South African life also has its limitations. In his Jerusalem Prize acceptance speech, Coetzee laments the way his circumstances have trapped him and narrowed his focus as a writer. Including his own work in his analysis, he posits: "South African literature is an enslaved literature. . . . It is a literature which is not fully human: being more preoccupied than is natural, with power and with the torsions of power, it does not know how to pass from the elementary relations of contestation, of domination, and of subjugation, to the vast and complex human world which extends beyond." He explains that what hinders the South African writer from writing about this larger life is "the *power* which the world (where his body lives) has to impose itself on him, and (in the last instance) on his imagination. . . . The *coarseness* of life in South Africa, the naked force of its seductions, not only on the physical level, but also on the moral level, its harshness and its savageries, its hungers and its furies, its greediness and its lies make it as irresistible as it is displeasing." Just as in the story of Don Quixote, the South African writer's efforts end with "the capitulation of imagination before reality" ("Apartheid" 58). Coetzee thus clearly acknowledges the impact of history on his writing.

Furthermore, his critical comments on other contemporary South African writers reveal his concern for the social and ethical implications of different narrative strategies. In his essay on Alex La Guma, Coetzee suggests "that the writer should not, so to speak, choose his tradition at random, but rather choose it with some sense of the social implications of his choice" (6). He makes such a suggestion after noting the irony of Nkosi's lament that black authors have failed to follow "the lessons of the masters" of modern Western experimental literary techniques. Coetzee himself considers social implications when he judges critical realism to be a more appropriate technique for the black South African novelist than naturalism: "we are entitled to ask what purpose a literature serves which only chronicles the lives and deaths of little people, the victims of social fates too dark for them to comprehend" (8). Rejecting the common classification of La Guma's *A Walk in the Night* as naturalistic, Coetzee identifies the "considerable weight of political statement" in the novel and applauds La Guma's "courageous and valuable literary act" (10, 11).

In a second essay on La Guma, "Man's Fate in the Novels of Alex La Guma," Coetzee takes up the dilemma of black South African writers in exile. Because their work is deprived of its social function, such artists may "retreat" to universalizing their work, to "transcending the world and the age out of which it grows" (16). Alternatively, artists in exile may be content to bear witness, to testify about the lie, as Brink advocates. Coetzee cryptically asks about this Sartrean stoic, "with, all the while, an eye on his moral relation to his obsessive story; is he merely fondling his wound?" (16). The image is not a positive one, and suggests a gratuitous rather than healing treatment of the ills of the country. As in his earlier essay, Coetzee admires how La Guma renders the political in his work but goes on to criticize the black author's "excesses of realism" (22). Citing La Guma's relentlessly weighted descriptions of "an *old* iron bed . . . *unwashed* bedding . . . a *backless* chair . . . a *chipped* ashtray," Coetzee demonstrates how wounds may be fondled (22).

Coetzee's most extended discussion of the ethical responsibilities of the South African writer appears in an essay published in the *New York Times Book Review* called "Into the Dark Chamber: The Novelist and South Africa." Written in conjunction with the Forty-Eighth International PEN Congress held in New York City in January 1986, this essay focuses on torture and how the writer should respond to its contemporary existence. Admitting that "torture has exerted a dark fascination" on himself and many other South African writers, Coetzee nonetheless cautions that the writer who depicts "the dark chamber" must be careful

(13). The novelist must resolve "how to justify a concern with morally dubious people involved in a contemptible activity . . . how to treat something that, in truth, because it is offered like the Gorgon's head to terrorize the populace and paralyze resistance, deserves to be ignored" (35). Coetzee objects to realistic depictions of torture in fiction because he thinks that the novelist participates vicariously in the atrocities, validates the acts of torture, assists the state in terrorizing and paralyzing people by showing its oppressive methods in detail. Excessive realism may again be merely a fondling of the wound, a gratuitous submission to the fascination of the forbidden chamber.

Yet the obscenities of the state must not be hidden either. The author has an ethical responsibility not only to refuse complicity with those in authority who practice torture but also to recognize the fact that torture is a sign, a word, that desperately needs the exposing light of interpretation. Coetzee claims, "Relations in the torture room provide a metaphor, bare and extreme, for relations between authoritarianism and its victims." The challenge thus faced by the author "is how not to play the game by the rules of the state, how to establish one's own authority, how to imagine torture and death on one's own terms" (13). Coetzee meets this challenge, as I discuss in Chapter 5, in his novel *Waiting for the Barbarians.*

Although Coetzee refuses to delineate the responsibility of the writer, or to prescribe a single way that the novelist should respond to the realities of South Africa, he is concerned to evaluate competing strategies that authors have employed in their response. Keenly aware of the special liabilities of traditional realism and naturalism, Coetzee has chosen an alternative narrative strategy to embody his responses. In his novels, he attempts to create his own terms, to avoid merely fondling the wound or retreating to a depoliticized timelessness, to deal with the reality of South Africa in a responsible and ethical fashion.

Language and Stories

We can begin to understand the kind of terms that Coetzee creates in his work by looking at his unusual contribution to a South African literary manifesto, *Momentum: On Recent South African Writing* (1984). Published by the University of Natal Press, this collection of essays includes several statements by prominent South African authors concerning their work. The compilers of *Momentum* described their purpose in a letter to the authors: "As matters become more than ever difficult for all writers in this crazy society of ours, and as writers themselves are debating publicly their role . . . it will be very valuable, especially to scholars, to have a firsthand account from writers of how they experience and conceive of their activity" (*Momentum* xii). Coetzee's response to such a request consists of an extremely brief essay (less than three pages long) that discusses the linguistic phenomenon of the "middle voice" that lies between active voice and passive voice in some verbs, particularly the verb "to write."

At first glance, this rather esoteric matter, clearly originating in Coetzee's formal training as a linguist, appears to have little to do with the role of the writer and seems only another example of Coetzee's tendency to sidestep the issue of responsibility. Yet in "A Note on Writing" Coetzee actually sounds the primary theme of his narrative practice, a motif that is transposed, expanded, and played in a series of variations in his novels. He introduces the idea of the middle voice, he tells us, because it "speak[s] a word of caution about constructions that we often run across in literary criticism in South Africa, particularly at the level of reviewing." Constructions such as "to use a language," "to write a book," "to create characters," "to express thought" all use transitive verbs and the active voice. "They reflect a common conception of the subject—a subject prior to, independent of, and untouched by the verb—and of the relation, or lack of relation, between subject and object" (12).

In other words, literary critics writing about South African literature too often assume the complete autonomy of the author in the face of his or her language or thought. Coetzee cautions us that it might be occasionally useful to consider these phrases as bearing a middle voice; in such a case, "to write" would involve carrying out the action of "doing writing" with reference to the self. He quotes from Roland Barthes: "today to write is to make oneself the centre of the action of *la parole;* it is to effect writing in being affected oneself; it is to leave the writer *(le scripteur)* inside the writing, not as a psychological subject . . . but as the agent of the action" (11). The subject "I" in the middle voice is both the one who acts as well as the one who is acted upon—by language, by thought, by the book.

Throughout much of his critical writing Coetzee is concerned to analyze the "dense complicity between thought and language" that appears in texts ("Newton" 9). While he rejects a simplistic Whorfian notion of language as sole determiner of thought, Coetzee does find Newton's semantics of agency and instrumentality bound up with his philosophical questions about causality in the same way that he finds (shifting from semantics to rhetoric) the colonial explorers of South Africa ill equipped to deal with a land which refused traditional social analysis and geographical perspectives (in his discussion in *White Writing*). Coetzee's writing, both critical and fictional, consistently focuses on the relationship of thought, language, identity, and history. The controlling question of his work is how one responds to the dual challenge of reality and the stories and language by which we apprehend that reality.

In wrestling with these issues, Coetzee does not acquiesce to the complete anti-realism of post-structuralist thought, but neither does he ignore the constitutive and constructive power of language. His concern is hermeneutical: how can the South African author "read" his or her country? Which methods of interpretation prove useful? Which are distorted and result in oppression and injustice? How can authoritarianism and colonialism be overcome in a world so governed by their myths?

In a talk given in 1987 in Cape Town, Coetzee indirectly addressed the charges that his writing irresponsibly turns away from the historical reality of South Africa. Noting that in contemporary South Africa there exists "a powerful tendency, perhaps even dominant tendency, to subsume the novel under history," he explains that those works which function in such a way as to "supplement" the history text are seen as carrying more truth than other kinds of works ("Novel Today" 2). However, Coetzee argues, novels can either supplement history or act as rivals to history, and perhaps there is equal value in those works that act as rivals. A novel that is a rival to history "operates in terms of its own procedures and issues in its own conclusions, not one that operates in terms of the procedures of history and eventuates in conclusions that are checkable by history . . . evolves its own paradigms and myths, in the process (and here is the point at which true rivalry, even enmity, perhaps enters the picture) perhaps going so far as to show up the mythic status of history." Speaking "as a member of a tribe threatened with colonisation," Coetzee says that "in South Africa the colonisation of the novel by the discourse of history is proceeding with alarming rapidity" (3). As more critics advocate social realism and critique imaginative works of literature in terms of their adherence to a materialistic dialectic, history swallows and subsumes literature.

Coetzee goes on to admit that he does not actually need to speak on behalf of his art, for storytelling "will always be able to take care of itself" (3). It has lasted throughout history, despite numerous attempts to transform it, eradicate it, domesticate it. The unique and enduring aspect of stories is "their faculty of making and changing their own rules. There is a game going on between the covers of the book, but it is not always the game you think it is" (3–4). Stories can never be simply summarized or paraphrased: "a story is not a message with a covering, a rhetorical or aesthetic covering." A story is always more. "Storytelling . . . is not a way of making messages more—as they say—'effective'. Storytelling is another, an other mode of thinking." Both storytelling and history are modes of discourse, and Coetzee refuses to privilege history. The point he is making is "that history is not reality; that history is a kind of discourse; that a novel is a kind of discourse too, but a different kind of discourse; that, inevitably, in our culture, history will, with varying degrees of forcefulness, try to claim primacy, claim to be a master-form of discourse, just as, inevitably, people like myself will defend themselves by saying that a history is nothing but a certain kind of story that people agree to tell each other" (4). Refusing to tell the same story that history does, imaginative storytelling provides a rival vision of reality. And in the South Africa of the twentieth century, who would not agree that a new story is necessary?

Inextricably connected to the reality of South Africa yet defiantly creating their own imaginative terms, Coetzee's stories provide an alternative to traditional Afrikaner discourse on South Africa. Without denying that his novels speak of profound, universal themes, I wish to examine Coetzee's fictions in terms of their conditions in and consequences for South Africa. Coetzee's work is able to transcend its historical situation only because it is in the first place linked to that historical situation. This study, then, will examine the complexly interwoven relationships of the material reality of South Africa, the various discourses that tell stories about that reality, Coetzee's narrative strategies, and his primary thematic concerns. All of these issues concern language, authority, and mythmaking.

· 2 ·

Naming the Other: History,
Language, and Authority

Coetzee's nonrealistic novels can be understood as instruments of ethical action when we examine them within what Jerome McGann terms their "networks of social relations" (18). In the previous chapter I considered the current debate over the role of the writer in South Africa. Now I will extend the analysis to the broader social and cultural institutions of South Africa, in an effort to understand *how* and *to whom* Coetzee speaks as an author, the particular social relationships that his work calls into existence. His fiction takes its place within a social context in which race is a key determining material condition. The unjust economic, political, and educational policies of the South African system of apartheid are well known. However, Coetzee's fiction also takes its place within a cultural context governed by a number of significant discursive practices, which embody strategies of power and subjection, inclusion and exclusion, voices and silences. These discursive practices encourage a psychological apartheid, in which whites become unable to see blacks as anything but Others, objects bereft of full human reality. In an essay in *The World, the Text, and the Critic,* Said points to "the power of culture by virtue of its elevated or superior position to authorize, to dominate, to legitimate, demote, interdict, and validate: in short, the power of culture to be an agent of, and perhaps the main agency for, powerful differentiation within its domain and beyond it too" (9). In its various discursive practices, South African culture has achieved this kind of differentiation with respect to blacks and whites.[1]

André Brink describes the kind of distancing apartheid creates. As a university student, he never had any kind of contact with blacks: "One could spend a lifetime in South Africa in those years, as many still do, living so exclusively within one of the many totally segregated microcosms that exist side by side in the country, without ever having contact—except on the most superficial level—with others. You hardly knew they existed. If other people did exist, they were *they:* the black masses; the other" (*Writing* 30). The anthropologist Vincent Crapanzano found similar attitudes in a group of white South Africans living in a village north of Cape Town that he calls Wyndal. In *Waiting: The Whites of South Africa,* he records their stories and concludes that the effect of the whites' role as dominators is a loss of what Keats called "negative capability." White South Africans have lost "the capability of so negating their identity as to be imaginatively open to the complex and never very certain reality around them." The loss of this ability results in mental isolation: "they create a kind of psychological apartheid, an apartness that in the case of South Africa is institutionally reinforced. In such circumstances there can be no real recognition of the other—no real appreciation of *his* subjectivity. He becomes at once a menial object to be manipulated and a mythic object to be feared. He cannot be counted in his humanity" (xxii). The physical and psychological distance created by apartheid prompts whites to think of the world of the coloureds and blacks as "a grotesque anti-world" of the exotic, the psychotic, the criminal, the violent (261–63).

In this chapter I will examine a few of the discursive practices that support and encourage this objectification and distancing of blacks. We will see how the physical reality of apartheid is reinforced by the myths of South African history, the silencing of black voices, and the employment of language as a tool of control. The South African world is one in which history, language, and authority have all been co-opted to serve the cause of oppression.

The Myth of History

Coetzee's insistence that "history is nothing but a certain kind of story that people agree to tell each other" takes on special resonance when we consider the mythical role played by history in South Africa ("Novel Today" 4). Although in common usage myth is a story that is not true, in anthropological or sociological usage a myth is defined more by its function than by its degree of veracity. According to the *Oxford English Dictionary,* a myth is "a tale which is told to justify some aspect of social order or of human experience." Henry Tudor elaborates, "The view of the world that we find in a myth is always a practical view. Its aim is either to advocate a certain course of action or to justify acceptance of an existing state of affairs" (124). History, as constructed by the Afrikaners, functions as such a myth, persistently endeavoring to justify Afrikaner nationalism and its ideology of apartheid. Coetzee charges that the story told by the "official" history of the Afrikaner is "an edifice constructed of selected fragments of the past by a historiography in the service of 20th-century nationalist politics. It was put together for precisely the purpose of buttressing and justifying the activities of a specific political grouping" ("Listening" 28). Afrikaner history silences blacks and casts them in the role of Other while simultaneously painting the Afrikaners as a heroic and wronged people.

Repeatedly, white South African myths attempt to erase or write out the native Africans from their own land and history. The most common historical myth is that South Africa was essentially uninhabited, with the exception of a few Bushmen (San) and Hottentots (Khoikhoi), when the Dutch first landed at the Cape in 1652. The Bantu (Xhosa), who were to become the major black group in South Africa, are alleged to be relatively recent immigrants, migrating from the north around the same time as the Boers began to trek into the interior in the eighteenth century. Official publications, South African textbooks, and governmental rhetoric all perpetuate this version of history. The official guidebook at the central national shrine, the Voortrekker Monument, tells the thousands of daily visitors: "It is nonsense to suppose that the interior of Southern Africa belonged to the Bantu and that the white man took it away from him. The Bantus penetrated from the north almost at the same time as the white man entered the south. They had equal title to the country. The Voortrekkers wished to partition the country and live in peace because they had already experienced enough trouble in the Cape. But the Bantu were not amenable to reason. He respected only one thing and that was force" (qtd. Harrison 15).

South Africa has attempted to perpetuate this myth in international discourse, as well. For example, *South Africa 1983*, the official yearbook distributed internationally by the South African Department of Foreign Affairs and Information, says, "It was not before 1770, at the Great Fish River, that [the Afrikaner farmer] encountered the vanguard of the Bantu (Black) peoples who, during the course of centuries, had been migrating slowly southwards on a broad trans-continental front" (38). Similarly, the South African Representative to the United Nations stated to the Security Council in October 1974: "Towards the middle of the

17th century the white and black peoples of southern Africa converged in what was then an almost uninhabited part of the continent" (qtd. Laurence 79). The implication of the myth of the empty land is that since both whites and blacks arrived at the same time, neither has a superior claim to South Africa. Yet this myth is also inherently self-contradictory, for it mentions the presence of the Bushmen and the Hottentots, only to negate that presence: the land was *almost* uninhabited."

For many years, scholars have been criticizing the misleading assumptions shaping Afrikaner history. Yet despite the accumulation of archeological, anthropological, and historical evidence to the contrary, the myth of the empty land continues to be propagated by the government and believed by Afrikaners.[2] Crapanzano's conversations with white South Africans in 1984 reveal the popular belief in this myth: "You think South Africa belongs to the Black man," one Afrikaner farmer told him, "But we came here before the Kaffirs were here. There were some Bushmen and Hottentots. The Hottentots died of smallpox, like your Red Indians, and the Bushmen, well, they're the Coloureds now, they and the Malays" (59). This farmer again obliterates the presence of the San and Khoikhoi, and ignores the presence of the Bantu in the east. A UNESCO study conducted by Marianne Cornevin and published in 1980 states, "South African historians, who know well that the blacks came first, have never intervened to have the official doctrine altered. Even though it is sometimes expressed in an attenuated form, the theory of simultaneous migrations of whites and blacks is still upheld nowadays in political speeches and recently published school textbooks. Still more serious, it has been defended so long and so vigorously that it has been uncritically repeated, even very recently, by foreign authors" (78). Although the Bantu-speaking Africans had not yet moved into the Cape area when the white settlers arrived, they had been settled farther east in South Africa since the fourth century.

When the indigenous people of South Africa were allowed into history, they were relegated to a subhuman position somewhere between animals and civilized people. The initial encounters with blacks set the tone and vocabulary for such descriptions. John Jordain wrote in 1608, "I think the world doth not yeild a more heathenish people and more beastlie" (Raven-Hart, *Before* 42). Colonial travel narratives repeatedly note the strange dress, language, and eating habits of the indigenous people. European visitors often used animal metaphors to describe the native customs, and many early travelers suspected (without grounds) that the blacks were cannibals. Ralph Standish's account in 1612 reveals how such a view of native South Africans served subconsciously to justify European colonization:

> The Counttrey being firtille ground and pleasantt and a counttrey verie temperatt but the people bruitt and salladg, without Religion, without languag, without Lawes or government, without manners or humanittie, and last of all withoutt apparell, for they go naked save onelie a ppees of Sheepes Skyn to cover their Members that in my opinion yt is a great pittie that such creattures as they bee should injoy so sweett a counttry. Ther persons are preporcionable butt ther Faces like an Appe or Babownne, with flat nosses and ther heads and faces both beastlie and fillthye to behoulde.[3]

Such descriptions fill written accounts throughout three centuries, such as those by Hondius (1652), Kolb (1719), Mentzel (1785), Barrow (1801), and Philip (1828). In the 1830s whites referred to themselves as "masters" and to the black menial laborers as "schepsels," which means creatures (van Jaarsveld 6). In *White Writing* Coetzee discusses the tendency of these accounts to focus on the Hottentots' idleness as evidence that blacks are underdeveloped or backward. Part of the threat that this poses, Coetzee suggests, is that the Hottentots generated relatively little material for the anthropological writer: "the almost universal denunciation among the travel writers represents a reaction to a challenge, a scandal, that strikes particularly near to them *as writers;* that the laziness of the Hottentot aborts one of the more promising of discourses about elemental man" (23). Those about whom anthropological discourse is not possible are truly Others.

The construction of black as Other begun in these early accounts is still rehearsed in twentieth-century textbooks, historical accounts, and official rhetoric. Cornevin includes among the ten common myths of white South African history that black leaders were nothing more than bloodthirsty despots, that only the appearance of the whites saved the blacks from internecine destruction, and that blacks' original political ideas were always inspired by whites (95–111). Another UNESCO study of South African textbooks carried out by a British team at the University of Leicester found that texts for both blacks and whites "stereotyped black people as incompetent, primitive, ignorant, unintellectual, warlike, and, indeed, innately and permanently inferior."[4] Stephen Biko, the Black Consciousness leader who died in police custody in 1977, complained,

> Colonialism is never satisfied with having the native in its grip but, by some strange logic, it must turn to his past and disfigure and distort it. Hence the history of the black man in this country is most disappointing to read. It is presented merely as a long succession of defeats. The Xhosas were thieves who went to war for stolen property; the Boers never provoked the Xhosas but merely went on 'punitive expeditions' to teach the thieves a lesson. . . . Not only is there no objectivity in the history taught us but there is frequently an appalling misrepresentation of facts. (44)

Historical accounts that repeatedly contrast "Christian" and "heathen," "civilized" and "uncivilized," or "Boer" and "barbarian" establish a hierarchical binary opposition, in which the term associated with the black represents a negative, lower order of existence. Such hierarchical oppositions, as deconstructionists have demonstrated, invariably oppress and silence the Other.[5]

As South African history effaced blacks either by omitting them or by referring to them as deviant, it simultaneously elevated and defined that strange mix of Dutch, German, French Huguenot, and other northern Europeans who settled at the Cape in the seventeenth century, gradually intermarried, and became known as Afrikaners. According to the dominant version of South African history, the Afrikaners are a heroic people who have endured over a century of wrong at the hands of the British while at the same time fighting off the threat of the country's indigenous peoples. Repressed and dominated by the British who began to rule the Cape at the beginning of the nineteenth century, thousands of Afrikaners banded together in small groups to make the Great Trek into the interior, seeking the freedom to establish their own way of life. Sheila Patterson explains, "In essentials, the modern legend of the Trek perpetuates the hostility, treacherousness and savagery of the African, the unwarranted interference and dog-in-the-manger attitude of the British authorities, and, as is only reasonable, the simplicity, piety, courage and endurance of the Trekker men, women and children" (22).

Perhaps one of the most important stories in Afrikaner history concerns a group of trekkers led by Piet Retief, who headed north across the Drakensberg mountains in 1838, traveling in rough ox-wagons together with their wives and families. After Retief was treacherously murdered by Dingane, the Zulu King, the Zulus attacked and slaughtered many of the Boers, including women and children. When the five hundred remaining Boers found themselves surrounded by fifteen thousand Zulu warriors, they swore an oath that if God would give them the victory, they would always celebrate that day as a sign of their covenant with him. The Battle of Blood River was fought on December 16, and the Boers won an overwhelming victory, killing three thousand Zulus. The annual Day of the Covenant is still celebrated in South Africa every December 16 with great reverence; it is "the key date in the Afrikaner calendar, the focal point of the whole of the sacred history" (Harrison 15). One alienated Afrikaner journalist told Richard John Neuhaus, "For the Afrikaner, Covenant Day is Christmas, Easter, and your Fourth of July rolled all into one" (16).

The Great Trek did not end the Boers' sense of beleaguerment, however. By the end of the century, the Afrikaners found themselves struggling to break free of British rule again. Encouraged by the discovery of gold and diamonds in the interior of South Africa, Britain again manifested its imperialistic drives. Leonard Thompson, one of the leading revisionist South African historians, explains that in the decade 1895–1905, "Joseph Chamberlain, British colonial secretary, and Alfred Milner, high commissioner in South Africa, in collaboration with British and Jewish mining capitalists, exploited the presence of the *Uitlander* (foreign) community on the Witwatersrand to provoke a war of conquest" (28). The Anglo-Boer War (1899–1902) resulted in a British victory and subsequent attempt to denationalize the Afrikaners and promote the English language and culture. Outraged by the inhumane treatment Boer women and children had received in British concentration camps and incensed by attempts to assimilate them to British ways, the Afrikaners stubbornly held out for their own cultural identity and gradually won political control away from the British during the early part of the twentieth century.

Defining themselves in opposition first to the British, and then to the people of various colors inhabiting the land with them, the Afrikaners developed a nationalistic mythology premised on their uniqueness. In an essay called "The White Tribe," Coetzee explains how the Afrikaners ironically possess a "tribal world-outlook," and consider themselves not so much individuals as members of a special social unit (490). This tribal mentality and the way that Afrikaners elevate themselves at the expense of others is epitomized in the rhetoric and philosophy of Afrikaner history. Taking the traditional Christian idea of history as a progression of events controlled and directed by God to establish his eternal kingdom, Afrikaners, in a distorted development of the Calvinistic notion of election, have come to believe that they are a Chosen People, specially selected by God to establish his kingdom in the modern world. The conjunction of their role as a Chosen People and the Otherness of the black pervades nationalistic rhetoric. Brink notes that in the Afrikaner's evolution toward nationhood, the negative aspect of his search for identity was "his attempts to assert himself—one of God's chosen people—against others" (*Writing* 18). We find an example of such an attempt in the words of an Afrikaner theologian: "Should the non-Whites then cruelly murder us and cut us into shreds, then that barbarism will triumph which was so wondrously checked at Blood River. But this, precisely, is for us a matter of faith: we believe that God in any case has made merciful provision for our people. But in any case, our choice remains that of rather perishing on the way of obedience than to melt into the non-Whites, to forfeit our identity and our sacred calling." (De Klerk 233). The Afrikaner mythology of the Chosen People promotes those hierarchical oppositions that resulted in oppression.

In this philosophy or typology of history, Afrikaner history corresponds to the history of Israel. In biblical hermeneutics certain events or characters of the Old Testament are read as "types" foreshadowing events and characters in the New Testament. In a similar way, Afrikaner typology interprets the Old Testament narrative as parallel to its own history. Afrikaners see themselves as a second Israel, specially chosen by God to fulfill his purposes. The Great Trek is another Exodus to the Promised Land. For example, in a characteristic speech made in 1871, President M. W. Pretorius called the original Voortrekkers "Fathers of Israel . . . who even as the Israelites had trekked from Egypt to escape Pharaoh's yoke, had themselves withdrawn from the yoke of the detestable English Government to found their own Government and administration."[6] The natives encountered during this journey are labeled "the sons of Ham" and must be subdued even as the tribes of Canaan were. The Day of the Covenant marks God's seal of approval for the Afrikaner tribe and its annihilation of the indigenous people. Such rhetoric uses only Old Testament biblical references and tends to overlook the Christological dimensions of the Bible.[7] Although historians differ as to when Afrikaners began employing this understanding of their own history, by the 1960s almost all Afrikaner nationalistic rhetoric employed typological references and was based upon the Chosen People theory.[8]

Silenced by the Afrikaner myth of history, blacks in the twentieth century began to realize that they needed to create their own myth and to tell their own story. In an essay called "Black Consciousness and the Quest for a True Humanity," Stephen Biko called for blacks to develop their own voice and construct their own myth: "a lot of attention has to be paid to our history if we as blacks want to aid each other in our coming into consciousness. We have to rewrite our history and produce in it the heroes that formed the core of our resistance to the white invaders" (44–45). Yet in the record of contemporary South Africa, the voice of the black continues to be systematically repressed and distorted.

The Voices That Are Dead

In his introduction to *"Race," Writing and Difference,* Henry Louis Gates, Jr., notes the Enlightenment interest in the question of whether or not Africans could produce works of literature. Without the ability to write, black people were seen as fundamentally different from Europeans: "Without writing, no *repeatable* sign of the workings of reason, of mind, could exist. Without memory or mind, no history could exist. Without history, no humanity, as defined consistently from Vico to Hegel, could exist" (11). Gates notes that throughout the nineteenth century, whites attempted to keep blacks illiterate (by instituting laws against teaching slaves to read and write, for example), while blacks attempted to gain the selfhood granted in "an authentic black voice" by writing (9–12). We find a tragically similar struggle repeated in contemporary South Africa.

A survey of events during the last four decades demonstrates that when black voices grow too loud, they have been promptly silenced. All kinds of black discourse have been greeted with banning, censorship, detaining, exile, or even death. After the Soweto uprising in 1976, Achmed Dangor wrote a poem expressing his frustration at the repeated silencing, entitled "The Voices That Are Dead":

> There is a silence
> upon the river tonight
> No great floods of song
> flow out into the darkness,
> our voices are dead.
> . . . . .
> Oh, my brothers—
> you too are dead,
> your voices rage barrenly

within the august halls
of the doomed,
but are not heard
by the cowherd who treads
his unknowing peace,
nor is it heard
in the ashen townships
where soon your memory
will flit unlovingly
from one darkness to the next.

In its closing lines Dangor's poem expresses the dogged persistence that characterizes the black attempt to speak: "from the ashes something stirs / new voices are being heard" (qtd. Barnett, *Vision* 40–41).

Numerous events in the 1960s extinguished the leading black political voices in South Africa. The nonviolent strikes, protests, and defiance campaigns of the African National Congress (ANC) and the Pan-Africanist Congress (PAC) were silenced when the government instituted a "new draconian legal system" and then employed it to outlaw both organizations and imprison their leaders (Davenport 293). Both the ANC and the PAC set up headquarters outside of South Africa, but the life sentences received by Nelson Mandela and Walter Sisulu removed two of the most viable black political voices from the public arena. Other leaders went into exile or were banned.

The unique South African practice of the "banning order" is the most twisted of the bureaucratic contortions used to silence black voices. It not only censors people's works, but also imposes a wall of silence around their lives. Banning was first instituted as part of the Suppression of Communism Act in 1950, which gave the Minister of Justice the right to limit the freedom of movement and speech of any person deemed to be furthering the goals of communism. Bannings do not require charges or proof, and are not subject to judicial appeal. Over the past forty years, the practice of banning has grown in complexity and application. Extended by the Sabotage Act in 1962, banning orders shut down all forms of human communication: a banned person may not write or publish anything, may not be quoted or cited in any publication, may not be with more than one person at a time other than family, may not communicate in any way with another banned person, is confined to a location (a magisterial district or even a particular address), and must report to the local police station once a week.[9] Such rules effectively silence both the spoken and the written voice. Nelson Mandela was not only imprisoned, he was banned. According to South African law, he could not be quoted in any publication and no one within the country could repeat his words, for three decades. Banning thus systematically deprives one of the ability to exercise one of the most fundamental human attributes: communication with others through language.

Black journalists and creative writers also have been silenced. What Lewis Nkosi terms "the fabulous fifties" of the black literary scene quickly became the silenced sixties as virtually all of the black writers who had flourished writing for literary magazines such as *Drum* or *The Classic* were suppressed. Their works censored or banned, most went into exile. The death blow occurred in 1966 with the Amendment to the Suppression of Communism Act, which put a blanket ban on all the work of most of the leading black writers. Forty-six authors were banned on April 1, 1966, including Ezekiel Mphahlele, Mazisi Kunene, Lewis Nkosi, and Bloke Modisane, who all left the country (Barnett, *Vision* 20). Other notable exiles include Dennis Brutus, Alex La Guma, Peter Abrahams, Nat Nakasa, Arthur Nortje, Bessie Head, Can Themba, and Alfred Hutchinson. The aberrant nature of the South African literary scene is suggested by the fact that in a recent volume featuring statements by South African writers about their art, an entire section was devoted to "South African Voices from Abroad." A contribution by Alex La Guma could not be used since he is banned in South Africa, and an essay on Dennis Brutus could not appear for a similar reason (*Momentum* xv).

Those who leave find themselves in a strange limbo. Unable to be read in one's own country yet obsessed with the need to address the social problems of South Africa, a banned writer becomes "a native of nowhere," as Nakasa describes it (*World* 169). Nkosi notes that few exiled black South African writers become "internationalists" like Naipaul or Nabokov; instead they continue to write about their home. Consequently, they end up speaking into a virtual vacuum:

> A writer needs his roots; he needs his people perhaps more than they need him in order that they should corroborate the vision he has of them, or at least, to dispute the statements he may make about their lives. These messages tossed away into the ocean thousands of miles away, written about a home one has not seen for fourteen years, begin to assume a strange unreality, if not features of a lunacy. Who reads the fiction, the poems and the biographies of South African writers in exile? Certainly Europeans, Americans, Indians and Chinese. Everyone but the people in whose name one is writing. (*Home* 93)

The silences imposed by exile can be costly. Some stop writing; others cannot live. Themba, Nakasa, and Nortje all committed suicide. Mphahlele found himself unable to write and felt increasingly guilty about his exile; in 1978 he returned to South Africa. His banning lifted soon after his return, Mphahlele now holds a senior research fellowship at the Institute of African Studies, located at the primarily white University of the Witwatersrand. He is able to teach only a few black students (Barnett, *Vision* 259–61).

Black writing appeared to undergo a small renaissance in the 1970s with the new emphases of the Black Consciousness movement and a turn to poetry and drama. Poetry was more closely aligned with traditional art forms, and, chanted at protest meetings and read at political funerals, was less subject to censorship. "Read-poetry" became popular, and drums, flutes, and other musical instruments were commonly used for poetry readings. Playwrights such as Matsemela Manaka, Maishe Maponya, and Zakes Mda developed plays in workshops that were presented in garages, community halls, and township churches.[10] Several independent presses also emerged in the 1970s, providing greater access for black readers, and making it unnecessary for black writers to look for British or American publishers. Renoster Press, Ravan Press, Ad. Donker, Bateleur Press, and David Philip all were committed to publishing black writers. Similarly, new journals such as *Staffrider, Wietie, The Bloody Horse,* and the *New Classic* published work written specifically for and by the people of the townships. Established writers, such as Coetzee and Gordimer, helped promote these new avenues for black expression. Gordimer serves as one of the trustees of Ravan Press, and Coetzee wrote a sympathetic description of *Staffrider* for *The African Book Publishing Record.*[11]

With the growth in black expression, however, came increased efforts to repress that renaissance. After Stephen Biko's death in police custody in 1977, the government instituted a nationwide crackdown. Seventeen Black Consciousness organizations were banned; forty-seven black leaders were arrested and held in detention. The World and the *Weekend World,* the two largest newspapers directed toward a black audience, were closed down.[12] As the protests in the townships grew and the South African security forces responded with greater violence throughout the 1980s, the voice of the black continued to be obliterated. The apparent relaxation of the censorship rules in 1980 was deceptive, as both Gordimer and Brink warned, for while both of these internationally respected writers had their work unbanned, black writers such as

Mtutuzeli Matshoba continued to be banned. The government censors had changed their standards only in order to clamp down more specifically on those works most likely to reach a black readership.[13]

Under the State of Emergency declared in 1985 by President P. W. Botha, the silence of black voices grew even more deafening. Gordimer relates in an article in *Africa Reports* published in 1987 that many South African booksellers—in Johannesburg, Cape Town, and smaller towns—had recently cleared their shelves of books published by the new controversial presses, fearing that the police might make trouble. She continues, "the aspect of the word which concerns writers so much, through imaginative literature, is completely withheld. There's no exposure at home where people live, as far as blacks are concerned. The schools have few or any books, the libraries are pitiful in the black areas" ("Censorship" 52). Similarly, Richard Rive describes the literary environment of 1988 in terms reminiscent of the sixties:

> The present then is a period of continuous political turmoil and confrontation. The situation has severely affected the quantity and quality of black writing, ironically at a time when publishers, almost all of whom are white, are more than ever prepared to publish their works, even if the subject matter is controversial. Staffrider and Classic, literary magazines catering predominantly to blacks, seem to have ceased publication. Some black writers have been jailed. Others have gone into exile. And many more are also busy attacking bastions and storming the castles.   ("Storming" 32–33)

In the recent turbulence, blacks are silenced not only by being detained or banned, but also by being written out of history once more, as a series of governmental rulings have restricted both the South African and the international press. In November 1985, the government banned TV, radio, and photographic coverage of black unrest in "emergency areas." In June 1986, these restrictions were extended to the coverage of violence in the print media. The restrictions were broadened again in December 1986, and finally, in January 1987, Police Commissioner J. Coetzee was authorized to ban publication of "any matter." That same month, South Africa ordered Alan Cowell, the Johannesburg bureau chief of the *New York Times,* to leave the country and refused a visa to his successor, effectively eliminating any first-hand coverage of South Africa by the American newspaper of record.

Consequently, while news of South Africa filled the broadcast and print media of the United States in 1985 and 1986, three years later one heard little about South Africa. Protests and repression continued; thousands of children were detained; moderate black leaders were arrested and detained. Yet the American media said little about these events, for their reporters could no longer cover events in the black townships, film crews were not allowed to tape any scenes of violence, and international reporters who reported too many negative things about the government soon found themselves expelled from the country. On March 1, 1987, Alex S. Jones reported in the *New York Times* that the sixteen-month campaign of steadily tightening press restrictions had succeeded in reducing the coverage of news from South Africa both in print and on television. An accompanying story by Neil A. Lewis noted that South Africa had significantly receded as a priority issue for the American government, according to officials. The curtain of silence had fallen effectively.[14]

Kept from self-expression by the silencing of black leaders and writers, deleted from current history by censorship, South African blacks were further objectified by the continued propaganda efforts of the official regime throughout the 1980s. The old stereotype of the inability of the black to develop independent political thinking was continued in the *ad hominem* charge of communist leanings. Any person who disagreed with governmental policy and the institution of apartheid was immediately branded a communist. In 1950 the South African Parliament enacted the Suppression of Communism Act, which, in addition to banning the Communist Party, also widened the definition of Communism to apply to any doctrine or party "which aims at bringing about any political, industrial, social or economic change . . . by the promotion of disturbance or disorder, by unlawful acts or omissions" or which "aims at the encouragement of feelings of hostility between the European and non-European races of the Union of South Africa" (Dugard 87–88). Thus, any group conducting a passive resistance campaign against the apartheid system, such as encouraging the burning of passbooks, was subject to the charges of promoting communism.

Alan Paton writes of the effects: "Many of my friends were banned from public life under this Act, although they were in fact opposed to communism. They were banned for one reason and one only, and that was because they were opposed to apartheid, a considerable number of them on moral and religious grounds" (*Journey* 38). Similarly, while communist countries have been one source of support among many for black resistance movements, the government frequently characterized all apartheid opponents as mere tools of international communism. For example, the *South Africa 1983* yearbook alleges that communism "manifested itself, *inter alia,* in movements launched by the African National Congress (ANC)" (50). The yearbook claims that the protests of the sixties were "instigated by communist leaders" (51), and that the continued agitation against apartheid conducted by a variety of black organizations is part of a communist plot: "The Government also realises that much of the animosity professed by its Black neighbours is caused by their distorted or deficient conception of the fundamental principles underlying the policy of multinational development, and that the prevailing misunderstanding is aggravated by communist countries whose tactics are to fish in troubled waters" (310).

In addition, the control exercised by the South African regime over international discourse promoted a picture of Africans as bloodthirsty, quarrelsome, and fragmented. The few news stories made available by official police statements since the tightening of press restrictions in 1987 often featured black-on-black violence or dissension. The South African government was not reluctant to allow reporters to chronicle the "necklacing" of suspected black informers in the townships, the violent activities of the Zulu youth brigade called the Inkatha, or the charges that Winnie Mandela's bodyguards killed a young black boy. The political labels and lopsided news coverage perpetuated a version of Otherness that has characterized white discourse since the days of the earliest European explorations of Africa. What Abdul R. JanMohamed terms "the fixation on and fetishization of native savagery and evil" continued to be propagated in official South African discursive practices (82).

The Power of Language

Afrikaner myths of history and elaborate systems of social control have silenced blacks and cast them in the role of Others. These myths and systems compose the cultural discourses that complement the material practice of the apartheid system. As such, they suggest the way that language and authority have been employed in South Africa to enforce injustice and oppression. Mythologies and discourse depend on language for their existence and take their shape in language, but also symbiotically affect and mold the very language that affects and molds them. Language exercises power in this way in any cultural and historical situation. In South Africa, however, the institution of language plays an even more particular role in the discourse of power. Language has been a crucial means of creating an identity and a tool of oppression.

For many different groups in South Africa, language has played an important role in the creation (and rejection) of ethnic identity. As the descendants of the original settlers of the Cape began identifying themselves as "Afrikaners," distinct from both the indigenous peoples and the politically dominant British, one of the key aspects of their emerging identity was their unique language. Between the end of the seventeenth century and the British occupation of the Cape in 1806, Afrikaans evolved from the Dutch language as Frisians, Nederlanders, Germans, and others employed a simplified form of Dutch in order to communicate, and as African and Malay slaves added their own words and inflections. In the 1870s, with the First Language Movement, Afrikaans became established as a written language and, along with skin color and religious affiliation, became an integral part of what it meant to be an Afrikaner.[15] During this period, S. J. du Toit wrote the first uniform Afrikaans grammar as well as the first nationalist history in Afrikaans, *Di geskiedenis van ons land in di taal van ons volk* (*The History of Our Land in the Language of Our People,* 1877). Du Toit's title reveals the important juncture between the Afrikaner myth of history and the unique language of Afrikaans.

By the 1890s the First Language Movement had lost its drive, and it appeared that High Dutch and English would become the primary written languages of South Africa. However, the events of the Anglo-Boer War and the subsequent attempt by Sir Alfred Milner, the British High Commissioner, to anglicize South Africa prompted the renewal of interest in Afrikaans. Smarting from military defeat and outraged over the high number of deaths that occurred in the British detention camps, Afrikaners began asserting their own identity and their own language. Irving Hexham writes: "Maintaining language was essential to preserve national identity. The future depended upon which language and culture would triumph in South Africa. . . . The idea that Afrikaans gave them their unique identity was an idea with far reaching consequences. Not only did Afrikaans distinguish Afrikaners from the English and the Dutch, it also made them a separate race" (*Irony* 133–34). The publication of the Afrikaans war poetry of J. D. du Toit (known as Totius); the establishment of the South African Academy for Language, Literature and the Arts (*Suid-Afrikaanse Akademie Vir Wetenskap en Kuns*); and the inaugural issue of the popular magazine *Die Brandwag* all contributed to the new flourishing of Afrikaans in the early twentieth century. Increasingly used in schools and churches, Afrikaans was declared one of the official languages of the Union of South Africa in 1925. The renewal of Afrikaans poetry in the work of the writers of the thirties (the "Dertigers") signalled to many white South Africans that they had fully achieved a national identity.

Given the mythical importance attached to the development of the Afrikaans language, it is not surprising to find that language has become an important issue of contention in discussions about the identity of black South Africans. Most feel a violent antipathy toward the language of the oppressor; in fact, the spark that set off the Soweto explosion in 1976 was a decree from the Department of Bantu Education that all black schools had to teach courses in Afrikaans instead of English.[16] Although some blacks have argued that English is also the language of the oppressor and that Africans should write in Bantu languages, most blacks today view English as the language of choice. Their reasons, like those guiding the status of Afrikaans, are political: English provides a medium in which the various ethnic groups can achieve a common identity, and it allows more effective communication with the international world. Nat Nakasa explains, "In their joint use of English, Africans reach with greater ease the various levels of common ground which are of importance in the process of eliminating tribal division with all its unwelcome consequences. To the African, English has become a symbol of success, the vehicle of his painful protest against social injustice and spiritual domination by those who rule him" (*World* 187).

The Afrikaans language not only is an embodiment of the Afrikaner nationalistic identity, but also is systematically used as a tool for oppression. By manipulating definitions and the meanings of words, governmental discourse has employed language to veil and distort many of its activities. In South Africa today, the government regularly practices a kind of "doublespeak" in which words mean something other than their literal definitions. Take, for example, the official names of some of the more important Acts of Parliament since the beginning of the Nationalist regime (which we will look at in their English translations). In 1950, the Immorality Act was passed, in which all interracial sexual relations, including those within marriage, were forbidden. The Abolition of Passes and Coordination of Documents Act, passed in 1952, rather than abolishing passes actually made them mandatory for more people. It required all Africans, including women for the first time, as well as those exempted under earlier pass laws, to carry "reference books" containing their photograph, birth information, and records of employment and encounters with the police. The Reservation of Separate Amenities didn't "reserve" places for blacks; it segregated movie houses, beaches, swimming pools, and post offices. The Extension of the University Education Act, rather than extending the University, ejected most blacks from the regular University of South Africa and required them to attend a newly established "tribal college" to be educated in a Bantu language.

Other terms of apartheid are equally corrupted. We have already seen how the official rhetoric has brandished the word "communist" in order to malign those seeking racial justice, regardless of their political beliefs. Perhaps the most meaningless word in official rhetoric is "homeland." Many blacks may never have seen the dry, barren, virtually uninhabitable regions of the country now designated as their homelands. No historical evidence supports the claim that the homelands correspond to the areas historically occupied by each black "nation."[17] Most urban blacks despise the homelands, feeling, as Mark Mathabane told his father during his first visit to his tribal reserve, "I'd rather die than live here" (90). The term "homeland," along with "separate development," "relocation," and "Bantu education," can no longer be employed meaningfully. Kenneth Parker notes "the curious power" that apartheid has to change the meaning of other words: "In the language of apartheid, political protest is a 'riot', humans are 'located' and the maintenance of the system is justified as the 'restoration of law and order'" (1–2). Controlled by the authority of the state, many words have become implicated in the corruptions of apartheid.

Language can be affected by history, as George Steiner points out about German:

> Use a language to conceive, organize, and justify Belsen; use it to make out specifications for gas ovens; use it to dehumanize man during twelve years of calculated bestiality. Something will happen to it. . . . Something of the lies and sadism will settle in the marrow of the language. Imperceptibly at first, like the poisons of radiation sifting silently into the bone. But the cancer will begin, and the deep-set destruction. The language will no longer grow and freshen. It will no longer perform, quite as well as it used to, its two principal functions: the conveyance of humane order which we call law, and the communication of the quick of the human spirit which we call grace. (124)

A similar decay has taken place in South Africa. With Afrikaans linked so thoroughly to a racist agenda and with official rhetoric employed so methodically to camouflage oppression, language in South Africa has become impoverished and inept. Nkosi claims, "South Africans are, as a nation, a speechless people whose fear of the spoken and the written word has created a horrible fatuity in their lives, both private and public" (*Home* 126). South Africans, Nkosi explains, are often at a loss for words because their language is not inhabited or enlarged. Such a loss of language reflects a loss of self, for despite the Afrikaner attempt to create an identity by means of marginalizing others, the institutions of marginalization dehumanize them as well.

Writing in South Africa

The myth of history, the methods of silencing black voices, and the corruption of language confront the South African writer with numerous challenges. The literary tradition is hemmed in on all sides by the social and discursive practices of apartheid. Both black and white authors repeatedly express a sense of intellectual claustrophobia. T. T. Moyana argues that a significant problem for a creative writer in South Africa is the impoverishment of the culture because of apartheid. Unlike Solzhenitsyn, South African writers have not found oppression creatively liberating: "where the oppressor has not taken away everything; in a situation where a Gordimer is permitted to operate in the half-light of spurious freedom, or in a situation where the black writer is permitted to operate piecemeal in occasional moments of repose from the grinding tortures of the law, the human spirit does indeed wither, the creative imagination drying with it" (94). Similarly, Brink states: "the loss of creativity, the loss of larger *dimensions* in much of this writing—directly attributable to apartheid—is one of the main arguments against the deliberate separation of cultures which leads, not to development, but to stagnation." The evidence of such stagnation is the narrowness of South African literature: "In most Afrikaans writing there is an irksome awareness of 'them' and 'us', a denial of the humanity of the Other; in much English writing the 'cause' is so important as to obscure an identification with living individuals" (*Writing* 78).

The claustrophobia grows even more intense and the challenges more difficult for the writer who is an Afrikaner. Besides the burden of belonging to the oppressing group, the Afrikaner writer also works in a tradition long associated with the ideology of apartheid. The birth of Afrikaans literature in the early twentieth century was closely related to the birth of Afrikaner nationalism. Commemorating the national suffering that took place during the Anglo-Boer War, the poetry of Jan

Celliers and Totius simultaneously bound Afrikaners together into a persecuted people and began the Afrikaner literary tradition. The widely read poetry of Totius in particular demonstrates a nationalistic and typological rhetoric. In *Potgieter's Trek*, Totius chronicles the trials of the Voortrekkers by casting the indigenous people into the role of Other:

> But see! the world becomes wilder;
>   the fierce vermin worsen,
> stark naked black hordes,
>   following tyrants.
> How the handful of trekkers suffer,
>   the freedom seekers, creators of a People.
> Just like another Israel,
>   by enemies surrounded, lost in the veld,
> but for another Canaan elected,
>   led forward by God's plan.[18]

Afrikaner literature encouraged the nationalistic drive even as the newly developing nationalistic spirit provided material for the development of the new literary tradition. With their own language and their own literature, Afrikaners became even more convinced of their status as a unique ethnic unit, a nation.

The evolution of the Afrikaans novel in the thirties and forties took place within this developing nationalism and also within a growing Afrikaner nostalgia for the simple life on the farm. As South Africa was becoming an industrial and urban country, Afrikaans fiction frequently depicted the recent rural past of most Boers. The novels of Jochem van Bruggen (1881–1957), M. E. Rothmann (1875–1975), and C. M. van den Heever (1902–1957) idealized pastoral life and suggested the evils of urbanization. Coetzee explains that the Afrikaans novel "is haunted, even into our day, by the idea of the *plaas (farm)*, the *plaas* that stands somewhere in the not too distant past of every Afrikaner." The implication of this dominant idea is that "the novel thus presents an 'official' view of South Africa as a settled land, a land whose soil belongs to its farmers and title-holders, a land that is someone's property. The profound feel for the land for which the *aardsheid* [earthiness] of the Afrikaans language equips the Afrikaans novel goes hand in hand with a proprietorial attitude towards the earth; and this proprietorial attitude has made of the black man a temporary sojourner, a displaced person, not only in the white man's laws but in the white man's imaginative life" ("The Great South African Novel" 79). Traditional Afrikaans fiction participates in the Afrikaner myth of history and perpetuates the oppressive depiction of blacks.

Partly because of their contributions to the formation of the national identity, Afrikaner authors and their work hold a special place in South African society. Parker explains some of the consequences: "To this day the literary intellectual within the Afrikaner group is invested by fellow Afrikaners with great respect, and it is against this background that those Afrikaans writers who in recent years have presumed to question the received tribal myth have been severely castigated" (5). One such author is André Brink, who elaborates on the position of the Afrikaans writer: "Because of the very nature of his situation—the fact that, through history, culture and the colour of his skin he is linked, like it or not, to the power Establishment, nothing he says or writes takes place in a vacuum: it always elicits a *response*." The possible responses vary: the authorities will probably overreact, younger Afrikaners may respond with enthusiasm, and black South Africans may find hope. Brink concludes, "Even more important: a book written by an Afrikaner dissident draws significant echoes from the silent world of the oppressed" (*Writing* 151).

The question of how one should write in the context of South Africa becomes even more problematic when we consider the state of discourse in South Africa and the particular position of the Afrikaner writer. How can a white, privileged author such as Coetzee refer to South African history with any credibility, or depict blacks without contributing to their marginalization? Is it possible to draw echoes from the silent world of the oppressed when blacks have consistently become Other by the very fact and tradition of representation? If the oppressed are unable to speak, how can we hear their silences? And how can an author speak for them without becoming an oppressor in that act? Finally, how can a writer employ language to convey law and grace, as Steiner puts it, given what has happened to language in South Africa? Adam Small, a South African poet officially classified as Coloured, whose native tongue is Afrikaans, admits, "The (white) Afrikaans writers of today . . . have to live with this cultural feeling of guilt, that the language in which they write is not 'innocent of the horrors' of apartheid" (264). Coetzee himself warns that the language in which an author writes sometimes "writes" the author, for example, when the author writes "in stereotyped forms and genres and characterological systems and narrative orderings, where the machine runs the operator" ("Note on Writing" 12–13).

Recent South African writers who have opposed the official regime have tended to follow one of two routes.[19] Some have written realistic novels in the liberal tradition centering on personal identity and relationships. Novelists such as Alan Paton, André Brink, and Jack Cope focus on the need for personal awareness and reconciliation. Since the 1960s, others—such as Alex La Guma, Harry Bloom, and Mtutuzeli Matshoba—have turned from the individual to consider issues of social struggle and the state's response. Both routes are types of realism, which seems to be the dominant genre of South African fiction.[20] But Coetzee has chosen a different path. In an interview in 1978 he comments, "The novel of character belongs to a certain stage in the history of the middle class. It is quite dead now. As for the 'typical' characters that a theorist like Lukács advocates, I would like to think that the novel today is after a bigger game than that" (Coetzee, "Speaking" 24). Coetzee's "game" is neither individual characters nor the power relationships of the state, but rather language and communication. His work concerns the difficulties of writing fiction, the impasses of language and relationships, the predicament of the authority of the author in an oppressive society.

A brief overview of the six novels published by Coetzee to date suggests the remarkably different genre in which he is working. Flatly rejecting both liberal and socialist realism, Coetzee opts for a non-realistic, self-referential fiction that constantly highlights its own unreliability. Usually employing a first-person narrator and narrated in the present tense, Coetzee's works depict situations of oppression along with the discourse that simultaneously accompanies, enables, and exposes that oppression. In his novels, Coetzee demonstrates a growing concern both with the question of how, as a white South African writer, he can depict the Other and with the imminent apocalyptic destruction of his country.

Dusklands (1974) is made up of two novellas about mythmakers: *The Vietnam Project* is the story of Eugene Dawn, a propagandist for the United States government attempting to convince the Vietcong to accept colonization; *The Narrative of Jacobus Coetzee* purports to be the travel narrative of an eighteenth-century South African explorer who encounters the savagery of the Hottentots during a journey into the interior. Coetzee's second novel, *In the Heart of the Country* (1977), is the meditation of a crazed young woman living on a remote farm in South Africa, who is completely dominated by her overbearing father and is searching for a linguistic way to overcome the patterns of oppression. *Waiting for the Barbarians* (1980) contains the reflections of the administrator of a frontier town who wrestles with his government's use of torture and military aggression toward a nomadic people known only as the Barbarians. With its vague setting and loose allegorical resonances, *Waiting for the Barbarians* is much more distant from the historical world than Coetzee's first two books.

Life & Times of Michael K (1983) distances itself in yet another way; although it takes place in South Africa, it is set in an unspecified future of civil war and chaos. This novel also is Coetzee's first attempt to center his narrative in a non-white character: it chronicles the experiences and thoughts of an urban coloured man who sets out to bring his ill mother back to her rural home. In *Foe* (1986) Coetzee turns to the colonial literary tradition in his retelling of the story of Robinson Crusoe, from the point of view of the woman who lived with Crusoe on the island but was written out of Daniel Defoe's account. *Age of Iron* (1990) returns to South Africa. Set in 1986 during the height of township violence and government repression, Coetzee's sixth novel contains the final confession of an elderly woman dying of cancer as her country's future turns to ashes.

Coetzee's novels clearly are not realistic; they neither reflect the social world as it appears to most readers nor give the reader the illusion of actual and ordinary experience. His fictional mode is difficult to label. His novels have been called modernist, postmodernist, fabulation, and metaphysical. But regardless of what we label his choice of genre, Coetzee's explorations of the relationships of language, authority, and history closely align him with postmodern criticism and discourse. Coetzee is fully aware that his fictional mode is quite unusual for a South African writer, and he claims that he doesn't see any South African writers as his forebears. Instead, he lists Beckett, Nabokov, Pound, Rilke, Herbert, Neruda, and Barthes as influences.[21] However, influences can be both positive and negative, and Coetzee's awareness of the traditions of South African writing and his concern with how discourse informs thought suggest that South African writing might actually influence his work more than he admits. In fact, we can see his first two novels as deliberate revisions of two of the most common South African genres: the travel narrative and the farm novel. Furthermore, while granting that his style is influenced by international modernism, we can also note the particular significance that kind of fiction has in the South African context.

Coetzee's rejection of realism can be seen as a political and ethical act. In moving beyond the conventions of the traditional novel and highlighting "the sheer act of telling or confabulating" (Christie et al. 162), he explores the impact of language and history on the act of telling. Thematically, his works often examine how Others have been kept from speaking; technically, his narrative strategies give silenced voices life, tell an alternative story of South Africa. Structurally, Coetzee's novels display an unusual openness. Rejecting the authoritative voice of either the omniscient author or the fully constructed narrator, his works are dialogical, in Bakhtin's terms, allowing a variety of voices to speak. Wayne C. Booth points out that the value of the dialogical is related to the rhetorical and political situation of the work and the reader; "for Mikhail Bakhtin, writing in the Soviet Union, it could seem self-evident that any genre that tends to combat single-voicedness is superior to those 'monophonic' works that can be used to reinforce convention and auto-cratic power" (70). Similarly, for J. M. Coetzee, writing in South Africa, the dialogic has a particular ethical import. Coetzee's rejection of realism and embrace of a self-referential and open text is a rejection of the oppressive discourse, manipulative myths, and corrupt language of South Africa. As Robert J. Green notes about a similar movement away from realism in the drama of Athol Fugard, "to the artist working in a society which defiles semantics, which rewrites, for instance, the rich associative power of the word 'homeland', the cybernetics of realism, a mode rooted in historical and verbal confidence, must appear problematic" (171). Coetzee's narrative technique both undermines the absolute authority associated with the author and affirms the more ambiguous and tentative authority embodied in storytelling, in non-linear discourse, in dialogic voices, and in gaps. His affirmation of what Alice A. Jardine would characterize as "modern" discourse and of what others might term *l'écriture féminine* is his answer to the oppression that prevails in his society.

Besides their postmodern concern for fictionality and language, Coetzee's novels also speak allegorically of the various manifestations of oppression in South Africa. As modern allegorical fables, his works participate in a tradition of dissent that has increasingly characterized contemporary writing. Lois Parkinson Zamora, in a most perceptive analysis of Coetzee's narrative strategies entitled "Allegories of Power in the Fiction of J. M. Coetzee," traces the tradition of allegory from its conservative and fixed mode in medieval and Renaissance writing to its modern manifestation as a radical critique of corrupt political and social orders. Zamora examines Coetzee's first four novels as allegories of the

Hegelian dialectic in which power shifts from the master to the servant. But she also notes Coetzee's tendency, particularly in *Waiting for the Barbarians* and *In the Heart of the Country,* to emphasize the indeterminacy and uncertainty of language and interpretation: "Coetzee repeatedly deconstructs the referential certainty upon which allegory has always stood. . . . He uses the forms of allegory to undo the traditional referentiality of allegory, undermining and ultimately dismissing interpretive determinacy within his own allegorical tale" (7). Coetzee thus takes a form which traditionally operates on a one-to-one correspondence and relies on fixed meanings and employs it in a far more allusive and suggestive way. Zamora associates his strategy with that of other Latin American and Eastern European writers in the tradition of dissent: "It is another irony that in a symbolic form abstracted from specific time and place, these writers have found an effective medium for their very specific protests against the simplifications of absolute power" (13).

Coetzee's postmodern allegories are not nihilistic, however, as some have suggested.[22] In his subversion of accepted modes of thought and experience, Coetzee does not suggest that existence (or fiction) is utterly meaningless, an abyss or a void. While he reveals that language is an uncertain medium, he does not deny that the use of language involves responsibility. And while he dramatically depicts the nightmare of the constraints of history, he does not rule out the possibility of change or transcendence. Coetzee continually exposes the way that language works in the world, the way that power and misused authority can co-opt language. His allegories vividly suggest the various ways that language and discourse in South Africa have been socially and historically constructed. The word can entrap, but it can also free. Coetzee's novels ultimately affirm the value of speaking and storytelling, as long as such discourse is done in a self-conscious and non-authoritative way. In his comments on the influences of modernist discourse, Coetzee is careful to hold on to the notion of storytelling as an essential part of the novel: "I certainly believe that narrative and story-telling are fundamental to the novel, and therefore that all attempts to eradicate story-telling from the novel are doomed—which is not to say that the efforts that have been made to write novels without stories—and here I think particularly of the Nouveau Roman—are futile and worthless, but I would regard these as philosophical experiments rather than novels . . . experiments from which we finally have to retreat, and if we are ever going to go back to the novel, go back to a story-telling enriched perhaps by the experiments of the writers I referred to" ("Interview" 5–6). That ability to tell stories, stories that contain unheard voices and work on an emotional and evocative level, provides one way to battle the monophonic and autocratic discourses of history. In a world with few models of non-oppressive discourse, Coetzee struggles to reclaim language and storytelling for responsible action.

Seen in the South African context, Coetzee's position as a writer is precarious. As Stephen Watson notes, "The one fact most important for an understanding of the apparent anomalies in his work is that he is not only a colonizer who is an intellectual, but a colonizer who does not *want* to be a colonizer" (377). Watson's provocative essay places Coetzee's works in the context of the problematic standing of "the Western-oriented English intelligentsia in South Africa," who have been deprived of a historically meaningful role (380). What Watson does not emphasize, but might, is the even more problematic status of Afrikaner writers, who, regardless of whether they write in English or Afrikaans, are informed by a significantly different set of cultural, social, and historical circumstances and roles. The person of British background who opposes the regime, such as Gordimer, is seen as a typical minority voice; Afrikaners who differ with it are aberrations, or worse, traitors to their own identity.

Coetzee says that he writes in English because, linguistically, Afrikaans is limited and "frankly dull." English has "a historical layer in the language that enables you to work with historical contrasts and oppositions in prose"; it also has a genetic diversity that facilitates contrasts in the etymological basis of words and thus allows macaronic effects not possible in Afrikaans ("Interview" 2). Coetzee wants a language that he can play with, that facilitates multiple meanings and evokes a diversity of meaning. What remains unspoken but nonetheless present in his discussion of his linguistic medium is the oppressive use to which the monologic Afrikaans has been put.

Coetzee's decision to write in English has meant that his works are more readily accessible to an international readership. Within South Africa, Coetzee's novels have a limited readership. Crapanzano states that among the Afrikaner farmers with whom he spoke, Brink and Breytenbach are condemned as apostates but Coetzee's work is simply ignored (95). Few black South Africans would have physical access to his novels. Those who do read Coetzee in South Africa are the intellectuals. But over the course of his career Coetzee has gradually found himself writing for an international audience. *Dusklands* originally appeared only in South Africa, issued by Ravan Press in 1974. But because South African publishers lack adequate distribution systems Coetzee began what has become his usual practice of publishing first in Great Britain and then in South Africa (Géniès 60). *In the Heart of the Country* was published in London and New York in 1977 and then came out from Ravan Press in 1978. Coetzee's subsequent novels were published by Secker and Warburg in London and Viking Penguin and Random House in the United States. French translations of *In the Heart of the Country (Au coeur de cepays)* and *Waiting for the Barbarians (En attendant les barbares)* have been published by Nadeau-Papyrus. *Life & Times of Michael K (Michael K, sa vie, son temps)* and *Dusklands (Terres de crépuscule)* were published by Seuil. This practice, born out of the restrictions of South African life, has given Coetzee his most enthusiastic and sizable audience. Particularly after the publication of *Waiting for the Barbarians* in 1980, Coetzee achieved a new status in the Anglo-American and French literary worlds. Although he has repeatedly denied writing with a deliberate sense of audience, characterizing himself as his ideal reader, his audience primarily consists of South African academics and well-educated Western readers concerned about oppression and injustice.[23]

Coetzee's novels dramatize for the international community the reality of South Africa and elaborate the way poststructuralist arguments about the power of discourse work in a particular historical situation. A chronological examination of the novels and Coetzee's career reveals how each work grows out of and takes its place in a specific historical and social context. Drawing on many common South African discourses and rhetorics, Coetzee's stories both expose the oppression at the heart of different uses of language as well as provide a re-vision of the reality of South Africa, a new method of apprehension and understanding. Ultimately, these stories are answers to the misuse of history, language, and authority that prevails in South African society. Coetzee's storytelling voice articulates the difficulties of articulation and provides us with a sense of the diversity belying the authoritarian tones of official South African discourse.

· 3 ·

The Master Myth of History:
Dusklands

In September 1965, J. M. Coetzee landed in New York on board a former Italian troop ship carrying foreign students arriving to study in the United States. He was twenty-five years old. Having recently left his position as a systems programmer in Bracknell, England, he was on his way to the University of Texas, Austin, to pursue graduate studies in English, courtesy of a Fulbright fellowship. He found an economically booming country clothed in miniskirts and Nehru jackets, impressed with the new technology of color television, and full of national faith in continued American prosperity and world leadership. President Johnson was proclaiming his vision of a Great Society, and the passage of the Civil Rights Act of 1964 suggested that racism might be abolished through legislation. But underlying this optimism lay the reality of the burgeoning involvement in Vietnam, which the American public was just beginning to recognize. Coetzee remained in the United States until 1971, first as a graduate student and later as an assistant professor of English at the State University of New York at Buffalo, witnessing the social and political upheavals of the late 1960s that transformed the nation.

The year that Coetzee arrived was a critical one in the history of the Vietnam War. American military involvement in Vietnam was increasing dramatically as President Johnson and the military began acting on the Gulf of Tonkin resolution passed in 1964. "The secret war turned into an open war in early 1965," Murrey Marder wrote in the *Washington Post* (25). By the fall of 1965, the United States had 148,300 troops in Vietnam and the first mass demonstrations against the war had begun. Both military involvement and civilian protest continued to escalate, reaching their height during 1967–1969. The relatively new medium of television, which expanded its evening news broadcasts from fifteen minutes to half an hour in 1963, displayed memorable coverage of both the war and the protest. Vietnam was the first televised war, and many families watched it daily in living color as they ate their dinner, prompting the *New Yorker* writer Michael Arlen to christen it "The Living Room War" (Stern 8).

The vivid visual images and heated public discourse on Vietnam surrounded Coetzee at the same time he was exploring the world of literary criticism and linguistics as a graduate student. In his autobiographical account of this period, "How I Learned About America—and Africa—in Texas," he tells of his courses in bibliography and Old English, his research into Beckett, and his seminar paper on the morphology of Nama, Malay, and Dutch. His research into the latter prompted him to read extensively in a popular seventeeth- and eighteenth-century form: the travel narrative.[1] In these narratives he found reports on the territory of South West Africa by explorers, accounts of punitive expeditions against the indigenous people, dissertations on the physical anthropology of the natives, makeshift grammars written by missionaries, and word lists compiled by sailors. He even found one narrative written by a distant ancestor, Jacobus Coetse. This research gave Coetzee a new respect for the coherence and complexity of so-called primitive languages, but it also caused him to think more seriously about the phenomenon and significance of "white writing," through which South Africa has been perceived and thought about by Europeans.[2]

These simultaneous encounters with the two worlds of America and Africa form the context for Coetzee's first book, *Dusklands,* which was drafted while he was in the United States.[3] The book opens with *The Vietnam Project,* the first-person narrative of the mental disintegration of Eugene Dawn, a minor functionary in a RAND-like corporation preparing propaganda for use in Vietnam. The second half contains *The Narrative of Jacobus Coetzee,* the first-person account of a South African explorer who travels into the interior in 1760 on an elephant hunting expedition, and who later returns to revenge himself on the servants and natives he believes have humiliated him. Together, the two stories explore the common psychology of colonialism and oppression, the dark mentality that informs the United States' involvement in Vietnam and the Dutch colonization of southern Africa.[4] With linguistic playfulness, the two narratives suggest that "the master myth of history"—the central story providing coherence to world events—is the myth of masters, the story of domination and oppression.[5] An equally important aspect of both novellas, though, is their emphasis on discourse, on the writing of the master myth of colonialism. "The myths of a tribe are the fictions it coins to maintain its powers," Eugene Dawn claims (24). Coetzee's first novel not only exposes some of those myths but also reflects on the mythmaking process.

The Discourse of Colonialism

Twentieth-century Vietnam War coverage and eighteenth-century South African travel narrative embody two ways that the master myth of history has been propagated. Vietnam represented the most important social and political context in which Coetzee found himself during his early years as a writer. He says that during "a long, crucial period of my life . . . the major emotional involvement, from a political point of view, was not with the South African situation but with the war in Viet Nam" (Coetzee, "Speaking" 23). In an interview conducted in South Africa soon after his first novel was published, Coetzee particularly notes the impact that the media coverage of the war had on him during his sojourn in America. The war "was sold" to the American public, and Coetzee believes "that all the talk about the war searing consciences was itself part of the sell" (Temple 3). The televised reports of the war may have had a special impact on Coetzee as a South African, for there was no television available in his native country until 1976. In his essay about his experiences in America, Coetzee remarks about the constant media focus on Vietnam: "Complicity was not the problem . . . the problem was with knowing what was being done. It was not obvious where one went to escape knowledge" ("How I Learned" 9). Coetzee's major concern, as he expresses it in these comments, was with the effects of the media coverage, how the discourse was "writing" Americans.

What knowledge was the American public absorbing? One important aspect was the exciting technological capability of the American war machine. Coetzee says, "I think particularly of the effect televised air strikes had on the small screen. The violence erupted at you, the massiveness of thousands of tons of high explosives dropped" (Temple 3). The epigraph to *The Vietnam Project* quotes Herman Kahn, one of the Pentagon's key defense strategy advisors and advocate of the "megadeath" concept, describing "films of fighter-bomber pilots visibly exhilarated by successful napalm bombing runs on Viet-Cong targets." Daniel C. Hallin, who has conducted an extensive study of media coverage of Vietnam, estimates that more than half of the television coverage from 1965 to 1967 focused on such day-to-day military operations (114). Stories about bombing raids emphasized the pilots' skill and technological achievements: "The pilots certainly *were* skillful, and one of the things that made them so appealing as television characters was that they fit one of the great hero-images of modern American culture: they were *professionals* who had mastered technology and could make it perform as they wanted" (137). In the fiction of Vietnam, the pilot played the role of hero.

Coetzee feared the psychological effects of such coverage, commenting that "once you have—and once a whole nation has—the technological capacity for destruction that the Americans have, that destructive ability becomes everyone's psychic possession." He continues, "I think people were given the kind of opportunity they've never been given before to participate by identification with massive acts of violence. . . . The war was an avenue through which a lot of pent-up aggression, sadism, let itself out, not only on battlefields but in people's livingrooms" (Temple 3). The media coverage enabled a kind of vicarious oppression as the American public watched their television screens. The discourse of Vietnam both enabled and embodied oppression. Early in his career, we find Coetzee doubting the efficacy of certain kinds of discourse and fearing that vivid realism may write the viewer—may by its very existence facilitate more aggression.

The media also propagated other myths, other ways of understanding the meaning of Vietnam. Hallin states that the prevailing notion of the nation as a family writ large prompted television stories that celebrated "the unity of the National Family" (125). Stories featured Americans in action rather than the country or people of Vietnam. Television coverage was governed by some common assumptions about the value of war: it is a national endeavor; war is an American tradition harking back to frontier days; war is manly, giving men the chance to show their toughness and professionalism; winning is what counts; war is rational (142–47). Finally, the media consistently depicted the enemy as Other: "television coverage of Vietnam dehumanized the enemy, drained him of all recognizable emotions and motives and thus banished him not only from the political sphere, but from human society itself. The North Vietnamese and Vietcong were 'fanatical,' 'suicidal,' 'savage,' 'half-crazed,'" Hallin writes, quoting from actual broadcasts (158).

Despite or perhaps because of this mythmaking, American public opinion concerning the war constantly shifted as the country experienced what Laurence Stern terms "national schizophrenia" (6). The national

schizophrenia, which lingers to this day, represents part of the psychological cost of this particular myth of masters. When American troops
were first deployed in Vietnam in large numbers in 1965, there was
widespread support for the war. But by October 1967, most Americans
believed the United States had made a mistake in becoming involved in
Vietnam. Public support of the war increased temporarily with the Tet
Offensive, but by the end of March 1968, growing numbers of people
felt that the United States was wrong to have entered the war.[6] Albert
Cantril, of the Institute for International Social Research, believes that
the public opposed the war on practical grounds when faced with the
financial cost, casualties, and lack of military success, but was still sus-
ceptible to "the strong appeals from the White House for support in the
name of patriotic anti-Communism" (Stern 6). Material realities con-
flicted with ideological justifications. A similar kind of schizophrenia is
delineated in the epigraph from Kahn: the audiences who see the films
react with "horror and disgust" to the pilots' jubilation, although Kahn
finds it "unreasonable to expect the U.S. Government to obtain pilots
who are so appalled by the damage they may be doing that they cannot
carry out their missions or become excessively depressed or guilt-ridden."
The disturbed responses to the war and the mythmaking of the media
are both reflected in *The Vietnam Project*.

Mythmaking and propaganda are also crucial to the second informing
context of *Dusklands:* the discourse of colonial South African travel
narratives. The Van Riebeeck Society, South Africa's most eminent
historical society, has been reprinting these early accounts since 1918, and
such accounts arguably constitute the beginnings of South African literature in written form. Whether overtly or covertly, travel narratives
assisted in the process of colonization. Many of the early accounts were
written for and under the editorial control of the Dutch East India
Company. The Dutch pastor François Valentijn, employed by the Dutch
East India Company, "wrote overtly to the glory and honour of the
Company, the Dutch people and Dordrecht," says his editor (Valentijn
7). A journal kept by Captain Rhenius during a trading expedition in
1724 was later rewritten at the Castle of Good Hope for official purposes
and sent to the Chamber of Seventeen in Holland. Similarly, in an effort
to earn a pardon, a deserter named Wikar produced an "improved" diary
for the use of the Cape administration based upon the account he kept
during his travels into the interior in 1779. The account of Baron A. Van
Pallandt, *General Remarks on the Cape of Good Hope* (1803), apparently

did not pass muster; his description of the settlers' cruel treatment of Hottentots and Kaffirs was quickly suppressed by the Dutch regime after only fifty copies were printed, and the Baron lost his job with General Janssens.[7]

Descriptions of official expeditions—organized to trade for cattle, search for minerals and other natural resources, or map out the unknown territory—could be useful propagandistic tools. The sanctioned accounts of travels into the interior were primarily factual, providing geographical, scientific, and anthropological information about the country that the Company was colonizing and governing. Typically, such accounts describe the terrain, the miles traveled per day, the weather, the flora and fauna, and the indigenous peoples. Similar factual narratives with less overt agendas were written by the numerous European botanists and naturalists, such as Thunberg, Paterson, and Sparrman, who descended upon the Cape throughout the eighteenth century. Many travel narratives implied that the natural resources were only waiting to be used by European settlers and often disparaged the society and character of the current inhabitants. As we have seen, these accounts were employed to support the ideas of Christian nationalism, and many depict the indigenous people as animalistic and brutish.

At the beginning of the nineteenth century, control of the Cape changed hands several times, with the Dutch and the British struggling for possession. The travel narratives from this time reflect this struggle in their descriptions and polemics. Perhaps most notorious was Sir John Barrow's *An Account of Travels into the Interior of Southern Africa* (1801), dedicated to Henry Dundas, the British Secretary of State under whose auspices the Cape was annexed to the British Empire. Barrow's depiction of the Dutch farmers was especially inflammatory: "Unwilling to work, and unable to think; with a mind disengaged from every sort of care and reflexion, indulging to excess in the gratification of every sensual appetite, the African peasant grows to an unwieldy size, and is carried off the stage by the first inflammatory disease that attacks him" (1:78). Barrow's scorn for the Dutch is accompanied by his defense of the Hottentots and Kaffirs, who, he insists, are not savage, treacherous, and cruel but are reasonable people with their own forms of society, culture, and religion (1:156–204). Barrow's account inspired many rebuttals in the following years, including an impassioned defense written by the German scientist, physician, and naturalist Henry Lichtenstein. Accusing Barrow of the "grossest injustice," Lichtenstein praises the African landowners' diligence, hospitality, and civility and sympathizes with the difficulties they have in controlling the native Hottentots and Bushmen (58, 85, 124–126).

Lichtenstein was attacked in turn by John Philip, of the London Missionary Society, for his false reports about the British missionary work in Africa. Lamenting "the want of candour and the rashness of most writers who have spoken incidentally of missionary labours," Philip notes the great progress made by the missionaries in "civilizing natives" and chronicles the barbarous treatment of the Bushmen by the Dutch commando squads, who attacked in order to obtain more land and servants (I:96, 40–49, 296). Many of these narratives provided detailed accounts of colonial violence against the Africans. Vaillant relates how Dutch commando units used prisoners as targets in a shooting competition (I:354–55); Mentzel describes a particularly cruel encounter with a group of Bushmen: "some of the soldiers proved that if they were free to do as they pleased, they could be wanton and savage. Some of the most brutal ones seized the small children by the legs and crushed their heads against the stones. Others killed the wounded women and cut off their long breasts, afterwards making themselves tobacco pouches from these as tokens of their heroism" (II:309).

Similar to the media's coverage of the Vietnam War, the colonial travel narratives—official reports on resources, scientific accounts of the countryside, detailed list of longitudes and latitudes, political or religious arguments—all were similar in viewing southern Africa and her people "from above," as Coetzee puts it. In reading travel narratives, he "followed the fortunes of the Hottentots in a history written not by them but for them, from above, by travelers and missionaries, not excluding my remote ancestor Jacobus Coetzee, fl. 1760" ("How I Learned" 9). This notion of viewing "from above" suggests both the objectification of the African people that occurs even in such essentially sympathetic accounts such as those of Barrow, Philip, and Mentzel, and the lack of an inside story, of a history written by an African. Throughout Coetzee's fiction, we find him attempting to discover ways to overcome these two problems inherent to discourse about Africa and her people.

What Coetzee has described as writing "from above" is characterized by Mary Louise Pratt as scientific, information-oriented travel writing. This kind of writing, Pratt explains, is normalizing and authoritarian, codifying difference and fixing the Other in a timeless present. However, Pratt also notes another kind of travel narrative, first emerging in the

1780s, which she terms sentimental or experiential. In the conventional travel narrative, the narrator must not talk about him or herself.[8] The sentimental, on the other hand, is a dramatic account of the traveler as protagonist and hero: "It narrates the journey as an epic-style series of trials and challenges, of various kinds of encounters—often erotic ones— where indigenous inhabitants occupy the stage alongside the European. If the other discourse is called informational, this one should be called experiential. It constitutes its authority by anchoring itself not in informational orders but in situated human subjects" (150). Sentimental accounts can be dialogical: "they represent the Other's voices in dialogue with the voices of the self and often tender the Other some credibility and equality" (151). The sentimental narratives sometimes also expose their own authority: "In contrast and in chorus with the monochromatic and self-effacing stance of information, then, [these] books . . . asserted multivalence, confusion, self-doubt, and self-parody" (158). In *The Narrative of Jacobus Coetzee,* Coetzee experiments with both the scientific and the sentimental travel narrative.

As we have seen, both African travel narratives and Vietnam War journalism participate in the formation of myths that distance and objectify Others. Similarly, the violence embodied in both provides a self-gratifying way for the reader or viewer to release aggression, whether in horror or delight.

The Myth of Masters

The first dark land we enter is America in the throes of the Vietnam War. *The Vietnam Project* is divided into five sections, four of which appear to be diary entries recounting events in the life of Eugene Dawn. In the opening section, Dawn recounts all of his paranoia: his supervisor—one J. M. Coetzee [9]—does not like his writing style; he suspects his wife, Marilyn, is having an affair; he loathes and feels trapped in his body. The second section, written in bureaucratic jargon with subheadings and references, contains Dawn's report for the New Life Project, a propaganda plan that his think tank is preparing for the Department of Defense.[10] An expert in mythography, Dawn argues that the United States should concentrate on forming a counter-myth to the current Vietnamese myth of the sons (Vietnam) banding together to rebel against the father (the United States). After turning this report in, Dawn is convinced that J. M. Coetzee is avoiding him, and he is troubled with bad dreams. Attempting to grasp reality, he runs away with his son, Martin, to a motel in the mountains. When Marilyn and the police come to reclaim the child, Dawn—in a remarkable passage written in the present tense and describing his sense of dissociation—stabs Martin. In the final section of the novella, Dawn writes from a psychiatric hospital, in which the doctors are analyzing his childhood and attempting to discover what made him perform such an atrocious act.

Like Dawn's account, *The Narrative of Jacobus Coetzee* has five sections, four of personal recollection and one official document. Dawn's story has numerical divisions; Jacobus gives his sections different narrative titles. In addition, the second half of *Dusklands* is accompanied by a framing device, a preface by a presumed translator (J. M. Coetzee) and an afterword by a South African academic historian (S. J. Coetzee). This framing device directs our attention to the ongoing propagation of the Afrikaner master myth of history.

Jacobus Coetzee, an eighteenth-century Dutch explorer and hunter, opens his narrative with a discourse on the Bushmen and then describes his "Journey beyond the Great River," accompanied by his six Hottentot servants. His "Sojourn in the land of the Great Namaqua" occurs when he becomes ill, and, delirious with a fever, finds himself being taken to a Nama village and nursed in a menstruation hut. While recovering, he is bathing in the river when a group of small boys steal his clothes and begin to mock him. Furious, he falls upon them, and in the ensuing fray, bites the ear off a boy. The Nama physically punish him and then expel him from the village for this savage act of mutilating a child. Accompanied by his faithful servant Klawer, who dies during the journey, Jacobus makes his way back to civilization, only to return with a small armed force to avenge himself on the people who had humiliated him. The final section of his personal narrative, "Second journey to the land of the Great Namaqua," unrelentingly details this cruel punishment. A final account of the first journey appears in the Appendix, which contains the deposition of Jacobus Coetzee, taken down in 1760 at the Castle of Good Hope to serve as the official governmental report. This deposition tells an entirely different story from the personal account, detailing the days of travel, the various natural resources found in the country, and several peaceful encounters with the Nama.

The juxtaposition of these two narratives immediately invites comparison. Both Eugene Dawn and Jacobus Coetzee are explorers. "I have an exploring temperament," Dawn explains. "Had I lived two hundred years ago I would have had a continent to explore, to map, to open to colonization" (31–32). In the twentieth century, however, what remains to be explored is the human psyche, and instead of mapping rivers and mountains, Dawn sets down body language, dreams, and myths. In their respective roles as government servants, Dawn explores the psychological interior of the Vietnamese rendered in their mythology, and Jacobus journeys into the physical interior of Africa. As explorers, both are driven to know the unknown, to encompass that unknown both mentally and physically. Touching the surface of a photograph of an imprisoned Vietcong, Dawn notes that it "is bland and opaque under my fingers, yielding no passage into the interior of this obscure but indubitable man. I keep exploring. Under the persistent pressure of my imagination, acute and morbid in the night, it may yet yield" (16–17). Similarly, Jacobus states, "I am an explorer. My essence is to open what is closed, to bring light to what is dark" (106). His "explorer's hammerblow" attempts to crack the bleak desert exterior to reach the "innocent interior" (77).

As Jacobus's imagery suggests, the explorer does not shrink from violence. During the course of their narratives, both Dawn and Jacobus physically harm a child, which indicates their disturbed estimation of human life. Similarly, they not only are unmoved by the physical atrocities performed by their respective colonial powers, but also contribute to or urge this kind of violence themselves. Dawn repeatedly examines three photographs that are part of his material for the Vietnam report: a Vietnamese prisoner in a tiger cage, a onetime Texas linebacker copulating with a tiny Vietnamese woman, two Special Forces sergeants holding the severed heads of Vietnamese "taken from corpses or near-corpses" (15). The "delicious shame" stimulated by these pictures provides his imagination with the "slight electric impulse" needed to stimulate his mythographical exploration (15, 13). Dawn's final solution to the problem of Vietnam is to destroy the land physically by intense bombing and chemical warfare, to "show the enemy that he stands naked in a dying landscape" (29). In mythological terms, he advises rape: "assault upon the mothering earth herself" (28).

With the exception of his attack on Martin, Dawn's violence is confined to discourse; Jacobus actually practices violent destruction. Returning to the Nama village, he coldly watches as his troops kill, rape, and burn. He personally supervises the punishment of the four servants who had abandoned him, and recounts the cruelty of these deaths in horrible detail: "I pushed the muzzle against his lips. 'Take it', I said.

He would not take it. I stamped. His lips seeped blood, his jaw relaxed. I pushed the muzzle in till he began to gag. I held his head steady between my ankles. Behind me his sphincter gave way and a rich stench filled the air. 'Watch your manners, hotnot', I said. I regretted this vulgarity. The shot sounded as minor as a shot fired into the sand. Whatever happened in the pap inside his head left his eyes crossed" (104). The phallic suggestiveness of this scene typifies the sexual terms in which the violent assault on interiors is described throughout both novellas. The rhetoric suggests the integral connection between political, economic, racial, and sexual oppression, a connection that Coetzee explores further in his later works.

Dusklands shows how the obsessive drive to explore and the inevitable acceptance of violence of both the propagandist and the elephant hunter are common elements of the master myth of colonialism. But rather than accepting a purely material basis for this behavior, Coetzee points to a metaphysical origin. In this respect his work differs sharply from the Marxist analysis of the roots of colonialism. *Dusklands* actually takes several oblique potshots at the materialistic focus of Marxism. Jacobus's animal references suggest the inhumanity of pure materialism. His dogs eat the flesh of the hare, but he obtains "metaphysical meat" from the death of the hare (79). Even more sarcastically, he wonders if when he dies, his organs will be thrown to "the economic pigs" (106). Dawn also notes the inadequacy of understanding all human behavior in Marxist terms, complaining about his supervisor, "His career has been built on the self and its interests. He thinks of me, even me, as merely a self with interests. He cannot understand a man who experiences his self as an envelope holding his body-parts together while inside it he burns and burns" (32). Beyond economics and self-interest, which Coetzee never completely discounts, are other human drives.

Both Dawn and Coetzee suffer from an ontological problem: they are uncertain about the nature of their own existence in relationship to the external world. Michael Vaughan observes: "They are identical, not in character or experience, but in the *mode of consciousness* by which they perceive their world, and their relation to this world" (123). As they struggle to understand the relationship of their own subjectivity to the objectivity of the world around them, both turn to exploration as a means of breaking through their philosophical impasse. Each moves between total objectivity and total subjectivity, the extremes of annihilation and solipsism. This desperate search for one's true position in the universe results both in their use of others as a means of asserting an identity and in the acceptance of violence as a copula, a means of establishing and bridging the gap between self and other. "The gun and its metaphors," Dawn states, are "the only copulas we knew of between ourselves and our object" (17). Similarly, Jacobus claims, "The gun stands for the hope that there exists that which is other than oneself. The gun is our last defence against isolation within the travelling sphere." Violence overcomes solipsism: "The gun saves us from the fear that all life is within us. It does so by laying at our feet all the evidence we need of a dying and therefore a living world" (79). The colonizing impetus, then, comes from this divided consciousness, which Stephen Watson identifies as originating with Descartes: "the colonizing project of the West was set in motion when this same man embarked upon his Cartesian project of separating subject from object, self from world in a dualism which privileged the first of the two terms and thereby assured his domination of nature and any other obstacle he might confront. . . . Just as Western people conquer nature in an effort to conquer their own self-division, so they cannot desist from enslaving other human beings who necessarily confront them as that Other, alien and forever threatening" (375–76).

The absence that looms for both protagonists is the failure of transcendence, the missing superstructure that controls the relationship of objects and subjects. Their search essentially is religious, as the rhetoric of each narrative reveals. Dawn says about the American presence in Vietnam, "Our nightmare was that since whatever we reached for slipped like smoke through our fingers, we did not exist; that since whatever we embraced wilted, we were all that existed. We landed on the shores of Vietnam clutching our arms and pleading for someone to stand up without flinching to these probes of reality" (17). He realizes that his desire for someone to stand up to reality, to draw a clear line of demarcation between the controlling subjectivity and the controlled object, is actually a "tragic reach for transcendence" (18). The subtext of his meditation is the loss of God:

We bathed them in seas of fire, praying for the miracle. In the heart of the flame their bodies glowed with heavenly light; in our ears their voices rang; but when the fire died they were only ash. We lined them up in ditches. If they had walked toward us singing through the bullets we would have knelt and worshipped; but the bullets knocked them over and they died as we had feared. We cut their flesh open, we reached into their dying bodies, tearing out their livers, hoping to be washed in their blood; but they screamed and gushed like our most negligible phantoms. We forced ourselves deeper than we had ever gone before into their women; but when we came back we were still alone, and the women like stones. (17–18)

The same religious reverbations appear in Dawn's search for a father. His advice that the United States employ "the father voice," the voice of authority, in its propaganda broadcasts to the Vietnamese reveals his own longing for transcendent authority (21). "The excluded orphan," he dreams of home, "the true home before whose barred gate I have spent this last orphan year" (34). In his orphan state, he is unable to touch the faces from his photographs of Vietnam that populate his dreams; without a home or father, he cannot love others. Instead, as he forces himself deeper and deeper into others in an attempt to reach their subjectivity, he turns them into objects. When guns, drugs, torture, or rape rip open the interior, the subject becomes a mere ghost or absence of self: "where they had once been is now only a black hole through which they have been sucked" (17). Without transcendence, Dawn is unable to escape a solipsistic world.

Jacobus, also, considers the possibility of "a universe of which I the Dreamer was sole inhabitant" (78). In a passage reminiscent of the desire of Melville's Ahab to "strike through the mask," Jacobus wants to discover the reality at the heart of the world. And like Ahab, he fears that perhaps nothing lies behind the material world:

Behind this familiar red or grey exterior, spoke the stone from its stone heart to mine, this exterior jutting into every dimension inhabited by man, lies in ambush a black interior quite, quite strange to the world. Yet under the explorer's hammerblow this innocent interior transforms itself in a flash into a replete, confident, worldly image of that red or grey exterior. How then, asked the stone, can the hammerwielder who seeks to penetrate the heart of the universe be sure that there exist any interiors? Are they not perhaps fictions, these lures of interiors for rape which the universe uses to draw out its explorers? (77–78)

The imagery of Jacobus's meditation echoes Dawn's frustration at "the women like stones." The intractable stoniness of the southwestern African terrain—in which Coetzee was raised and Jacobus Coetzee made his discoveries—no doubt contributes to this rhetoric. However, its wildness also helps to form the solipsism of the explorer: "In the wild I lose my sense of boundaries. This is a consequence of space and solitude. The operation of space is thus: the five senses stretch out from the body they inhabit, but four stretch into a vacuum. The ear cannot hear, the nose cannot smell, the tongue cannot taste, the skin cannot feel" (78). Only the eyes are free, and Jacobus becomes an Emersonian "spherical reflecting eye moving through the wilderness and ingesting it." Everything that he sees is included "in his traveling sphere. What is there that is not me? I am a transparent sac with a black core full of images and a gun" (79). The search for the interior is a metaphysical hunt, provoked by the human need to understand the self in relationship to the world.

The fatal loss of transcendence, the obsessive drive to explore, and the recourse to violence are common elements in the colonialism of both the propagandist and the elephant hunter. Jonathan Crewe notes that "we are looking at *recto* and *verso* of the same coin—the Western consciousness in its exploded and imploded condition" (94–95), and Vaughan implies that Dawn and Jacobus represent two different colonial eras: "the contemporary intellectual . . . of latter-day imperialism" and "the early explorer-coloniser . . . in the epoch of the youthful vigour of Western imperialism" (122). However, *Dusklands* also demonstrates how the practice of colonialism takes different forms in different times and places. While Coetzee's narrative rejects a pure materialism, he nonetheless acknowledges the contributions of material circumstances to the embodiment of metaphysical questions. Different cultural conditions cause the loss of transcendence to manifest itself in different ways, as well as provide different social and discursive structures within which that loss may be understood. In this respect, the differences in the depiction of Dawn and Jacobus are as significant as the similarities. Their contrasting reactions to the loss of transcendence are particularly noteworthy. Jacobus takes on himself the role of the missing God, exalting in his strength and solipsistic power, but Dawn physically and psychologically disintegrates with the loss of the father. To a certain extent, each is a metonymy of his era and country—Jacobus typifying the physical dominance and religious arrogance of the Afrikaner settlers; Dawn typifying the rhetorical dominance and psychic disturbance of contemporary American society. In an early review of the novel published in South Africa, Lionel Abrahams points out how one part of *Dusklands* is "a story about our origins" while the other is "a story about our possible destination" (3).

In the self-aware twentieth century, the myth of masters results not in physical control but in self-doubt and alienation.

Eighteenth-Century Mythmaking

Although the passages detailing Jacobus's dreams and feverish reveries reveal the similarity of his philosophical dilemma to that of Eugene Dawn, Jacobus embodies that dilemma in markedly different ways. Unlike Dawn, Jacobus is a self-possessed man of action. Most of his narrative is matter-of-fact in tone and supremely confident. With a master myth that lends validity to his actions, Jacobus never doubts himself. The social conditions of eighteenth-century southern Africa—a sparsely populated wilderness, the absence of a strong central political authority, the distortions of typological thinking, the technological mastery of the Dutch, and the radical difference of the indigenous African culture—all contribute to the particular manifestation of oppression practiced by Jacobus. His master myth is the South African myth of history. His narrative displays not only his deep-seated prejudice and inability to see the African people as human beings but also his self-aggrandizing appropriation of divine sanction.

On a conscious level, Jacobus clearly understands his story in terms of the Afrikaner myth of the Chosen People. Both the opening and the closing of his narrative point to this theological reading of history. Fearing that "everywhere differences grow smaller as they come up and we go down," Jacobus begins his story maintaining that Christianity is "the one gulf that divides us from the Hottentots." He confidently claims, "we are Christians, a folk with a destiny" (57). At the conclusion of *The Narrative,* Jacobus reveals the underlying metaphysical motivation for his revenge as well as the standard Afrikaner explanation. His punishment of the Nama serves to reaffirm his identity, and it is part of God's larger plan. "Through their death I, who after they had expelled me had wandered the desert like a pallid symbol, again asserted my reality." But such personal reasons are informed by divine reasons for the man who believes he acts on behalf of God: "Who knows for what unimaginable crimes of the spirit they died, through me? God's judgment is just, irreprehensible, and incomprehensible. . . . I am a tool in the hands of history" (106). Jacobus's master myth justifies all his actions.

His constant characterization of the indigenous peoples as animalistic is informed by this myth and echoes the common eighteenth-century stereotypes. Hottentots, even if they claim to be Christians, have no conception of the afterlife and care only for the food they can stuff down today, Jacobus claims. Bushmen are even lower on the chain of being. Jacobus repeatedly describes them in animalistic terms, comparing them to dogs, jackals and baboons: "a wild animal with an animal's soul . . . the only way to treat them is like beasts" (58). His detailed advice on how to hunt Bushmen resembles one of those informative passages, detailing the practice of hunting elephants or trapping rhinoceroses, typical of the travel narrative. Similarly, he advises the reader on breeding techniques as though the human beings involved are cattle: "If you want profit out of women you must make them breed you herders off the Hottentots (they do not breed off white men). But they have a very long cycle, three or four years, between children. So their increase is slow" (61). Approaching the indigenous people of Africa with European structures of understanding, Jacobus fails to perceive their humanity.

Jacobus's fascination with Bushman sexuality and his assessment of its deviant nature is another element commonly found in travel narratives.[11] "Both men and women are sexually misformed," he asserts, "The men go into death with erections." Raping "a wild Bushman girl" is a particularly satisfying expression of one's mastery. A Dutch girl is connected with an entire system of property relations, but a Bushman girl has no economic or social reality: "She may be alive but she is as good as dead. She has seen you kill the men who represented power to her, she has seen them shot down like dogs. You have become Power itself now and she nothing, a rag you wipe yourself on and throw away" (61). In Jacobus's account, Bushmen have no human reality; they exist merely as a cipher, or an absence.

Given these attitudes toward the African people and his assurance that he has a God-ordained destiny, Jacobus's subsequent behavior comes as no surprise. His master myth generates not only his physical oppression of the Nama but also the structure and rhetoric of his narrative, in which he claims to recount the truth of history objectively and omnisciently. Both the final punishment and the narrative of the tale represent his attempt to encompass the Africans by inserting them into his history, his master myth. For the deepest threat of the savage, according to Jacobus, is the alternative history he proposes: "He threatens to have a history in which I shall be a term. Such is the material basis of the malady of the master's soul" (81). Such a history might better be termed "annihilation," Jacobus believes. So he constructs his own heroic plot: a benevolent man travels into the wilderness, is cruelly betrayed by his hedonistic servants, and is brutally imprisoned and tortured by the animalistic natives. Against all odds, the man travels back to civilization and returns to deliver a just punishment on his persecutors. Jacobus's narrative demonstrates his need to control history, to write history in such a way that *his* master myth is maintained.

When he first encounters the Nama, Jacobus realizes that his adventure could take many different routes, and he calmly considers the outlines of different common travelers' tales that his own might follow:

> Tranquilly I traced in my heart the forking paths of the endless inner adventure: the order to follow, the inner debate (resist? submit?), underlings rolling their eyeballs, words of moderation, calm, swift march, the hidden defile, the encampment, the gray-beard chieftain, the curious throng, words of greeting, firm tones, Peace! Tobacco!, demonstration of firearms, murmurs of awe, gifts, the vengeful wizard, the feast, glut, nightfall, murder foiled, dawn, farewell, trundling wheels, the order to follow, the inner debate, rolling eyeballs, the nervous finger, the shot, panic, assault, gunfire, hasty departure, the pursuing horde, the race for the river . . . (65–66)

This sketches two possible scenarios; the complete passage includes at least three other possible plots for his encounter with the Nama. All these possible stories are romantic insertions of the Nama into a European fiction. Allan Gardiner calls these stories "amusing reductions of the plots of typical imperial adventure stories of the Haggard/Kipling kind" and notes that "this aspect of colonial discourse does not originate as a representation of actual colonial experience, but rather is generated from the (European) public symbolic order" (181). Jacobus thus enacts the colonial ordering of reality through stereotypical discourse.

Jacobus's control of these narrative options is made manifest when he describes Klawer's death in two contradictory tales. In one version, Klawer drowns attempting to cross the Great River; in the other, Jacobus abandons him in the mountains when he becomes ill. The competing versions of Klawer's death are not only devices to highlight the narrative's fictiveness but are also, as Peter Knox-Shaw explains, "intended rather to alert us to the ease with which a sole witness may falsify facts prejudicial to his self-presentation" (30).[12] As the all-powerful chronicler of history, Jacobus can construct his story in any way he pleases, and we are helpless before his narrative power. The contradictory accounts of Klawer's death and the entirely different story told in the deposition remind us that we have no way of knowing what actually took place on Jacobus's journey; we can only know the story he chooses to tell us.

Another way that Jacobus exercises control is through his self-characterization. Repeatedly, he uses typological imagery to designate himself as a god. On the journey into the land of the Namaqua, his divine stature is manifested in his superior knowledge and control, much like God's patient dealings with the Israelites during the journey through the desert: "It was I who saw that every man had food. It was I who, when the men began to murmur on those last terrible days before we reached the Great River, restored order with a firm but fair hand. They saw me as their father. They would have died without me" (64). During the first encounter with the Nama he wonders whether "on my horse and with the sun over my right shoulder I looked like a god, a god of the kind they did not yet have" (71). He increasingly characterizes himself as a divinity in his vengeance. When the Nama children steal his trousers, his retribution would be almost comical in its severity if it did not all too accurately predict the narrative's conclusion: "Roaring like a lion and enveloped in spray like Aphrodite I fell upon them. My claws raked welts of skin and flesh from their fleeing backs. A massive fist thundered one to the ground. Jehovah I fell upon his back" (90). On his return to civilization, he similarly exercises his mastery over an animal: "Like God in a whirlwind I fell upon a lamb, an innocent little fellow who had never seen his master and was thinking only of a good night's sleep, and slit his throat" (100).

Jacobus again casts himself as God in the sermon he delivers to his mutinous servants on his return to the Nama. However, his version of the gospel demonstrates how distorted his understanding of traditional Christianity is. The sermon is based upon the text of Matthew 10:29, "Are not two sparrows sold for a penny? Yet not one of them will fall to the ground apart from the will of your Father." Jacobus turns this assurance of God's providential care into a cold statement of God's impartial knowledge: "the sparrow is cheap but he is not forgotten." As a Christian explorer, Jacobus tells his captive audience, he has always attempted to preach "the gospel of the sparrow, which falls but falls with design" (101). Like the sparrow, the servants are cheap animals, but they have not been forgotten. For Jacobus has nourished himself for months on his memory of their actions and his plans for their death. Their existence depends on him: "They died the day I cast them out of my head" (106).

With the exception of his misleading citation of the passage in Matthew, most of Jacobus's biblical allusions refer to the Pentateuch and emphasize God's power and knowledge, rather than the love and mercy revealed in the Prophets and Gospels. "We do not require of God that he be good," he says, "all we ask is that he never forget us" (101). Jacobus's understanding of God both molds and justifies his actions. Yet the insufficiency of this master myth emerges during his feverish meditations. Jacobus's God, lacking love and mercy, does not provide a coherent center to the universe, a meaningful means of interacting with others and nature. Pure power and knowledge ultimately become solipsism: "A world without me is inconceivable." The conclusion of Jacobus's narrative demonstrates his final, confident self-absorption: "If the worst comes you will find that I am not irrevocably attached to life. . . . when the day comes you will find that whether I am alive or dead, whether I ever lived or never was born, has never been of real concern to me. I have other things to think about" (107). Jacobus's master myth and its accompanying rhetoric have written him in such a way that he has lost all contact with objective reality.

Twentieth-Century Mythmaking

In the twentieth century, the process of mythmaking has become increasingly institutionalized and self-conscious. Coetzee suggests this in a parodic fashion both in his creation of the department of Mythography in *The Vietnam Project* and by means of the academic trappings affixed to *The Narrative*. Business, government, and education all consciously employ the discourse of myth to maintain power. In our time, the presence propagating and enforcing such myths is the media. Dawn describes the authority of the media with vivid imagery suggesting that its powerful coercion is the contemporary version of torture:

> Radio information, I ought to know from practise, is pure authority. It is no coincidence that the two voices we use to project it are the voices of the two masters of the interrogation chamber—the sergeant-uncle who confides he has taken a liking to you, he would not like to see you hurt, talk, it is no disgrace, everyone talks in the end; and the cold handsome captain with the clipboard. Print, on the other hand, is sadism, and properly evokes terror. The message of the newspaper is: "I can say anything and not be moved. Watch as I permute my 52 affectless signs". Print is the hard master with the whip, print-reading a weeping search for signs of mercy. (14)

Television is equally demanding. Dawn recalls, "I was being taken over. I was not my own man. It was insupportable. Guilt was entering our homes through the TV cables. We ate our meals in the glare of that beast's glass eye from the darkest corner" (48). Discourse has become a weapon, as Dawn's description of his attack on his son unconsciously reveals: "Holding it like a pencil, I push the knife in" (42). Jacobus hunts elephants and Africans with his gun in the desert; Dawn does his hunting with his pencil in the library.

The controlling national myth also takes slightly different forms in the two halves of *Dusklands*. Colonial Afrikaners viewed their world through typological lenses; the American media preferred the sociological concept of the country as family. Dawn's mythographical proposal is based upon creating a new family myth for American-Vietnamese relations. His country, Dawn complains, has not been using the voice of the father in its propagandistic broadcasts but rather the voice of "the doubting self": "The father is authority, infallibility, ubiquity. He does not persuade, he commands" (20, 21). In Dawn's version, the United States embodies this father-God, the master of the myth, and must marry the daughter of technology and destroy the mother earth to effectively subdue the enemy. While the traditional South African master myth envisions the Afrikaners acting on behalf of God, in its contemporary American version, the country itself embodies the father-God.

Both the institutionalization of mythmaking and the national myth proposed by Dawn can be seen as further developments of eighteenth-century phenomena. However, Dawn's greater self-awareness of the process of mythology and his conscious effort to scrutinize himself are significantly different from Jacobus's unconscious revelations. Dawn's metaphysical search has professional and national implications, but most of his narrative concerns his precarious mental state and crumbling personal relationships. At times, Jacobus experiences the same kind of despair as Dawn, but his narrative is more concerned with his actions and his place in history. These differences suggest the different genres of the two narratives. Following the categories delineated by Francis R. Hart, we can term one a memoir and the other a confession. A memoir is "personal history that seeks to articulate or repossess the historicity of the self"; a confession is "personal history that seeks to communicate or express the essential nature, the truth, of the self" (Hart 227). Jacobus is concerned to construct history and claim his own historicity, but Dawn's primary concern is to find and express his essential nature. Even the report within the narrative becomes confessional as the formal subdivisions, references, and diction break down. "Tear this off, Coetzee, it is a postscript, it goes to you, listen to me," Dawn pleads in its final sentence (30). His exploration of the Vietnamese psyche increasingly takes second place to his obsessive exploration of himself. Self-analysis is his primary goal in constructing his narrative: "There are significances in these stories that pour out of me, but I am tired. They may be clues, I put them down" (32). If he is unable to solve the mystery of himself, perhaps others, such as his editor or his readers, might be able to read his confession.

Dawn writes a confession rather than a memoir in part because he has no firm master myth against which to judge himself or to use in constructing his narrative. Jacobus has his society's controlling myth of God-ordained white rule to give shape to his experiences; the mythologically attuned society in which Eugene Dawn lives no longer has a single controlling myth but rather is characterized by a number of competing myths, several of which emerge in Dawn's account. While Jacobus knows where authority lies (but fails to recognize the responsibility that comes with authority), Dawn knows, as a postmodern man, that authority is merely constructed and is quite illusory. In such a world, one's identity and sense of responsibility become confused. Dawn begins his account by saying, "My name is Eugene Dawn. I cannot help that." By the end of the narrative, he has not yet determined who *can* help it: "In my cell in the heart of America, with my private toilet in the corner, I ponder and ponder. I have high hopes of finding whose fault I am" (49). The phrase "in the heart of America" suggests the metonymic resonances of Dawn's character as a typical American.

Instead of the master myth of the chosen people, Dawn unconsciously constructs himself upon various fragments of popular culture. He refuses Marilyn's "novelettish reading" of his problems and claims, "Nor, if I were to commit myself body and soul to some fiction or other, would I choose any fiction but my own. I am still the captain of my soul" (10). However, these words only demonstrate the way that American individualism has written him. His account abounds with references to and echoes of films, comic books, dime novels, fashion catalogs, popular psychology, women's magazines, *Playboy,* and contemporary literature. He often sees both himself and others as characters enacting certain roles. In her "tall blondeness, clear brown lines, hauteur and mystery of the swimwear model I married," his wife evokes the mystique of Marilyn Monroe, whose first name she shares (39). When he suspects that she is having an affair, Dawn phones her, breathing heavily "as described in the newspapers," and spies on her through their bedroom window as in "a novel in which a householder is arrested for peeping at his wife" (33). He even judges their sexual relationship by what he has read: "Though like the diligent partners in the marriage manuals we attend to each other's whispers, moans, and groans, though I plough like the hero and Marilyn froth like the heroine, the truth is that the bliss of which the books speak has eluded us" (7–8). Dawn's propensity to view his life in the context of popular culture emerges even at his most desperate moments: "Here I stand in the middle of a dark room with police whispering outside. Out of what movie is it?" (41). The narratives of his society, as Dawn fears, have formed him. He consciously casts himself as the betrayed husband, the dedicated professional, the caring father, the victim of war; yet he also knows that each pose is just that—a pose.

Unable to identify a transcendent reality and trapped in the tyranny of his consciousness of myths, Eugene Dawn falls apart, both physically and mentally: "There is no doubt that I am a sick man. Vietnam has cost me too much. I use the metaphor of the dolorous wound. Something is wrong in my kingdom. Inside my body, beneath the skin and muscle and flesh that drape me, I am bleeding. Sometimes I think the wound is in my stomach, that it bleeds slime and despair over the food that should be nourishing me. . . . At other times I imagine a wound weeping somewhere in the cavern behind my eyes. There is no doubt that I must find and care for it, or else die of it. That is why I have no shame about unveiling myself" (32). His narrative unveiling, or confession, reveals his lack of confidence, his inability to sustain a loving relationship with his wife, his fear and dislike of his supervisor. His "sickness unto death," his malaise, emerges in all aspects of his life. Increasingly, he feels a loathing of and distance from his body. "From head to foot I am the subject of a revolting body," he says, referring to his penis as "the length of gristle that hangs from the end of my iron spine" (7). His sexual encounters, much like Jacobus's, manifest his metaphysical search, but unlike Jacobus he is disillusioned by the experience of an interior nothingness: "Before the arrival of my seed her pouch yawns and falls back, leaving my betrayed representative gripped at its base, flailing its head in vain inside an immense cavern, at the very moment when above all else it craves to be rocked through its tantrum in a soft, firm, infinitely trustworthy grip" (8). Failing to exult in the power such an encounter gives him, Dawn longs for the comfort of otherness and the infinite trustworthiness of transcendence.

Dawn reacts to his inability to understand and touch reality with paranoia, paralysis, and dissociation. When he first runs away with Martin, he believes that he is finally breathing the "bracing air of reality" (35). He longs to learn the names of birds, plants, and insects, and closely studies *Herzog* and *Voss,* "puzzling out the tricks which their authors perform to give to their monologues . . . the air of a real world through the looking-glass" (37). But human contact, an escape to nature, and concrete nouns provide only temporary relief. "I am still unliberated," he admits. "Whereas I had hoped to sink through circle after circle of wordless being, under the influence of birdsong and paternal love and afternoon walks, until I attained the rapture of pure contemplation, I find myself merely sitting in the Loco Motel drenched in reverie and waiting for something to happen" (38). When Marilyn and the police arrive, he completely loses contact with reality: "This man is still walking towards me. I have lost all heart and left the room and gone to sleep even and missed certain words and come back and here the man is still walking across the carpet towards me." After stabbing his son, Dawn realizes what he holds in his hand: "That is what he was talking about, the thing he wants me to put down. It is the fruit-knife from the bedside table" (42). Jacobus's violence is premeditated and self-justified; Dawn scarcely knows what he is doing.

In the final section of his story, Dawn appears to be reordering his life and making contact with concrete nouns again, "the clear, functional words" (43). The plot of his story appears to follow the neat structure of Freytag's pyramid: rising action of mental disturbance, climax of his attack on Martin, falling action of regaining sanity. As his doctors sedate him with medication, isolate him from the outside world, probe his childhood, and "explicate . . . the labyrinth of [his] history," Dawn cheerfully and willingly cooperates (47). Their theory about his break-down has a surface plausibility and echoes Marilyn's earlier charge that Dawn's job is dehumanizing him: "The hypothesis they test is that intimate contact with the design of war made me callous to suffering and created in me a need for violent solutions to problems of living, infecting me at the same time with guilty feelings that showed themselves in nervous symptoms" (48). Yet the very patness of the explanation and the inauthenticity of the jargon suggest the limitations of this hypothesis, the partial nature of the story that it constructs for Dawn. He admits, "I am open to this theory, as I am open to all theorizing, though I do not believe it will turn out to be the true one" (46). Modern psychology provides a fairly convincing way of understanding the self, but it still fails to provide the missing transcendent, for one can never completely reach the inner self. The very premise of modern psychology is that there is always a significant gap or absence in one's conscious understanding. The secular mode of confession offered by psychology has no way of breaking out of the circle of self-consciousness, of establishing the truth about the self without being self-deceived. Absolution is impossible.[13] Knowing that the author of *The Psychology of Gesture* identifies curling and clenched fingers as a sign of depression, Dawn consciously flexes his fingers and relaxes his hands to demonstrate that he is not depressed. Or is he? The self-aware mythmaking of the twentieth century allows for no escape from fictions to reality; as Vaughan says about the divided consciousness, "Awareness is no transcendence" (124). However, the differences between Dawn and Jacobus do suggest that awareness might be a necessary beginning for the end of oppression.

Coetzee's Mythmaking

As the author of *Dusklands,* Coetzee himself is engaged in mythmaking, and throughout the text he deliberately calls attention to that fact. In posing as the "editor" of *The Vietnam Project* and the "translator" of *The Narrative of Jacobus Coetzee,* Coetzee exposes his own role as the constructor of discourse. Although Jacobus Coetzee may present himself as a reliable, omniscient, and objective narrator, his twentieth-century son is very aware that, as the epigraph to *The Narrative* states, "What is important is the philosophy of history." A closer examination of Coetzee's own mythmaking, an examination that his own structuring of the work almost begs us to conduct, further demonstrates how the discourse of history, particularly the discourse of the travel narrative, is controlled by ideology and structures our perceptions of reality.[14]

Coetzee drew on a number of historical sources to write *The Narrative of Jacobus Coetzee,* many of which are noted in its footnotes and references.[15] Coetzee uses these sources very subjectively to construct a certain kind of narrative. The primary source is *The Relaas of Jacobus Coetsé Jansz,* a deposition taken down in the Castle of Good Hope by the Political Secretariat in November 1760 and containing an account of the journey the elephant hunter Jacobus Coetse made into the land of the Great Amacquas that year. The illiterate Coetse told his story to the secretary, who then wrote the account up in Dutch, using the third-person "den Relatant," the narrator, to refer to Coetse. No contemporary copy of the *Relaas* has survived; a transcription was first published in the Netherlands in *Zuid Afrika in de Holandse Tijd* (The Hague, 1916). The South African Van Riebeeck Society later published the *Relaas* in Dutch with an English translation by E. E. Mossop in *The Journal of Wikar, Coetsé and Van Reenen* (1935). These publication facts suggest the numerous filters through which the account passed even before it reached Coetzee.

The deposition appearing at the end of *The Narrative of Jacobus Coetzee* is based upon the *Relaas,* but contains several significant differences that show us Coetzee's mythmaking at work.[16] Coetzee has provided his own English translation of the deposition, and has both added to and taken away from the original account. The fictional deposition appears to be a straightforward informational account describing some of the people, animals, and vegetation encountered during a long journey into a new territory. It contains no mention of the protagonist's illness, "captivity," or expulsion; these details appear only in the extended fictional narrative. According to the fictional deposition, the Narrator quickly convinces the Nama he comes in peace, and they allow him to continue his expedition without incident. In the terms Pratt uses to describe travel narratives, the deposition is "scientific" rather than "sentimental." Yet the many changes that Coetzee has made from the original deposition hint at and support the dark narrative of the other tale.

A few facts have been changed to correspond with the fictional narrative. Instead of the two wagons and twelve Hottentots the historical Coetse traveled with, the fictional deposition has one wagon and six Hottentots. The conclusion of the fictional deposition briefly notes that the narrator was deserted by his servants on his return journey, while in fact all twelve servants returned with Coetse. Several omissions efface the friendly interactions that took place between Coetse and the Nama. Coetzee's version omits an exchange of gifts and the fact that one of the Great Amacqua who wanted to travel returned to the Cape with Coetse. Furthermore, Coetzee eliminates the following comment found in the original document: "The narrator found this nation, particularly those members living deepest inland, of a friendly disposition. This was evident from the fact that after being assured that his arrival was not associated with any evil intention, they allowed him to journey through their country without any trouble, and to return in like fashion" (285). The final significant omission is a paragraph describing another nation named the Enequas, who "live in continuous enmity with the Amacquas" (287).

By omitting the friendly disposition of the Nama toward the white traveler and the intertribal hostility that was their primary defensive concern, Coetzee's "scientific" account gives further credence to his "sentimental" one. This effect is heightened by other changes and additions. In the first encounter with the Namaqua, Coetse remarks that his arrival was viewed "niet sonder bevreemding" (280)—not without astonishment, or surprise. Coetzee, however, translates this phrase somewhat inaccurately as "not without suspicion."[17] In Coetse's deposition, he verbally convinces the uncertain Amacqua that he means them no harm. In the novella's deposition, on the other hand, the narrator demonstrates his weapons in order to convince the natives to allow him to proceed. One significant addition that Coetzee made clearly points to the story contained in the fictional narrative. A second troop of Nama tell the narrator about the eloquent Damroquas, who have yellow skin and long hair, and wear linen clothes. To this fact from Coetse, the fictional deposition adds "that the Envoy of the Damroquas had not long ago met a treacherous end at the hands of servants afflicted for lack of pursuits with the Black Melancholy; that these servants had fled to the Namaquas he the narrator had first met and dwelt yet among them; wherefore he should treat warily with the lastmentioned and look always to his Person."[18] Reading the deposition in conjunction with the narrative, the reader sees the narrator's experiences reflected in the subtext of confrontation, enmity, and threats. The complementary scientific and sentimental accounts demonstrate Jacobus's writing of the Nama as Other.

The flesh-and-blood Coetse returned to Namaqualand in 1761–62. Intrigued by his story of the fair people clad in linen, the Cape administration sent out an expedition led by Captain Hendrik Hop and guided by Coetse to search for this nation. The section of Jacobus's *Narrative* describing his return to the Nama purports to be the "expedition of Captain Hendrik Hop" (100). But again Coetzee has constructed a fiction around a historical event, since we have an account of this expedition in the journal of Carel Frederik Brink, who was the group's official cartographer and scribe. Brink's journal, as Knox-Shaw notes, provided Coetzee with many geographical details that he used in constructing the first part of Jacobus's story (27–28). It also describes the death of a Great Nama who accompanied Coetse a year before during his visit to the Little Nama: "Yesterday, when crossing the river with his cattle, he had the misfortune to fall into the stream and was drowned" (*Journals of Brink* 29, 31). Coetzee took this brief account and turned it into one of the two versions of Klawer's death. Jacobus's rendition again demonstrates his tendency to dramatize himself as the noble master of a loyal servant: "With horror I watched my faithful servant and companion drawn struggling downstream, shouting broken pleas for help which I was powerless to render him, him whose voice I had never in all my days heard raised, until he disappeared from sight around a bend" (93–94). The second version of Klawer's death resembles an incident described in another travel narrative, written by William Paterson in 1779: "Towards the evening Mr. Pinar arrived with three of the Hottentots who were dreadful to look at, having travelled five days through sultry desarts, over sandy hills and rocky mountains, without eating or drinking. The fifth day they found a small fountain where they left one of the Hottentots who they expected could not live one day longer" (Forbes and Rourke 152). Jacobus abandons the ill Klawer in a similar situation, again depicting the scene in a romantic light. When Klawer tells Jacobus that he must go on without him, it was "a noble moment, worthy of record." Klawer says goodbye, weeping, and Jacobus writes, "My eyes were wet too. I trudged off. He waved" (95). Jacobus both writes and is written from a heroic perspective.

The account of Brink's journal given in the Van Riebeeck edition may have also suggested to Coetzee how official accounts may have effaced incidents of colonial brutality and murder. As Knox-Shaw states, "there is no record of racial friction on the journey" (33), but nonetheless an ugly racial incident did occur. The editor of the Van Riebeeck edition, E. E. Mossop, has shown that during Hop's expedition, a mentally disturbed Dutchman killed a Hottentot servant for refusing to obey him. Mossop has reconstructed this event from other documents, such as depositions and court records, but the surviving version of Brink's journal fails to mention this murder. Mossop argues that the existing manuscript of the journal is not an exact copy of what Brink actually recorded during the expedition, but rather either what he was ordered to write in a clean copy or what some other person put down before the document was sent to Holland. Athough the murderer was tried and convicted, the Cape administration obviously did not want news of the murder to reach Holland in Brink's report (*Journals of Brink* 1–2, 116–17). In a similar fashion, although its subtext reveals his preoccupation with betrayal, Jacobus Coetzee's official deposition contains no mention of his conflict with the Nama or of his crazed murder of his unfaithful servants.

Coetzee's exposure of the politics of history-making is not merely confined to eighteenth-century narratives, however. His most scathing attack on twentieth-century mythmaking occurs in the afterword to *The Narrative,* supposedly written by "my father, the late Dr. S. J. Coetzee, for the Van Plettenberg Society" (55). The afterword is "drawn from a course of lectures on the early explorers of South Africa given annually by my father at the University of Stellenbosch between 1934 and 1948" (55). Coetzee's father, Zacharias, actually was an attorney, and Coetzee said in an interview, "the false historical link that has been inserted . . . simply has to do with my conception of the way in which the founding fathers of the South African state have run the history of the country since the seventeenth century" (Penner 47–48). The afterword, the accompanying footnotes, and the translator's preface and acknowledgments all clearly parody the methods and style of the Van Riebeeck Society.[19] However, the attitudes expressed in the afterword reflect the conservative, authoritarian, and uncritical Christian nationalism that burgeoned in the thirties and forties and are sometimes still characteristic of the Afrikaans-language universities such as Stellenbosch.[20] Jacobus Coetzee and S. J. Coetzee together represent an all-too-common "white writing" of South Africa. Coetzee remarked to the publisher of his first book that he was "one of the 10,000 Coetzees, and what is there to be said about them except that Jacobus Coetzee begat them all" (Barnett, "South Africa" 460). The use of the persona of S. J. Coetzee thus expands Coetzee's exposure of mythmaking to encompass the traditional academic and politically sanctioned histories of South Africa.

S. J. decries the scientific emphasis of the official account; his history claims to describe a deeper reality: "Mere circumstances, notably the truncated account of Coetzee's explorations hitherto current, have conspired to maintain the stereotype and hide from us the true stature of the man." The deposition was written by "a Castle hack," who was primarily concerned about "mineral ore deposits and about the potential of the tribes of the interior as sources of supply." Discounting such commercial and materialistic foci, S. J. is more interested in the heroic stature of the Afrikaner farmer: "The present work ventures to present a more complete and therefore more just view of Jacobus Coetzee. It is a work of piety but also a work of history: a work of piety toward an ancestor and one of the founders of our people, a work which offers the evidence of history to correct certain of the anti-heroic distortions that have been creeping into our conception of the great age of exploration when the White man first made contact with the native peoples of our interior" (108). Jacobus is heroic, according to S. J., because he typifies the perseverance and courage of the frontier farmer who explores and takes possession of the new land. S. J.'s account is decidedly anti-British and anti-Cape. The British, typified by "that supercilious English gentleman Barrow," wrongly see the Dutch farmers as ignorant, slothful, and brutal peasants (109). The British missionaries also come under attack for "collusion in the imperial mission." S. J. concludes, "We hunt in vain for a British exporter of the virtues of humility, respect, and diligence. In the things of this life, said Zwingli, it is the labourer who stands nearest to God" (111). The Cape administration is interested only in "easy profit" and does not provide the frontier farmers with protection from marauding Bushmen. The brave, isolated, silent frontiersmen are the true heroes, as in this romantic picture of "pastoral beauty": "dropping from his saddle, first the right foot then the left, beside the carcase of a freshly killed gemsbok, the cobalt smoke from the muzzle of his gun perhaps by now wholly mingled with lighter blue of the sky" (110). His account, Penner notes, "is a model of unconscious ironic romanticizing" (48).

S. J.'s chauvinism emerges also in his comments on the indigenous people. That the tribes of the interior sold their cattle to the Company for trinkets is "a necessary loss of innocence," as he patronizingly explains: "The herder who, waking from drunken stupor to the wailing of hungry children, beheld his pastures forever vacant, had learned the lesson of the Fall: one cannot live forever in Eden. The Company's men were only playing the role of the angel with the flaming sword in this drama of God's creation. The herder had evolved one sad step further toward citizenship of the world. We may take comfort in this thought" (110). This theological explanation in some odd way absolves the white people of all responsibility. The atrocious treatment of the Bushmen by frontier farmers is similarly justified. Because the Bushmen attacked their cattle and because they lacked the resources adequately to police the zone between the farms and Bushmen territory, "the instrument they reluctantly adopted to keep it free was terror" (114). The Hottentots, "perforce divorced from the indolence of a degenerate tribal culture," gradually fall into a paternalistic relationship with their superior Dutch master, "another of those durable relations in which farmer and servant dance in slow parallel through time," in S. J.'s approving description (115).

The afterword is erratic in nature, radically shifting topics and tone, and without clear organization. On one page S. J. might be describing the picturesque paternalism of colonial life—"the quiet farmhouse on the slopes, the quiet huts in the hollow, the starlit sky"—and on the next giving the Latin terms for certain flora and fauna (115, 116). He moves easily from romantic posturing to a mechanical listing of latitudes and longitudes. Although his account has a facade of learning with its many footnotes and foreign words, his use of sources is sloppy at best and deliberately misleading at worst. Many of his footnotes contain slight inaccuracies: the wrong page cited, several words omitted from quotes, two accounts conflated and presented as one.[21] He claims that Barrow "records" an instance of a farmer lighting a fire under a span of oxen, but Barrow actually reports a *story* he has heard about a farmer lighting a fire under *one* oxen (Barrow 183–84). S. J. claims that Jacobus's own son was murdered by his slaves and cites Lichtenstein's *Travels in Southern Africa* as his source. Lichtenstein does tell of the death of a Coetzee, but it is not the son of Jacobus Coetse (Lichtenstein 124–26). A little bit of historical research easily establishes that S. J. Coetzee is not the best of scholars, even by traditional methods of judgment. The afterword thus both subtly and not-so-subtly debunks the nationalistic historicism of South Africa and its romantic glorification of the past.

Dusklands ultimately is about the dangers of discourse. Even if it does not romanticize or consciously construct myths, discourse can participate in the marginalization of others and facilitate oppression. Coetzee's comments on the displaced aggression and sadism facilitated by televised depictions of events in Vietnam suggest some of the dangers. The pure presentation of the camera turns flesh-and-blood human beings into marks on a paper, flickering lights on a tube; Dawn giggles at the picture of a severed head and labels a picture of an American sergeant copulating with a childlike Vietnamese woman "Father Makes Merry with Children" (13). Speaking of Dawn's responses to his Vietnam photographs, Knox-Shaw states, "the idea that distanced documentary (particularly that of the camera) can corrupt response is convincingly projected" (32). Such distanced documentary reporting also reveals the inability of the reporter to see Others. When Jacobus forgoes his romanticizing and becomes purely descriptive, the effect is even more chilling: "A man, a sturdy Hottentot, began running after us clutching an enormous brown bundle to his chest. A Griqua in green jacket and scarlet cap came chasing after him waving a sabre. Soundlessly the sabre fell on the man's shoulder. The bundle slid to the ground and began itself to run. It was a child, quite a big one. Why had the man been carrying it? The Griqua now chased the child. He tripped it and fell upon it. . . . The Griqua was doing things to the child on the ground. It must be a girl child"(102). Jacobus's camera-eye rendition of the destruction of the Nama tribe uncovers his own sadism and the objectification of descriptive discourse. Both novellas demonstrate the basic similarity between physical violence and, as Tobin Siebers puts it, "the forms of violence that injure human beings by creating categories or ideas that risk depriving them of rights" (7).

The media coverage of Vietnam, the histories written "from above," and the themes and techniques of *Dusklands* all demonstrate the colonizing effects of discourse. The Cartesian visual metaphor, in which the subject perceives the object, immediately suggests the authority of the subject to assign meaning and the consequent distancing and objectifiction of the Other. As "a colonizer who does not *want* to be a colonizer" (Watson 377), Coetzee is experimenting in how to escape the colonizing effects of discourse. The ultimate paradox of *Dusklands* is that in exposing the ways in which discourse is used to empower and enable oppression, in revealing some of the master-myths of history, Coetzee necessarily employs his own discourse and constructs his own myth. But throughout the text, he attempts to expose himself, to call attention to the fictionality of his fiction, to disclaim the authority that is traditionally awarded the author. The self-conscious narrative of Eugene Dawn—"A convention allows me to record these details" (42)—and the elaborate layers of narrators and narratives found in the second half of *Dusklands* make us aware of the fictional structure. Coetzee never pretends to offer an unbiased, objective, natural view of the facts of the past. In effect, he is practicing a kind of New Historicism in his self-conscious construction of the story. In the multivalence, confusion, repetition, and narrative doubt of *Dusklands*, Coetzee attempts to sidestep the superior angle of vision suggested by his authority as author.

Stephen Watson suggests that "The novel is surely constructed on the principle that it is through language itself, through those conventional representations which come to be accepted as either 'natural' or 'universal,' that we are colonized as much as by any overt act of physical conquest. The deconstruction of realism, then, is evidently intended, at the most basic level of language itself, as an act of decolonization, and, as such, is very much part of its political meaning" (374). And Teresa Dovey states, "As self-referential allegories, Coetzee's novels draw attention to their own position within a set of institutionally authorised discursive practices. . . . Once again the novel does what its critiques fail to, as it takes into account the material conditions of its own production" ("Coetzee and His Critics" 25). She points out that those critics who charge that Coetzee's novel is symptomatic of the very forms of consciousness that it criticizes often overlook the formal and structural devices of the novel, its own metacommentary on the process of discourse (16). In both its themes and its narrative strategies, *Dusklands* gropes for an alternative for the colonizer who doesn't want to colonize. The significant differences between Eugene Dawn and Jacobus Coetzee—the former consumed with guilt and self-awareness, the latter self-assured and blind to his own culpability—suggest that self-awareness is a necessary first step, a step we find Coetzee taking in his self-aware construction of the novel. In his first work, we find Coetzee exposing the mythmaking and objectifications of South African discourse, but he has not yet come to terms with the problem of how the Other might speak, how Africans can write themselves and their own histories.

· 4 ·

A Feminine Story:
In the Heart of the Country

In *Dusklands* Coetzee exposes the white writing of eighteenth-century colonial history and the mythological use of this history by the "fathers" of South Africa. His second novel, *In the Heart of the Country,* reflects a later stage of South African history in its account of a crazed woman, Magda, who lives on an isolated sheep farm in the Cape desert at the beginning of the twentieth century. This novel is made up of 266 numbered sections, written in the present tense, narrated by Magda. Some readers have referred to these segments as diary entries, since they proceed in chronological order and loosely follow the events of Magda's life. Magda does call herself "a spinster with a locked diary," but near the end of her account she laments that she did not have the foresight to keep "a journal like a good castaway" (3, 123). In her narrative, Magda does not comment on the fact that she is writing, in the way that Eugene Dawn did, but she does comment on the fact that she is thinking. Consequently, it seems more accurate to speak of the numbered sections as segments of her thoughts, or meditations. She does not write retrospectively, like Jane Eyre, looking back on her life and understanding its events in light of some coherent order. Rather, she writes "to the moment," much like Richardson's Clarissa or Pamela. As Magda thinks about her life, in a text emphasizing that act by its use of the present tense, she creates or recreates that life.

Because meditations are concerned with the activities of the mind rather than the historical events of a story, we find it difficult to trace exactly what takes place during the period of Magda's life covered in the narrative. Her meditations begin with an account of her father's return with a new bride, Magda's jealousy, and her hatchet-murder of the father and his bride in their bed. However, we soon discover that these incidents have only been imagined by Magda—they exist only in her meditation—

and we begin to wonder about the historicity of the subsequent account. Magda's next plot concerns her father's growing interest in and eventual seduction of Anna, the newlywed black wife of their servant, Hendrik. Firing a shotgun into his bedroom window in protest, Magda mortally wounds her father. She then invites Anna and Hendrik to live with her in the house, and she attempts to talk to and become friends with Anna. Hendrik, however, physically abuses and rapes her. When the neighbors begin inquiring about her father, Hendrik and Anna flee, leaving Magda on the decaying farm. We are never sure whether this part of her account is another fiction or not. In her final meditations, Magda lives on the farm, caring for her aged father, who is apparently still alive, and pondering the messages she believes she receives from the sky gods.

Magda's story is set during a crucial period of South African history: the decades of change at the conclusion of the nineteenth and beginning of the twentieth century. Although *In the Heart of the Country* is not a realistic representation of an African stock farm, it does include enough particulars to identify the novel's historical setting. Transportation is by horse, donkey, bicycle, and train. The house has no electricity or running water. Magda herself is not always sure about the accuracy of these details, and the many uncertainties of her narrative include uncertainty over its historical setting and facts. As she imagines exploring a trunk in the loft, she thinks of finding "ornamental fans, lockets and cameos, dancing slippers, favours and souvenirs, a baptismal frock, and photographs, if there were photographs in those days, daguerreotypes perhaps" (38). Other references identify Magda's colonial ancestors. Speculating about the origin of the abandoned schoolhouse on their farm, she says, "Someone must have built and stocked a schoolhouse, and advertised for a schoolmistress in the *Weekly Advertiser* or the *Colonial Gazette*" (46). By the end of the novel, the twentieth century is upon Magda: she receives a letter printed in two languages "requesting the payment of taxes for road maintenance, vermin eradication, and other marvels I had never heard of," and she receives messages from voices "out of machines that fly in the sky" (124–25, 126). The novel thus spans the period of approximately 1870 to 1960.

Even though it is not precisely dated, *In the Heart of the Country* nonetheless evokes a certain epoch in Afrikaner history, an epoch most notable for witnessing the formation of Afrikaner national identity. Looking back to colonial ancestors, the Afrikaners at the turn of the century began to construct the myths of their national identity. *The Oxford History of South Africa* explains, "Before the 1870s, the Afrikaner people lacked a national consciousness" (Wilson and Thompson 2:301). The conscious development of the Afrikaner myth of history and the consequent sense of national identity were first articulated by S. J. du Toit and the other intellectuals associated with the Genootskap van Regte Afrikaners (Society of True Afrikaners) and the First Language Movement in the seventies and eighties. As we have seen, the events of the Anglo-Boer War (1889–1902) served as the final catalyst to transform this cultural myth into a viable political entity, with the foundation of the National Party after the war. S. J. du Toit's son, J. D. du Toit or "Totius," carried on the nationalistic mythmaking of his father in his Afrikaans poetry about the war. With a unique language, history, and literature, the Afrikaner people began constructing a political and social state founded upon their newly formed national consciousness.

In the Heart of the Country mirrors this epoch's preoccupation with identity in Magda's "fight against becoming one of the forgotten ones of history" (3). Magda, bearing the name of the long-suffering and heroic wife of the Great Trek leader Piet Retief, is one of the "mothers" of South Africa, the feminine counterpart to Jacobus Coetzee.[1] Just as the Afrikaners struggled to find a national consciousness at the turn of the century, so Magda struggles to discover her identity. But Coetzee's account of the "turn" of the century completely effaces what is commonly thought to be the most important event of this period of South African history: the masculine Anglo-Boer War. Magda's character and narrative further rewrite the nationalistic myth in their subversion of Afrikaner patriarchal discourse. By centering his novel in Magda, Coetzee reinscribes the figure of the woman that is commonly employed to validate the Afrikaner myth. Envisioning herself as one of "the daughters of the colonies" who will be ignored by scholars, "lost to history," Magda attempts to articulate the silenced voice (3). Her feminine history attempts to break out of the patriarchal hierarchies on which traditional Afrikaner identity is based. Her narrative presents an alternative version of South African national consciousness as she struggles to find her identity in relationship to the land, her father, and the Africans of color with whom they share the land. The meditations of Magda—with their contradictions, fluid quality, and feminine imagery—embody a counter-myth, an alternative story to the patriarchal history of Afrikaner nationalism.

The Discourse of Patriarchy

The Afrikaner consciousness that developed during the waning of the nineteenth century was patriarchal and authoritarian, as the *Oxford History*'s summary indicates: "Their central concept . . . was that the Afrikaners were a distinct people or nation, occupying a distinct fatherland, South Africa, speaking a God-given language, Afrikaans, and endowed by God with the destiny to rule South Africa and civilize its heathen peoples" (Wilson and Thompson 2:301–302). Women played an idealized role in this scenario. In his study of the "Afrikaner civil religion," as he terms the national consciousness, T. Dunbar Moodie notes, "the civil faith reserved a special place of pride for the figure of the Afrikaner woman" (17). In Chapter 2 I considered the tendency of this national consciousness to privilege its own religious and ethnic identity at the cost of writing out the indigenous peoples of Africa. The depiction of women by this patriarchal discourse may prove useful for understanding *In the Heart of the Country.*

The central and elevated role of Afrikaner women is suggested by two of the most revered national shrines of the Republic of South Africa: the Voortrekker Monument and the Vrouemonument, or National Women's Monument. These structures commemorate the two central historical events around which the Afrikaners have constructed their national mythology—the Great Trek and the Anglo-Boer War—and both prominently feature women in their massive free-standing bronze sculptures and marble bas-reliefs. Together they emphasize the Afrikaner woman's purity, martrydom, and central role as progenitor. The mythology of the Afrikaner woman always stresses her role as *Vrou en Moeder,* wife and mother.

Designed by Anton van Wouw and located near Bloemfontein, the Vrouemonument is dedicated to the women and children who died in the British-run concentration camps during the Anglo-Boer War. Because the British destroyed Boer farms, burning their crops as a means of keeping the Boer commandos from resupplying, some provision needed to be made for the farm women and children who remained behind. Consequently, the British moved thousands of women and children, most against their will, into a vast system of concentration camps, which were very poorly run and supplied. Rations were inadequate; fuel was limited; sanitary arrangements and water supplies were unhygienic. Popular Afrikaner legend holds that the British deliberately adulterated the inmates' food with ground glass and fishhooks.[2] "Deaths in the concentration camps reached extraordinary proportions," S. B. Spies states, estimating that the 27,927 civilians who died in the camps were approximately double the number of men on both sides who were killed in action (170). Thomas Pakenham notes, "The camps have left a gigantic scar across the minds of the Afrikaners: a symbol of deliberate genocide" (524). The Vrouemonument provides a physical symbol for this psychic scar. Its central sculpture shows one woman standing and looking out into the distance, and another woman sitting patiently, an emaciated child on her lap. Bas-relief panels depict additional scenes associated with the suffering at the camps. On one, women and children enter the camp under the inscription "for freedom, *volk,* and fatherland." Another depicts women and children gathering around a tent in which a child lies dying at its mother's side.[3] The nationalistic myth is thus inscribed through the figures of women and children, defiant in their death.

The popular poetry of Totius, written to finance and promote the Vrouemonument, also capitalized on the figure of the Afrikaner woman.[4] His first volume of poetry, *By die Monument* (At the Monument, 1908), was dedicated to the women and children who died at the camps, and provided a theological interpretation of their suffering as the way in which God had bound the Afrikaners together into a covenant people. A later volume, *Ragel* (Rachel), appeared shortly before the opening of the monument and celebrated the biblical Rachel as the archetypal suffering mother for the Afrikaner woman in the concentration camps:

> Thus I think, Rachel,
>   of your lot and will
> recall your suffering,
>   your greatest grief,
> cruelly taken by surprise,
>   as long as the world remains.
>
> Thus I think of
>   the Rachels of my land,
> who without home or house

were cruelly surprised—burnt
out of their homes,
    pushed out into the veld.[5]

Ragel appeared with a foreword written by M. T. Steyn, a former President of the Orange Free State, founder of the Women's Monument organization, and promoter of Afrikaner identity. Steyn called Totius's poems "a three-fold tribute to Afrikaner women. The mother who is not ashamed or frightened by her destiny, who is always ready to offer herself and her children for their People and Fatherland" (qtd. Hexham, *Irony* 39). Motherhood, sacrifice, and nationalism again characterize women in this discourse. The poetry of Totius and the activities of the Women's Monument organization, according to Irving Hexham, were the "two major factors that created and spread [the] new awakening of an Afrikaner identity" in the postwar days ("Afrikaner Nationalism" 396). Between fifteen and twenty thousand people traveled to Bloemfontein on December 16, 1913, to attend the opening of the Vrouemonument, which received extensive coverage in *Het Westen,* the pro–National Party newspaper (Hexham, *Irony* 183).

Twenty-five years later another memorable national celebration was held when the cornerstone of the Voortrekker Monument was laid on December 16, 1938, as part of the centenary celebration of the Great Trek. One hundred thousand people attended the ceremony, "the biggest gathering ever known in South Africa" (Harrison 9). Before this ceremony, nine official ox-wagons, followed by hundreds of people in private ox-wagons and automobiles, on horseback and bicycles, retraced the journey of the original trek from the Cape to the site of the Monument. Moodie describes how during this journey the official wagons were "baptised" at different historical sites along the way and given names taken from major events of Trek history. Eight of the wagons bore proper names—the five legendary (male) Trek heroes and three children who played a significant role in the ordeals of the Trek. The remaining wagon was generically named "Vrou en Moeder," again emphasizing the prescribed role of the Afrikaner woman (Moodie 178).

Located in Pretoria, the Voortrekker Monument is the central icon commemorating the Boers' rejection of British Cape rule in 1838 and their trek inland to found their own republics. In the completed monument, a huge bronze statue of the Voortrekker Mother has the place of honor, standing against the main wall, flanked by the steps leading to the Hall of Heroes. Clad in a simple dress and traditional kappie, she gazes into the distance as her son and daughter cling to her skirts and gaze up at her. The official guidebook states, "The woman suffers but she does not look down. She looks straight ahead. The children do not look back. They look up" (Harrison 12). Special guides from the Transvaal Education Department explain to visitors, "The place of honour has been given to the woman because she made everything possible by trekking with her husband . . . by giving up her home, by bringing her children, by being ready to face sickness and danger she helped bring civilisation to the heart of this black continent" (Harrison 11, 13). Inside the Hall of Heroes, the twenty-seven marble bas-reliefs of the history of the Voortrekkers depict women cooking, caring for children, driving the ox-wagons, loading rifles, and encouraging the men. The Monument was officially unveiled in 1949 as part of yet another great festival, and remains South Africa's most important national symbol. "It has become the shrine where the faithful come for inspiration from the past, where those who have doubts about the present may be reassured. . . . To this Afrikaner temple are brought bus-loads of young South Africans to learn their lessons of the past" (Harrison 10).

The tendency of Afrikaner iconography to employ the figure of the woman for inspiration and validation is longstanding. Even during the height of the Anglo-Boer War, Afrikaner leaders pointed to the symbol of the *vrou*. On December 16, 1900, the Boers celebrated the Day of the Covenant at a farm forty miles from Pretoria. The British were prevailing, holding all the main towns and railway lines, but thousands attended the celebration, despite the danger. In his speech, General Smuts evoked the courage of the women of the Great Trek: "He reminded the men how it was the Boer *vrouws* to whose heroism they owed so much. The women had insisted that the men should trek out of Natal, although they could have stayed there in peace and plenty; they preferred to go barefoot over the Drakensberg and endure nameless sufferings among the Kaffirs, rather than submit to the British flag. This must remain the inspiration of the men, the refusal of these heroines ever to submit" (Pakenham 509–510). As resolute pioneer and defiant prisoner, the Afrikaner woman was elevated into a potent symbol around which nationalistic forces could rally.

As the myth of Afrikaner identity unfolded during the first decades of the twentieth century, it became permeated with the notion of an ideal "golden age" of Afrikaner life. Sheila Patterson explains, "this golden age is still represented as the 'lekker lewe' [good life] of the farmer, the Boer, in the old Republics; a life when land was there for the taking, where the veld grass grew tall, where the fountains never failed and the game thundered in uncounted herds. A life where men were strong and God-fearing, their women fair and brave and where the Kaffir knew his place" (239). The pastoral family had strictly defined hierarchical roles. African workers depended on the paternal white farmers for work, food, and advice. The Afrikaner father was a distant and aloof patriarch, farming, hunting, and fighting; the mother raised numerous children and cared for the house, keeping the fires of Christianity and civilization burning. This tendency to valorize the domestic sphere as the moral realm resembles similar tendencies in nineteenth-century American discourse. But Afrikaner gender roles took on theological and typological overtones, as Moodie notes: "If the Afrikaner man was indeed the instrumental agent who worked out God's will in Afrikaner history, the woman provided a deep well of moral fortitude which complemented and even surpassed her husband's more practical exploits" (17).

This patriarchal discourse includes a strong emphasis on childbearing. In bearing and raising children, women are responsible for both continuing the Afrikaner race and sustaining its purity: "it was because of her willingness to accompany her husband into the wilderness that the racial purity of Afrikanerdom had been preserved. It was to the woman that God had entrusted the task of bearing and raising Afrikaner children in the true civil faith" (Moodie 17). From colonial times on, visitors to South Africa have noted the extremely large size of the typical Afrikaner family, and even into the twentieth century the birth rate of Afrikaners has continued to be one-third higher than the birth rate of the English-speaking white population (Patterson 67). Pakenham explains how the exorbitant birth rates of the Afrikaners worked to Kruger's advantage in the political and military struggles against the British: "If the Boer commandos had a secret weapon in the shape of the spade, the nation as a whole had a secret weapon in the shape of the cradle. Demographers rubbed their eyes when they tried to measure the Transvaal birth rate. . . . The dedication of the Boer *vrou* was epitomized by Kruger's own family. In 1900 he had one hundred and fifty-six surviving children, grandchildren, and great-grandchildren." One of the cornerstones of Kruger's state, Pakenham concludes, was "the indomitable *vrouw*" (271).

In her elevation as wife and mother, the Afrikaner woman came to represent the ultimate symbol of purity for the Afrikaner race. Her properly regulated sexuality not only propagated the chosen race, it preserved that race undefiled. Patterson says, "A strong element in the ideal picture of the vrou is the concept of her as a white woman, chaste and aloof amongst a coloured sea" (242). A similar picture emerges in Moodie's description of how "the Afrikaner woman in her faith and purity took on certain attributes of the Holy Virgin in Catholicism" (17). Graphic visual evidence of this kind of mythologizing is found in an illustration that appeared in *Die Transvaler* (a National Party organ) during the 1938 election, depicting the pure Voortrekker woman above a mixed couple. The implication was that the United Party's policy of allowing mixed marriages would undermine the purity of the Afrikaner woman (Moodie 246).

Nineteenth-century legislation in southern Africa reflected that concern to preserve the white woman's purity. Although some areas allowed mixed marriages, all specifically forbade illicit sexual intercourse between white women and any "native"; no similar law forbade such sexual relations between white men and black women (Patterson 242). Twentieth-century legislation in the Union was not as gender bound. In 1927, the Immorality Act made all illicit intercourse between Europeans and Africans illegal. Further legislation in 1949 and 1950 prohibited both marriage and sexual intercourse between whites and all non-whites. Community mores, however, still demonstrated a greater concern for feminine purity. Patterson says, "As far as casual sexual relations between non-whites are concerned, Afrikaners, and indeed all whites, may admit that white men occasionally stray across the colour line, but consider it unthinkable that a white woman could be involved by choice. Any sexual passage between a white woman and a non-white man is therefore translated in terms of rape or assault" (243). The laws, mores, and iconography that consider the Afrikaner woman as pure, white, separate, and morally superior mask her submissive and subordinate role in the Afrikaner patriarchal system. Within Afrikaner society the woman is decidedly inferior. Both church and state refuse her equality with men, and even within the family structure her role is strictly defined and subordinate.

Despite the many social changes that have occurred throughout the Western world as a result of the feminist movement, women in modern Afrikaner society for the most part remain confined to strictly limited roles. Statistics gathered between 1936 and 1951 demonstrated that

Afrikaans-speaking women were far less likely to have professional occupations than English-speaking women (Patterson 70–71). The family structure is still very patriarchal. One white South African told Vincent Crapanzano, "The father is very strong in the Afrikaner family. Right or wrong, his opinion is laid down as law. It's backed up by the church, and the church by the government. The Afrikaners have a strong-knit family. A child is subservient to the father right through almost to his father's death. If you step out of line, you get hammered physically" (114). Statements coming from the Dutch Reformed Church, according to Patterson, suggest that "the ideal unit of private life remains the old-style Boer family, with its strong pattern of paternal authority. Large families are desirable, birth control is condemned and it is not thought advisable that the mother should go out to work" (189). Reviewing Sheila Fugard's novel *A Revolutionary Woman,* Coetzee comments that South Africa is "a patriarchal society that worships a patriarchal God, a society whose women are never visible" ("Satyagraha" 12). Once again, religion and politics work together.

Few Afrikaner women in recent decades have become involved in anti-apartheid activities, and the major Afrikaner women's organizations tend to focus on helping black women with domestic matters, such as home management, needlework, nutrition, and hygiene. The oldest women's organization is the Afrikaanse Christelike Vrouevereniging (ACVV), which was founded in 1904 to continue the work of the women's committees set up in the Cape to do relief work in the concentration camps during the Anglo-Boer War. Patterson says, "The ACVV has remained primarily a welfare organization, in keeping with the traditional role of the Boerevrou" (261). The northern societies of the ACVV jointly publish a magazine called *Vrou en Moeder,* recalling yet again the terms in which Afrikaner women exist in their society. Crapanzano comments on the various women's organizations: "They are, so to speak, a daytime activity, when men are away at work. Theirs [the men's] is the realm of economics and politics and not that of everyday social understanding and domestic welfare" (264–65). Even in the 1980s, Afrikaner society and culture dictate very distinct gender roles.

Besides the elevation and consequent marginalization of women, the discourse of Afrikaner identity upholds several other patriarchal norms. One key element is its twisted emphasis on submission to authority in the form of humiliation. In a review of the *Notebooks* of Athol Fugard, Coetzee says, "the humiliation of the weak by the strong has been a characteristic practice of the Afrikaner within his own culture, a practice underpinned by a perhaps perverted reading of Scripture which gives inordinate emphasis to authority and its converse, abasement" ("Art and Apartheid" 27). The practice of humiliation pervades Afrikaner culture: "The humbling of children by parents, of students by teachers, and generally of the younger by the older (the uninitiated by the initiated)— humbling that does not cease till face has been lost—is part of the life experience of most Afrikaners, and is kept alive, against liberalizing counterforces, by such institutions as the armed forces, which reach into most white households" (27–28). Those who have been humiliated merely wait their turn to hold authority and continue to participate in the same authoritarian system. Coetzee states, "Fugard knows the castrating urge behind South African *baasskap* [literally, boss-ship], knows that the castrated, the unloved, usually takes his place at the forefront of the castrators" (28).

This mentality explains the curious paradox of Afrikaner history that has been noted by many of its chroniclers: the Afrikaner people perceive themselves as mistreated, persecuted, and marginalized by the British and yet simultaneously mistreat, persecute, and marginalize the African people. Speaking of "the irony of Afrikaner history," W. A. de Klerk describes how "a people who in their heroic age were the victims of a succession of imperial onslaughts on their life, might now suddenly discover themselves to be . . . the new imperialists. How strange, how contradictory it all is" (319). The reciprocal practice of the humiliation of the weak by the strong also sheds light on Afrikaners' deep-rooted fear of losing political power.

Patriarchal discourse also appears in one of the most important genres of Afrikaner literature, the *plaasroman* or farm novel. Dominating the development of Afrikaner literature between 1920 and 1940, *plaasromane* were written by authors such as D. F. Malherbe, Jochem van Bruggen, Johannes van Melle, Mikro (C. H. Kuhn), C. M. van den Heever, and Abraham Jonker. Although the *plaasroman* sometimes is seen as part of the pastoral tradition of farm novels written in English by South African writers such as Olive Schreiner and Pauline Smith, in *White Writing* Coetzee argues that the English farm novels drew upon the British aristocratic novel of rural life while the *plaasroman* had more in common with the German *Bauernroman* in its romanticism and anti-capitalism. Written during a period when years of poor rainfall and economic depression pushed more and more Afrikaners off the land and into the city, the *plaasroman* "celebrated the memory of the old rural values" (83) and emphasized the romantic, natural bond between humans and the land. "By and large, the programme espoused by the *plaasroman* is one of a renewal of the peasant order based on the myth of the return to the earth" (79).

Such novels united nationalistic discourse with romantic discourse, as a few lines from a novel by C. M. van den Heever suggest: "Where the slumbering might of all national culture lies: [in] man with his ties to the earth, with which he is mystically united by a dark love" (qtd. in *White Writing* 79–80). As Coetzee notes, the romantic bond between Afrikaner and land is depicted in the *plaasroman* as more than an individual feeling; it also arose from and was dependent on the handing down of the farm from father to son, on a "lineal consciousness" rather than an "individual consciousness" (109). Women are once again inscribed as fertile reproducers, either symbolized by the mother earth bringing forth the fruits of the farm or embodied by the farm wife, responsible for the continuation of the line. The *plaasromane* "buttress Afrikaner patriarchalism in order that a heightened significance should be attached to the acts of the founding fathers, to maintaining their legacy and perpetuating their value. Thus we find the ancestors hagiographized as men and women of heroic strength, fortitude, and faith, and instituted as the originators of lineages" (*White Writing* 83).

The patriarchalism of the *plaasroman* also encompasses black-white relationships. Although in many *plaasromane* black laborers are conspicuous by their absence, the pastoral idyll does include the idea of Africans taking their proper place as workers of the earth and childlike beneficiaries of European supervision.[6] Mikro's Toiings trilogy and van Melle's *Dawid Booysen,* for example, both dramatize how the return to the farm frees white landholders and black serfs alike to live in harmony, uncorrupted by the urban world. The dream of a rural South Africa made up of family farms on which Afrikaner farmers and African laborers live together in paternalistic harmony continues to haunt the South African consciousness. Crapanzano repeatedly encountered it among the white farmers of Wyndal. He says that one woman "gives at times the impression that the old Afrikaner farmers, as yet uncorrupted by the ways of the city, and their workers formed one big happy family" (246). Afrikaner cultural discourse thus upholds a patriarchal world of paternalistic land owner, supportive wife and mother, and obedient and grateful Africans—all "mystically united by a dark love" with the earth.

The discourse of patriarchy in South Africa has many texts and many facets, and we have only touched upon some of its most prominent features. As inscribed in literature and legend, history and marble, social practice and community norms, the Afrikaner patriarchal system marginalizes the weak and employs the feminine—the woman and the land—to further masculine power and authority. The Afrikaner identity, as evolved over the centuries and articulated in poems, speeches, novels, monuments, holidays, and legal statutes, is resolutely masculine. *In the Heart of the Country* challenges that oppressive identity by changing the very language of identity, by allowing the feminine to speak.

Magda's Search for Identity

Viewed against the ideal Afrikaner woman extolled in national mythology, Magda clearly is a parody, an anti-heroine. She is neither *vrou* nor *moeder,* and she is a solitary social being with neither a mother nor siblings. Her physical and emotional characteristics are antithetical to the Afrikaner ideal. The images with which Magda characterizes herself are negative and perverted; she repeatedly describes herself as black, scrawny, dried-up, and sterile. She is full of venom like a black widow spider (39); her womb is a withered apple (50); she is a black flower (108). Her rhetoric frequently runs counter to the traditional discourse of Afrikaner womanhood. "I am not a happy peasant," she says, "I am a miserable black virgin" (5). The bride she imagines her father bringing home is a "glutted woman" with "full lips," but unlike the typical *vrou* of history and literature, Magda carries neither physical nor moral weight: "Even decades of mutton and pumpkin and potatoes have failed to coax from me the jowls, the bust, the hips of a true country foodwife" (4, 21). The patient, long-suffering, and willingly subordinate women of the Trek and the War have no parallel in Magda's defiant rebellion against her father and her destiny. Neither her thoughts nor her actions are pure: she imagines murdering her father, fantasizes that Hendrik will rape her.

Traditional Afrikaner discourse holds that a moral domesticity makes women the "heart" of the country, but Magda represents a very different kind of heart: "instead of being the womanly warmth at the heart of this house I have been a zero, null, a vacuum towards which all collapses inward, a turbulence, muffled, grey, like a chill draft eddying through the corridors, neglected, vengeful" (2). The rigid strength and perseverance of the Afrikaner woman as captured in the massive sculptures of the Vrouemonument and the Voortrekker Monument are in stark contrast to Magda's discourse of feminine emptiness: "I move through the world not as a knifeblade cutting the wind, or as a tower with eyes, like my father, but as a hole, a hole with a body draped around it. . . . I am a hole crying to be whole. . . . I think of myself as a straw woman, a scarecrow, not too tightly stuffed, with a scowl painted on my face to scare the crows and in my centre a hollow." Pondering that anatomy is destiny, she is "not unaware that there is a hole between my legs that has never been filled, leading to another hole never filled either. If I am an O, I am sometimes persuaded, it must be because I am a woman" (41).

Magda has no hope of ever performing the sacred duty of contributing to lineal preservation of the race: "who would give me a baby, who would not turn to ice at the spectacle of my bony frame on the wedding-couch, the coat of fur up to my navel, the acrid cavities of my armpits, the line of black moustache, the eyes, watchful, defensive, of a woman who has never lost possession of herself?" (10). This meditation continues with a dark parody that echoes the typology of Afrikaner history:

> Who could wake my slumbering eggs? And who would attend my childbed? My father, scowling, with a whip? The brown folk, cowed servitors, kneeling to offer a trussed lamb, first fruits, wild honey, sniggering at the miracle of the virgin birth? Out of his hole he pokes his snout, son of the father, Antichrist of the desert come to lead his dancing hordes to the promised land. They whirl and beat drums, they shake axes and pitchforks, they follow the babe, while in the kitchen his mother conjures over the fire, or tears out the guts of cocks, or cackles in her bloody armchair. A mind mad enough for parricide and pseudo-matricide and who knows what other atrocities can surely encompass an epileptic Führer and the march of a band of overweening serfs on a country town from whose silver roofs the sunfire winks and from whose windows they are idly shot to pieces. They lie in the dust, sons and daughters of the Hottentots, flies crawl in their wounds, they are carted off and buried in a heap. (10)

This imagined history is no worse, however, than Magda's rendition of colonial history. Again employing typical Afrikaner discourse, Magda ironically chronicles the "great moment" when the first sheep is brought to South Africa, "bleating with terror, unaware that this is the promised land where it will browse generation after generation on the nutritious scrub and provide the economic base for the presence of my father and myself in this lonely house where we kick our heels waiting for the wool to grow and gather about ourselves the remnants of the lost tribes of the Hottentots to be hewers of wood and drawers of water and shepherds and body-servants in perpetuity and where we are devoured by boredom and pull the wings off flies" (19). An anti-Mary who gives birth only to an imaginary anti-Christ, a bored and cruel spinster, Magda represents the untold side of Afrikaner history, the feminine absence that completes the masculine presence. "The land is full of melancholy spinsters like me," she thinks, "lost to history, blue as roaches in our ancestral homes. . . . Wooed when we were little by our masterful fathers, we are bitter vestals, spoiled for life" (3). Corrupted and ruined by the dominating myths of her father, Magda sets out to inscribe her own story and write a new history of Afrikaner consciousness. She refuses to be the pure woman who sustains the patriarchal hierarchy as wife and mother, and instead becomes the woman who seeks to undermine that hierarchy in both her actions and her narration.

Rejecting the facile definition of womanhood provided by the national myth, Magda struggles throughout *In the Heart of the Country* to answer the question, "Who am I?" The cover of the Penguin edition pictures her staring at herself in a mirror, as she does in section 43, poring over her reflection in an attempt to see herself. Her meditations are her psychological mirror, her means of viewing her own consciousness. Longing to free herself from the shadow of her father, Magda nonetheless is tempted to blame her lot in life on her history. Pondering who is responsible "for my ugly face and my dark desires," she considers the culpability of her father, her mother, her four grandparents, eight great-grandparents, sixteen great-great-grandparents, and "so forth until we come to Adam and Eve and finally to the hand of God." Despite these centuries of spiritual deformation, Magda clings to a hope that change can occur. "It is up to me," she resolves (23). She can treat her complexion with a fruit diet and take brisk morning walks; she can learn how to channel her dark desires in non-oppressive ways.

Magda thus endeavors to write herself by constructing her own history. She writes herself not only in her act of composing the meditations and creating the story of her father's murder, but also in her feeble attempts to recover an alternative past. Her meditations are not merely a "retreat into language" and a "shrinking away from a genuine exploration of history," as Hena Maes-Jelinek contends (90, 91). Rather, Magda shrinks from the history bequeathed her by her father and attempts to find an alternative. She winnows her memories and ransacks her surroundings in an attempt to find "evidence of a credible past" (38). She searches the loft, pores over family documents and old photographs, and envisions former times in the decrepit schoolhouse. She quests for a past of connections: she imagines what her mother must have been like; she creates a large happy family of brothers and sisters, including a golden boy named Arthur; she conjectures about her father's courtship of her mother. The past that she creates reflects her longing for human interconnectedness as well as her essential isolation: "If I have brothers and sisters they cannot be in the city, they must all have been swept away by the great meningitis epidemic; for I cannot believe that fraternal intercourse would not have left its mark upon me, and it has all too plainly not left its mark upon me, the mark that has been left upon me instead is the mark of intercourse with the wilds, with solitude and vacancy" (47). Alternatively, she imagines that her siblings were actually stepbrothers and step-sisters, children of her father's first wife, who scorned her and were taken away to live with a maternal uncle. Nonetheless, she still loved them, especially the golden Arthur, who ignored her. Magda's imaginary families, like Huckleberry Finn's similar narrative clans, reveal her frustrated desire for human community. Her reflections on her identity in relationship to her history and her attempts to reconstruct that history prove defeating at worst and inconclusive at best.[7]

Magda also struggles to understand her identity in relationship to her natural surroundings. The solitary wasteland of her desert environment appears to reflect her own hollowness, but Magda's frequent meditations on the natural world invariably conclude that the romantic identification and bond between human beings and the land extolled in the Afrikaner *plaasroman* are impossible. The natural world exists only as being; she exists as consciousness. Although the unreflective existence of insects, flowers, and stones appeals to her, Magda cannot escape her human attributes of voice and choice, language and morality: "Though I may ache to abdicate the throne of consciousness and enter the mode of being practised by goats or stones, it is with an ache I do not find intolerable" (26). In other passages she is less phlegmatic: "I can never be the rapture of pure self that they [flowers, stones, bushes] are but am alas forever set off from them by the babble of words within me that fabricate and refabricate me as something else, something else. The farm, the desert, the whole world as far as the horizon is in an ecstasy of communion with itself, exalted by the vain urge of my consciousness to inhabit it" (48–49). Articulation precludes pure being. A black widow spider in metaphor only, she is "faced with a choice that flies do not have to make"—whether to give herself over to sensation or speech (78).

The significance of the desert and the farm is not the natural bond between them and Magda but the opportunity with which they present her: "The world is full of people who want to make their own lives, but to few outside the desert is such freedom granted. Here in the middle of nowhere I can expand to infinity just as I can shrivel to the size of an ant. Many things I lack, but freedom is not one of them" (50). Yet the freedom offered by the wide, solitary expanses of Magda's surroundings is paradoxically confining. Free to create her own history and identity through her articulations and choices, Magda nonetheless is trapped by the social structures of parent and child, master and servant, in which she exists. Asked about the image of the country as a desert that frequently appears in South African literature, Coetzee replied: "I think the desert archetype is about a lack of society and a lack of shared culture, a feeling of anomie, a feeling of solitariness, a feeling of not having humanities with the people around one" (Coetzee, "Speaking" 22). Magda's desert neither embodies nor shelters the loving mother and sister for whom she searches. Her meditations on her personal history and on the natural world point to her essential loneliness, her longing to find the "humanities" she shares with those around her.

Magda primarily attempts to define herself, then, through human relationships. However, the patriarchal oppositions of Afrikaner society and its tradition of the humiliation of the weak by the strong impair the formation of true community, as she continually discovers. These traditions breed oppression for both masters and slaves, the strong and the weak. As Coetzee has said, "In a society of masters and slaves no one is free. The slave is not free because he is not his own master; the master is not free because he cannot do without the slave" ("Apartheid" 57). As the submissive daughter of a domineering father, as the weak woman raped by an abusive man, as the white mistress of two black servants— Magda finds herself in a complex web of oppressive relationships. In her attempts to escape the master/slave dichotomy that characterizes all of these relationships, Magda tries to learn to live in reciprocity, in equality, in true freedom. The situation in both *Dusklands* and *In the Heart of the Country,* according to Coetzee, is that "of living among people without reciprocity, so that there's only an 'I' and the 'You' is not on the same basis, the 'You' is a debased 'You'" ("Speaking" 23). Unable to "create a society in which reciprocity exists," Magda condemns herself to "desperate gestures towards establishing intimacy" ("Speaking" 23). Her gestures ultimately end in violence and futility. Until the culture and society change, efforts of individual will are not enough. Individual efforts are necessary but insufficient means to the redemption of South African life.

The first master/slave dichotomy on which Magda meditates is her warped relationship with her father. With his heavy black boots, his ramrod-stiff posture, and "the black hole of the mouth from which roars the great NO," Magda's father epitomizes masculine domination (51). As Penner points out, Magda associates her father with the authoritarian and retributive god of the Old Testament (61). The fantasy of the first thirty-five sections demonstrates that Magda both fears and loves him. Their life together is devoid of love, words, or touch:

> Sundown after sundown we have faced each other over the mutton, the potatoes, the pumpkin, dull food cooked by dull hands. Is it possible that we spoke? No, we could not have spoken, we must have fronted each other in silence and chewed our way through time, our eyes, his black eyes and my black eyes inherited from him, roaming blank across their fields of vision. Then we have retired to sleep, to dream allegories of baulked desire such as we are blessedly unfitted to interpret; and in the mornings vied in icy asceticism to be the earlier afoot, to lay the fire in the cold grate. Life on the farm. (3)

The ironic echoes of the *plaasroman* suggest the moral bankruptcy of the patriarchal Golden Age.

Magda's desperate search for some kind of intimacy with her father results both in oedipal longings and in imagined acts of violence. In her story of her father bringing home a new bride, Magda depicts this woman as fertile and sensual, able to arouse and satisfy all of her father's baulked desire, quite unlike herself. Yet Magda's subsequent fantasy does not fit the standard Freudian interpretation, as Josephine Dodd explains: "Magda is supposed to desire her father as representative of the law and custodian of reason and language, but it is *only male children* who are suppose[d] to fantasize the killing of the father, only male children can hope to accede to that position of power" ("Naming" 159). In fantasizing about murdering her naked father in the forbidden bed, Magda empowers herself with masculine tools: she bludgeons his body with an axe;

in a later scene she (either literally or imaginatively) blows out his guts with a shotgun. From a position of helplessness and oppression, Magda reverses the dichotomy to become the masculine force that imposes its will on others, humiliating the weak to become the strong.

Her father's affair with Anna presents even more of a threat of marginalization. Anna appears to achieve a degree of intimacy with her father for which Magda longs in vain. As they sit in the kitchen eating peaches and bread, Magda listens at the door: "It is a love-feast they are having; but there is one feast which is nobler than the love-feast, and that is the family meal. I should have been invited too" (52). Beyond these laments of the loveless child lurks a greater fear, for in his relationship with Anna, Magda's father has subverted the white/black hierarchy. If Anna can become his mistress, perhaps Magda will become the servant. "I should be seated at that table," she continues about the love-feast, "at the foot properly, since I am mistress of the household; and she, not I, should have to fetch and carry. Then we might break bread in peace, and be loving to one another in our different ways, even I" (52). Similarly, "If she ceases to be the servant who will be the servant but I" (53). Apparently unable to visualize this relationship from the perspective of Anna—physically, economically, and socially dependent upon the father for her existence and thus essentially raped by the white master—Magda's sole concern is for her own further oppression. Again she turns to violence, "randomly" shooting the shotgun through the bedroom window and fatally wounding her father.

The death of her father and of the past he embodies frees Magda, she thinks, to go beyond the patriarchal system to establish new relationships with Hendrik and Anna. Yet the difficulties that she has with disposing of her father's body and the assistance she must have from Hendrik reveal that the burden of the patriarchal system is not so easily removed. Even before her father's death, Magda had begun to search for humanity in the desert of her life by turning toward the two black servants. Her initial interest takes the form of numerous imaginative journeys into their lives, creating in her meditations their wedding journey, Hendrik's ancestral golden past, Hendrik's first arrival on the farm, his desire to start a line by having children, the couple's morning routine. Despite these imaginative forays, however, she feels stymied in her attempts to achieve connection and relationship. "I know nothing of Hendrik," she admits (24); listening to his guitar music on the night air, she thinks, "we might as well be on separate planets, we on ours, they on theirs" (28).

However, following her father's death, Magda believes she can establish a new kind of intimacy with Anna and Hendrik. Dressing Anna in
the "sad noble clothes of bygone times" that she finds in a wardrobe (85),
Magda watches her promenade, dreaming that Anna will become the
sister she never had:

> I would like to stroll arm in arm with her of a Saturday night dressed in
> my gayest clothes, whispering and giggling like a girl, showing myself off
> to the country beaux. I would like to hear from her, in a quiet corner, the
> great secrets of life, how to be beautiful, how to win a husband, how to
> please a man. I would like to be her little sister, I have had a late start in
> life, the years behind me are as if passed in slumber, I am still only an
> ignorant child. I would like to share a bed with her, and when she tiptoes
> in at midnight peep with one eye at her undressing, and sleep all night
> cuddled against her back. (87)

Their intimacy would involve both speech and touch, sharing secrets and
strolling with arms entwined. Her casting of Anna as the elder sister
suggests Magda's sense that Anna has a superior wisdom concerning "the
great secrets of life." Yet Magda is able to envision this relationship only
within the stereotypical norms of Afrikaner farm life complete with
country beaux, feminine wiles, and bedroom confidences. Her imaginative transformation of Anna into a colonial belle is not true intimacy,
and Magda's fantasy remains firmly within the patriarchal order. Her
inability to recognize Anna in her own right is suggested immediately
following the promenade scene when she asks or orders Anna and
Hendrik to spend the night in the house with her, on a mat on the
kitchen floor. She wants them to share her living space, but she still
automatically relegates them to an inferior position. Similarly, as she
struggles to bury her father's body, she continues to give Hendrik orders,
and, when the body falls off the wheelbarrow, she resorts to the age-old
words, "You damned *hotnot*, it's all your fault, you and your whore!"
(91).

The patriarchal system is also perpetuated by Hendrik, who demands
to be paid for his labor on the farm. Magda idealistically wants the three
of them to live in a pre-capitalistic Eden, but Hendrik insists, "We did
our work, miss . . . Now we must get our money" (94). Hendrik's
reliance on hierarchical relationships is epitomized when he dresses
himself in her father's clothes and begins to preen on the loft platform.
Magda orders him to take the clothes off, and he threatens to expose

himself: "Hey, look! Look, our miss, look! . . . Come on, don't be scared, our miss, it's only a man!" (98). When Magda's attempt to withdraw money from her father's account fails, Hendrik demands the "something else" she can pay instead of money (97). His brutal possession of Magda's body perpetuates the master/slave relationship by merely reversing the terms. During his nightly visits he refuses to talk to her and continually humiliates her physically. Magda pleads, "Must I weep? Must I kneel? Are you waiting for the white woman to kneel to you? Are you waiting for me to become your white slave? *Tell me! Speak!*" (118). Clothed in the outward garb of the master, wielding the weapon of the male organ, Hendrik has become the new father who rules the farm. His history of economic and cultural deprivation and the perverted structure of the society in which he lives do not allow him to escape the master/slave relationship.

Magda acquiesces to his new role, longing to believe that it is the path to the intimacy for which she has been searching. She thinks, "In the heart of nowhere, in this dead place, I am making a start; or, if not that, making a gesture" (110). She invites Anna and Hendrik to move into the guestroom, and she asks Hendrik if she is "doing it right" during his nocturnal visits. "All I want is a little peace between us," she says to Hendrik (112). Magda believes that an individual act of the will is sufficient to escape the history that confines them all: "You are so bitter that you are completely blinded. I am not simply one of the whites, I am *I*! I am I, not a people. Why have *I* to pay for other people's sins?" (118). However, Magda cannot escape her existence as a social being; she remains a part of a people, trapped by that social role. The equality that she can offer is not sufficient, as events soon demonstrate. When the neighbors begin to inquire about Magda's father, Hendrik knows that he will bear the guilt: "one of these days they will be back, sooner than you think," he tells Magda. "Then they will see that you are living with the servants in the big house. Then *we* will be the ones to suffer—not you—she and I! . . . when they say I shot him, who will believe me, who will believe a brown man?" (117). Both psychologically and socially, Hendrik cannot escape the master/slave dichotomy.

With Anna, Magda achieves little more success. She both vocalizes and physically enacts her desire for intimacy, telling Anna she thinks they might have been something like sisters and lying beside her on the mat in the kitchen. As in her relationship with Hendrick, she attempts to reach the other both by means of the body and by means of speech.

She asks Anna to call her "Magda," but Anna continues to address her as "Miss" (102). Their physical intimacy is awkward and forced: "I find her head and press my lips against her forehead. For a moment she struggles, then stiffens and endures me. We lie together, at odds, I waiting for her to fall asleep, she waiting for me to go. I grope my way out of the kitchen to my own bed. I am doing my best in this unfamiliar world of touch" (103). In her insistent pursuit of equality, Magda ironically distances Anna even further, as she finally realizes, "Anna is oppressed by my watching eyes. She is oppressed by my invitations to relax, to sit by my side on the old bench in the shade of the sering-tree. She is oppressed particularly by my talk" (113). Another meditation concludes sadly, "There has been no transfiguration. What I long for, whatever it is, does not come" (114).

Magda's longing has been for true communion to take place between her and Hendrik and Anna. Yet she has no idea how to achieve this communion; neither her acquiescence to Hendrik's rape nor her perseverence in talking to Anna brings her the intimacy for which she longs. In one of her final meditations she describes her attempt at reconciliation: "The medium, the median—that is what I wanted to be! Neither master nor slave, neither parent nor child, but the bridge between, so that in me the contraries should be reconciled" (133). The failed transfiguration exemplifies the culmination of South African history as expressed in Alan Paton's *Cry the Beloved Country*. "I have one great fear in my heart," says one black character, "that one day when they are turned to loving, they will find we are turned to hating" (40). Although Magda has failed with Hendrik and Anna, she does express a tentative hope: "Is it that Hendrik and I are, in our different ways, ruined for love? Or is it simply that the story took a wrong turn somewhere, that if I had found a more gradual path to a gentler form of intimacy we might all have learned to be happy together? Or is this desert of fire and ice a purgatory we must pass through on the way to a land of milk and honey? And what of Anna? Will she come too? Will she and I one day be sisters and sleep in the same bed? Or will she, when she finds herself, scratch my eyes out?" (118–119).

As *Dusklands* did, *In the Heart of the Country* suggests that behind the impossibility of relationship lies the lack of transcendence. Magda reflects, "God has forgotten us and we have forgotten God. There is no love from us toward God nor any wish that God should turn his mind to us. The flow has ceased. We are the castaways of God as we are the castaways of history. *That* is the origin of our feeling of solitude" (135). The "gods" of the flying machines do not provide a satisfactory substitute with their obscure philosophical statements. Magda claims, "I am not a philosopher. Women are not philosophers, and I am a woman. A woman cannot make something out of nothing" (119). Reason is not enough. Women need relationships and dreams and purpose and physical reality: "I need people to talk to, brothers and sisters or fathers and mothers, I need a history and a culture, I need hopes and aspirations, I need a moral sense and a teleology before I will be happy, not to mention food and drink" (120). She puzzles over the cryptic messages delivered in a pure Spanish that she understands even though she does not speak Spanish, and she attempts to apply the messages to her life. Yet she refuses to accept their rational judgment of the inescapability of the master/slave consciousness. "Where, unless compassion intervenes, does the round of vindictiveness end?" she wonders (130). To the "indictments of the voices" she writes a poem in six parts: "DESERTA MI OFRA—ELECTAS ELEMENTARIAS—DOMINE O SCLAVA—FEMM O FILIA—MA SEMPRE HA DESIDER—LA MEDIA ENTRE" (133). Her poem holds out the possibility of hope:

> You offer me a desert
> elementary choices
> master or slave
> woman or daughter
> I have always desired
> the medium between

Answering their philosophy with her poetry, she concludes her meditations with an account of her maternal care for her father: carrying him out to sit in the sun, reminiscing about pastoral life on the farm, changing his diaper. In her voluntary care for her father, Magda seems to at last glimpse a way out of the desert, a medium between master and slave, woman and daughter. Whether or not she has actually killed him or if this final tender behavior is only imaginary is not important. For it is in her discourse that she killed him and now it is in her discourse that she loves him.

Most readers have seen Magda's story as ending in futility and madness, and so conclude that this is Coetzee's bleak prediction about the future of white South Africa. Sheila Roberts writes, "There is no change, no movement, no development in the life lived on 'the stone farm'—a symbol of the whole country" (30). And although Dick Penner sees Magda's compassionate care for her father as a change, he concludes, "No Messiah appears to fill the void left by the passing of the old order, the old language of hierarchy, which the father represents." Instead, we are left in a condition of "inertia, stalemate, deadlock, cul-de-sac, stasis, entropy—conditions common to modern and postmodern literature since Kafka's cockroach first limped on the scene, and certainly characteristic of most Absurdist fiction and drama" (72). Such conclusions oversimplify the complex achievement of *In the Heart of the Country*. Magda's search for the land of milk and honey redirects Afrikaner typological history and ends in affirmation, albeit tentative and subtle. This affirmation is perhaps made more visible or audible in the quality of Magda's discourse, which rejects patriarchy and authority.

Magda's Feminine Discourse

In the Heart of the Country subverts Afrikaner patriarchal discourse in a number of ways, both on a representational level and on a generic level. The character of Magda is, as we have seen, a subversion of traditional Afrikaner ideas about women. Similarly, the setting of the novel and its chorus of "life on the farm" parody the traditional *plaasroman* and so reveal the inadequacies of the pastoral vision in the face of South African realities. Paul Rich comments, "*In the Heart of the Country* emerges as an 'anti-pastoral' novel in that it takes an idealised rural situation . . . and subjects it to a merciless scrutiny in order to try and reveal some inner truth about the nature of real social reality" ("Tradition" 70). Rich terms the novel "a landmark" in the South African search for a genre to break with the pastoral colonial tradition beginning in eighteenth-century British literature, but we can also see how *In the Heart of the Country* breaks with the more narrow and specifically Afrikaner tradition of the *plaasroman* and so rebuts the Afrikaner identity associated with that tradition. Reviewing the novel in the South African quarterly *Contrast,* Jean Marquard writes that it "articulates an ironic, anti-pastoral approach to life-on-the-farm, thereby debunking the central theme of South African literature" (85).

Further generic subversion occurs in Magda's rejection of philosophy for poetry. Although lyrical landscape poetry is perhaps the oldest genre of South African literature, playing an important role in both the English and Afrikaans traditions, Magda refuses to speak in this voice also:

"There are poems, I am sure, about the heart that aches for Verlore Vlakte, about the melancholy of the sunset over the koppies, the sheep beginning to huddle against the first evening chill, the faraway boom of the windmill, the first chirrup of the first cricket, the last twitterings of the birds in the thorn-trees, the stones of the farmhouse wall still holding the sun's warmth, the kitchen lamp glowing steadily. They are poems I could write myself" (138). Instead, Magda says, "I have uttered my life in my own voice throughout . . . I have chosen at every moment my own destiny, which is to die here in the petrified garden, behind locked gates, near my father's bones, in a space echoing with hymns I could have written but did not because (I thought) it was too easy" (139). The traditional elegies to the landscape written by Jan F. E. Celliers, Eugene N. Marais, Thomas Pringle, and Guy Butler are rejected for Magda's own voice and own identity.[8] Marquard says, "In using the novel as a critical tool, aimed not only at South African way-of-life, but at the literature which has traditionally reflected it; he creates for the tradition a new direction" (85). But in subverting and refusing the traditions of the *plaasroman* and landscape poetry, Coetzee also employs his novel as a critical tool aimed at the Afrikaner identity created in and sustained by the cultural texts of these traditional genres.

Artists in South Africa, Coetzee claims in *White Writing,* have been on a quest for an authentic language, a quest impeded by the various social practices and physical realities of life in South Africa. "It is no oversimplification to say that landscape art and landscape writing in South Africa from the beginning of the nineteenth century to the middle of the twentieth revolve around the question of finding a language to fit Africa, a language that will be authentically African" (7). In Magda's voice, we hear Coetzee experimenting with a new language, a new mode of discourse. Magda's narration subverts patriarchal discourse, traditional Afrikaner language, in its anti-linear, anti-rational construction. The texture of her discourse is in itself an attempt at a medium, a median, between the mastery of logic and the enslavement of irrationality. In her final meditation Magda admits that she has not yielded to "the spectre of reason" and explained all of the details of her story—why she did not flee the farm and return to civilization, what exactly has happened during the course of her history (138). Yet neither does she give up reason entirely. Dodd argues that the novel demonstrates "the apparent un-supplantability of male discourse" because "to speak is to participate" (159, 160), but Magda's narration, with its blatant inconsistencies, alter-

native histories, self-awareness, and metafictions, does attempt to sup-
plant male discourse even as it refuses patriarchal norms.

Magda's unusual and fluid account in many ways resembles *l'écriture
féminine* as defined by French feminists such as Luce Irigaray, Hélène
Cixous, and Julia Kristeva. Associating rational and representational
discourse with the symbolic realm of the Law-of-the-Father (as defined
by Lacan), these critics describe feminine discourse as subjective and
instinctive. Feminine discourse refuses the traditional (masculine) values
of clarity, logic, and linear continuity, questioning the supposed superiority of rational unified discourse over instinctive discontinuous discourse. The stylistic characteristics "widely recognized" as forming
l'écriture féminine, according to Ann Jones, are "double or multiple voices,
broken syntax, repetitive or cumulative rather than linear structure, open
endings" (88). Additionally, for many feminist thinkers, feminine discourse is a language of the mind and the body, conveying both ideas and
the reality of the body itself.

Some believe that such discourse can be produced by both men and
women, even though western civilization has inscribed it as "feminine."
Kristeva claims, "All speaking subjects have within themselves a certain
bisexuality which is precisely the possibility to explore all the sources of
signification, that which posits a meaning as well as that which multi-
plies, pulverizes, and finally revives it" (165). She argues that the avant-
garde poetry of Lautréamont, Mallarmé, and Céline breaks with the
symbolic realm of the Law-of-the-Father for the pre-linguistic realm of
what she terms "the semiotic." Toril Moi explains, "The modernist poem,
with its abrupt shifts, ellipses, breaks and apparent lack of logical construction is a kind of writing in which the rhythms of the body and the
unconscious have managed to break through the strict rational defences
of conventional social meaning" (11). Irigaray's and Cixous's emphasis is
more biologically bound to the female body, and Gilbert and Gubar note
how many women writers have used images of female sexuality and
childbirth to counter the prevalent imagery of the pen as metaphorical
penis. Although feminist critics disagree over the ability of male writers
to engender feminine discourse, all emphasize the importance of the
female body as a site for such discourse.

Magda's account employs the repetitive structure, double voices,
abrupt shifts, and open ending of *l'écriture féminine.*[9] Her lyricism and
imagery further exemplify her feminine discourse, and in her language
she attempts to write the body even as she attempted to communicate to

Hendrik and Anna through the body. "Lyric is my medium, not chronicle," she states (71), and many readers have agreed, finding lyrical beauty in individual passages of In the Heart of the Country but remaining confused and sometimes bored by the narrative as a whole. Two particularly striking passages explore the possibility of reaching the other by means of a bodily identification, as Magda attempts in her poetry what she has found impossible in her history. Confined by language, she nonetheless attempts to go beyond language, to capture the instinctive pre-verbal realm of the semiotic within the symbolic, as indeed all *l'écriture féminine* must. The first passage occurs as her father lies dying:

> Oh father, father, if I could only learn your secrets, creep through the honeycomb of your bones, listen to the turmoil of your marrow, the singing of your nerves, float on the tide of your blood, and come at last to the quiet sea where my countless brothers and sisters swim, flicking their tails, smiling, whispering to me of a life to come! I want a second chance!   (71)

The second follows her rape, when she longs for a resolution to her struggle in a remarkable lyrical stream-of-consciousness passage:

> I want a home somewhere else, if it has to be in this body then on different terms in this body, if there is no other body, though there is one I would far prefer, I cannot stop these words unless I cut my throat, I would like to climb into Klein-Anna's body, I would like to climb down her throat while she sleeps and spread myself gently inside her, my hands in her hands, my feet in her feet, my skull in the benign quiet of her skull where images of soap and flour and milk revolve, the holes of my body sliding into place over the holes of hers, there to wait mindlessly for whatever enters them, the song of birds, the smell of dung, the parts of a man, not angry now but gentle, rocking in my bloodwarmth, laving me with soapy seed, sleeping in my cave.   (108–9)

Both passages express Magda's longing to go beyond the realm of words and language to a different kind of communication, a physical union in which the master/slave dichotomy is overcome, a oneness of harmony. And in their existence as written discourse, both passages achieve this (momentary) resolution.

In both passages, Magda achieves union with her father and Anna, not as the opposite force within the sexual act but nonetheless within the sexual act. Both passages characterize this unity with imagery of the sea, a common image pattern in modernist works and one that is often linked with feminine writing, particularly by Cixous, as Moi remarks: "For

Cixous, as for countless mythologies, water is the feminine element *par excellence:* the closure of the mythical world contains and reflects the comforting security of the mother's womb" (117). As Prufrock "lingered in the chambers of the sea / By sea-girls wreathed with seaweed red and brown," so Magda repeatedly invokes the sea as a place of peace and resolution. She admits, "I do not know the oceans," but she promises herself that someday she will board a train and spend an idyllic day at the seashore: "I will take off my shoes and crunch through the seasand, wondering at the millions of tiny deaths that have gone to make it up. I will roll up my skirts and wade in the shallows and be nipped by a crab, a hermit crab, as a cosmic joke" (44).[10] In her final scenes of peace with her father, it is this (imaginary?) day that she recalls in detail (136).

Magda's meditations on suicide also evoke the sea, but in these passages, we see her ambivalence about a total submersion in the semiotic. In section 31 she describes a suicide attempt: "Far down in the earth flow the underground rivers, through dark caverns dripping with crystalline water, graves, if only they could be reached, for all the family secrets in the world. I wade out into the tepid dam looking for the sinkhole which in our dreams beckons from the deep and leads to the underground kingdom" (13). Yet when she dives, "the elegiac trance passes and all the rest is cold, wet, and farcical. My underwear balloons with water. I strike bottom all too soon, as far from the mythic vortex as ever" (13). Similarly, in a later passage she explores "the pleasures of drowning, the feel of my body sliding out of me and another body sliding in, limbs inside my limbs, mouth inside my mouth" (53). Again the peace is only temporary: "For when I wake on the ocean floor it will be the same old voice that drones out of me, drones or bubbles or whatever it is that words do in water." The fluidity of the subconscious and the mystical diffusion of the self again is confronted with physical reality: "I pinch this flesh and it hurts. What more proof could I want? I am I" (54). Magda's sea meditations temporarily enter the semiotic realm, but she is always pulled back by reason.

Other metaphors of Magda's are also typical of feminine discourse. She uses imagery of sewing to describe the construction of her narrative, speaking of "embroidering" her story (1), "weaving" the details (6), "picking a hem" as she undoes her account of the axe-murder (17), and the "weave of reminiscence" (43). Another feminine metaphor Magda ironically invokes is that of childbirth. Although on the representational level Magda epitomizes the sterile spinster, on the linguistic level she gives birth to the text. On yet another level, her murder of her father and disposal of his body are described with images of maternity and birth. "Until this bloody afterbirth is gone there can be no new life for me," she thinks about the bodies of her father and his bride (15). And as she tries to carve out a hole large enough for his body, she becomes a maternal figure, placing him into the womb of the earth: "The bundle, hauled out again, lies like a great grey larva at the graveside, and I, its tireless mother, instinct-driven, set again about stowing it in the safe place I have chosen" (92). Magda's revision of Afrikaner patriarchy casts the woman not as the passive and submissive womb sustaining the Christlike race but rather as the industrious ant giving birth to a new kind of identity, a new nation.

Finally, Magda's discourse emphasizes dialogue as opposed to monologue. In the original South African edition of *In the Heart of the Country,* published by Ravan Press in 1976, this dialogic quality was linguistically embodied. Magda's meditations were written in English; the passages of dialogue in Afrikaans. The text itself thus conducted a dialogue between the two primary South African forms of discourse. The issue of dialogue also is of great concern to Magda as she attempts to break down the barriers between herself and Hendrik and Anna. The solitary voice leads to solipsism and to oppression, as Coetzee suggests in *Dusklands.* "This monologue of the self is a maze of words out of which I shall not find a way until someone else gives me a lead," Magda says (16). The most extensive dialogues recorded are those between Magda and the two blacks, yet eventually Magda feels even these conversations are monologic. "Why do you never *say* anything?" she asks Hendrik (118). When a conversation with Anna turns into another monologue, Magda thinks, "I only wanted to talk, I have never learned to talk with another person. It has always been that the word has come down to me and I have passed it on. I have never known words of true exchange" (101). The language she has inherited from her father, the word that has come down to her, does not facilitate the longed-for dialogue. The language of patriarchy does not bridge the gap: "The language that should pass between myself and these people was subverted by my father and cannot be recovered. What passes between us now is a parody. I was born into a language of hierarchy, of distance and perspective. It was my father-tongue. I do not say it is the language my heart wants to speak, I feel too much the pathos of its distances, but it is all we have. I can believe there is a language lovers speak but cannot imagine how it goes. I have no words left to exchange whose value I trust" (97). Magda's desire for a language of the heart, a language of lovers, with which to engage others in dialogue demonstrates again the inadequacies of the patriarchal discourse of South Africa.

As feminine discourse, Magda's meditations do not come to a neat and tidy conclusion. Her non-linear narrative is emotionally evocative rather than philosophically logical. Although she says "I want my story to have a beginning, a middle, and an end, not the yawning middle without end" (42–43), *In the Heart of the Country* never reaches any kind of closure. Hence the many readings of the novel as bleak, pessimistic, and alienating. Its indeterminate ending refuses the authority of patriarchy, but it also is indicative of the distortions of South African culture. Coetzee notes in a review of Njabulo Ndebele's fiction, "It seems to me that a feature of the South African novel for some while has been that its writers have not known how to end what they have begun, or what the times they are representing have begun for them. It is as though the end, the true and just end, has assumed the aspect of that which cannot be imagined, that which can be represented only in fantasy, whether dire or wishful" ("Tales out of School" 38). Nonetheless, in Coetzee's second novel Magda's meditations tentatively evoke and affirm the gentle touch over the violent blow, the instinct of compassion over the rigor of hatred, the lyrical flow over the reasoned philosophy, the exchange of dialogue over the rigid monologue. In his Jerusalem Prize speech, Coetzee claims, "At the heart of the absence of freedom for hereditary masters of South Africa, there is a deficiency of love" ("Apartheid" 57). Magda's narrative ends with questions and doubt, but the reader has no difficulty in ascertaining where Coetzee's heart lies.

· 5 ·

The Novelist and Torture:
Waiting for the Barbarians

In his third novel, Coetzee moves away from exposing the way historical discourses have worked to construct and reinforce the hierarchical systems of oppression in South Africa, and turns to a more allegorical rendition of the dynamics of contemporary life in South Africa. Although he continues to echo certain elements of Afrikaner discourse in *Waiting for the Barbarians,* throughout the novel Coetzee is more concerned with a specific issue looming over South African political life: the question of torture. Ever since the National Party gained control in 1948, there have been accusations of state-sponsored torture in South Africa. But the public outcry and debate over the issue of torture reached new heights in the late 1970s. At that time the issue of torture in South Africa filled public discourse of all kinds—from government reports to protest poems, from United Nations declarations to novels.

South African writers were audible voices in this discourse. As Coetzee notes, "Torture has exerted a dark fascination on many . . . South African writers" ("Into" 13). The problem of torture is unquestionably a timeless and transcultural phenomenon, but particular South African events of the seventies stimulated this dark fascination.[1] The revelation of facts about state-condoned torture, the litany of accusations and denials, the soul-searching of many white South Africans—these events provide the context for what I believe to be Coetzee's most powerful novel, first published in 1980.

The Rhetoric of Torture

The spark that ignited the bonfire of rhetoric concerning torture was the death of Stephen Biko. Following the Soweto uprising in June 1976, unrest spread throughout South African townships. Horrified by police shootings of unarmed schoolchildren and unable to tolerate the oppression of apartheid any longer, urban blacks boycotted schools, vandalized official buildings, marched in the streets, and organized stay-at-home strikes. During sixteen months of chaos, "recorded deaths numbered some six hundred but were thought to be nearer a thousand—all but two of them black, and most of them school pupils shot by police. Nearly four thousand were injured; thousands more vanished into detention, some to spend five years in solitary confinement, some never to be seen by their parents again" (Benson 190). The mass arrests included not only participants in the protests but also many leaders of the Black Consciousness movement, including the charismatic young leader of the Black People's Convention, Stephen Biko. After almost a month in detention, Biko died under mysterious circumstances on September 12, 1977.

Both the government and those opposed to apartheid immediately turned to public discourse to influence further developments. In a statement made by Police Minister J. T. Kruger, the government announced that Biko had died of a hunger strike, but their account was called into question by Donald Woods, a close friend of Biko's and the outspoken white editor of the English-language *Daily Dispatch*. In a series of editorials and public speeches, Woods challenged the hunger strike theory and accused the Security Police of responsibility for Biko's death. On October 19, 1977, the South African government responded to the outcry over Biko's death and the continued unrest in the townships with an iron fist. Seventeen Black Consciousness organizations, the anti-apartheid Christian Institute, and three prominent newspapers were banned. Forty-seven black leaders were arrested and held in detention, and seven prominent whites, including Dr. Beyers Naude, director of the Christian Institute, and Donald Woods, were banned (Hachten and Giffard 5–6). But the continued public campaign to uncover the facts of Biko's death finally resulted in an inquest held over thirteen days in November 1977.

In the weeks before the inquest, the international press began to pay attention to the case, and the South African government geared up its spin-control efforts. Woods notes that before the inquest "government propagandists were hard at work to condition the public through the medium of the State-controlled radio and television service" (173). While the pro-government Afrikaans newspapers continued to echo the official statements, the English-language newspaper *The Citizen,* which had begun publication in September 1976, also supported the governmental line. In response to the details of the autopsy, which revealed brain damage, *The Citizen* suggested that Biko had killed himself by banging his head against a wall (Hachten and Giffard 241). That *The Citizen*'s editorials were part of covert governmental efforts to influence opinion emerged in 1978 with the uncovering of the Muldergate scandal, which established that the paper had been secretly financed by the South African government with taxpayers' funds (Hachten and Giffard 244).

The inquest itself made public many grim facts about the treatment of political detainees in South Africa. The Security Police and attending doctors testified that Biko had been kept naked in isolation and was shackled in leg irons and handcuffs. The head of the Eastern Cape Security Police hypothesized that Biko's head injury occurred when he deliberately fell in the bathtub in an attempt to commit suicide. Another policeman suggested that the injury occurred during "a violent struggle" in which Biko physically attacked the investigation team. Three medical doctors who had examined Biko in custody admitted that they had submitted false reports about his state of health. The final verdict issued by the presiding magistrate declared that Biko died of a head injury "probably sustained on September 7 in a scuffle in the Security Police offices in Port Elizabeth." Furthermore, he determined, "on the available evidence the death cannot be attributed to any act or omission amounting to a criminal offense on the part of any person."[2]

Besides confronting white South Africans with the horrible facts of the mistreatment of detainees, the inquest also gave many South Africans their first glimpse of the Security Police. Wendy Woods, who attended the inquest alone since her husband Donald had been banned, explains, "The inquest provided a new experience for South Africans. We got a chance to get a good long look at Security Policemen. Millions of people could read what they had to say at the receiving end of interrogation and could see pictures of them in the papers. We at the inquest could see their faces, could watch their demeanor under cross-examination and could hear their words—their version of the story" (Woods 179). Consequently, many South Africans were confronted with the moral enigma prompted by torture: how could anyone perform such deeds on another human being? Wendy Woods's account shows her own struggle to understand:

These men displayed symptoms of extreme insularity. They are people whose upbringing has impressed upon them the divine right to retain power, and in that sense they are innocent men—incapable of thinking or acting differently. On top of that they have gravitated to an occupation which has given them all the scope they need to express their rigid personalities. They have been protected for years by the laws of the country. They have been able to carry out all their imaginative torture practices quite undisturbed in cells and rooms all over the country with tacit official sanction, and they have been given tremendous status by the government as the men who "protect the State from subversion." To all this, add the sort of personalities which enjoy inflicting pain on their fellow humans, and we see that they are men with diminished responsibility, victims of a collective mutated psyche, and—with the power they wield— very dangerous people. (179–180)

The public controversy over Biko's death epitomized the broader issue of state-condoned brutalization, torture, and murder. Biko's death was only one of many. Amnesty International reports that at least ten other political detainees died in detention in 1977. The Security Police claimed that five hanged themselves, two were killed by falls from upper-story windows, and three died of natural causes. The evidence produced at several inquests suggests that many prisoners might have been physically abused before their deaths. For example, between forty and fifty abraded bruises and other marks were found on one body. Both former detainees and defendants at a number of major trials in 1978 testified of being beaten, kicked, and subjected to electric shocks while under interrogation (*Amnesty Report 1978* 80). Official South African figures state that between 1963 and 1978, thirty-nine detainees died: nineteen by suicide, nine of natural causes, and two of unknown causes (*Amnesty for Terrorism* 62). Other accounts are higher. Woods lists the names of forty-five South Africans who are known to have died while being held in detention by the Security Police.[3]

Because Biko was articulate, personable, and well known, his death came to symbolize the continual mistreatment of detainees. The campaign for an investigation into the circumstances of his death soon became a rallying point for those opposed to all atrocities committed by the Security Police. One speech given by Woods at the University of Natal in Pietermaritzburg indicates the extent to which Biko's death became representative of widespread corruption:

Prime Minister Vorster and Justice and Police Minister Kruger . . . have presided over a system of detention under whose dispensation helpless people can be seized, tortured and assaulted without ever having had access to lawyers or friends or family—access not even denied to a criminal. Yet the government can see no reason for a judicial inquiry into deaths in detention.

There are several reasons: the numerous complaints of torture in detention. Whether or not Mr. Vorster regards these allegations as untrue, I can tell him that literally millions of South Africans believe that Security Police interrogation is often accompanied by torture, including torture by shocks with electrical apparatus and including beating up and tightening of material about necks until a point of near-suffocation is reached. It is also believed that that point has on occasion been exceeded—hence the number of alleged hangings in detention. (171–72)

Similarly, in its 1978 *Report,* Amnesty International notes, "Steve Biko's death, coming after so many other deaths in detention in recent years, had a very great effect on South Africa's Black majority population and led to outbursts of popular protest" (77).

The unsatisfactory conclusion of the inquest only added more fire to the public rhetoric. As a result of the events of 1977, the United Nations proclaimed 1978 International Anti-Apartheid Year. In January 1978, Amnesty International distributed internationally a special report, *Political Imprisonment in South Africa,* which details the ill-treatment of political prisoners and detainees in South Africa. Complete with graphic pictures of the injured bodies of those who died in detention, the report also includes the testimony of five former prisoners who were tortured. The report concludes, "To accuse any government of sanctioning the torture of its own citizens is a most serious matter; it is not a charge which Amnesty International would make lightly. However, Amnesty International is convinced that such a charge against South Africa is fully justified. All the evidence indicates that torture is extensively inflicted on political detainees, and that the Government sanctions its use" (56). In conjunction with this report, Amnesty began "a worldwide campaign for the release of prisoners of conscience, the repeal of discriminatory and repressive legislation and an end to the use of torture in South Africa" (*Amnesty Report 1978* 76).

Within South Africa, several different factions continued to agitate for better treatment of prisoners. The South African Institute of Race Relations reports that in 1979 both the United Congregational Church and the National Synod of the Gereformeerde Kerk spoke out against the massive detentions and criticized the police restrictions on visits by an ordained minister. In January 1989, during a Human Rights Conference held in Cape Town, Professor John Dugard called for "a full scale judicial enquiry into methods of interrogation used by the security police" and complained that "magistrates had consistently declined to examine methods of interrogation." Similarly, the Annual Conference of the Black Sash, held in March that year, cited the "horrifying callousness and inhumanity" of the treatment of prisoners and detainees and demanded "a prompt and full investigation of all allegations of ill-treatment and torture" (*Survey of Race Relations 1979* 148). The issue of torture had become both a national and an international scandal.

T. R. H. Davenport notes that the disclosures about Biko's death "were immensely damaging to South Africa's reputation, and led directly to the West's decision to support a mandatory arms embargo against the Republic in the U.N." (311). The South African government still carried on the rhetorical war, however, by releasing in June 1978 an offical report entitled *Amnesty for Terrorism*. This report, which was widely distributed by South African embassies in Europe and the United States, attempted to discredit the Amnesty International special report by suggesting that the organization was using a "tried and proven Marxist technique" in its criticism of the South African Security Police (59). *Amnesty for Terrorism* was compiled by the South African Department of Information, another governmental organization disbanded in the aftermath of Muldergate because of its illegal diversion of public funds for propaganda purposes.

The rhetoric about torture extended beyond the publications of organizations and institutions to form the basis of many personal accounts, lamentations, and fictional attempts to understand. The banned Donald Woods fled with his family to England, taking with him the manuscript of *Biko*, which was published to great acclaim in 1978. In a poem called "In Detention" (Brink and Coetzee 50) Christopher van Wyk explored the senseless official accounts of deaths of detainees:

> He fell from the ninth floor
> He hanged himself
> He slipped on a piece of soap while washing
> He hanged himself
> He slipped on a piece of soap while washing
> He fell from the ninth floor
> He hanged himself while washing
> He slipped from the ninth floor
> He hung from the ninth floor
> He slipped on the ninth floor while washing

He fell from a piece of soap while slipping
He hung from the ninth floor
He washed from the ninth floor while slipping
He hung from a piece of soap while washing

The Afrikaner novelist André Brink published *'n Droe wit seisoen* in 1979, a realistic novel about a white teacher who gradually realizes the corruption of his society when a black friend is unjustly arrested and then alleged to have committed suicide in police custody. The English translation, *A Dry White Season,* appeared in Britain in 1979 and in the United States in 1980. Perhaps one of the most striking facts about the novel is that Brink began writing it immediately after the initial Soweto uprising, almost a year before Biko's death ("Brink" 55). *A Dry White Season* first was banned in South Africa, but later was released following an appeal. Other fictional treatments of government-sanctioned torture that appeared following Soweto include Sipho Sepamla, *A Ride on the Whirlwind* (1981) and Mongane Serote, *To Every Birth Its Blood* (1981).

Torture and *Waiting for the Barbarians*

Coetzee spent 1979 in the United States and wrote most of *Waiting for the Barbarians* there.[4] Like other South African writers, Coetzee in this novel both laments and speaks prophetically of the practices of his country. However, his work is remarkably different from the other novels produced during this time in its non-specific historical setting and loose allegorical style. These unique qualities emerge from Coetzee's postmodern concern with the implications of torture for the writer. Should authors depict torture in their works, and if they do, how should they portray this incomprehensible act? *Waiting for the Barbarians* not only protests against the horrors of some South African practices, it also represents a working out of some tentative strategies for the novelist confronted with the question of torture. Seen in the light of the conditions of its production and reception, this novel represents Coetzee's contribution to the international discourse on torture in South Africa. Coetzee exposes how torture and other South African myths function in the creation of Others. The themes and the techniques of *Waiting for the Barbarians* suggest that a complete binary opposition of self and Other is both oppressive and false.

The novel is narrated by a man known only as the magistrate, the chief administrator of a small village on the frontier between the civilization of the Empire and the wastelands inhabited by the nomadic barbarians. When the novel opens, Colonel Joll, a stormtrooper-like Security man, arrives to investigate the rumored attack of the barbarians upon the Empire. As Joll interrogates and tortures barbarian prisoners, the magistrate becomes increasingly sympathetic toward the victims. When the Colonel leaves the outpost, the magistrate takes a barbarian woman, crippled as a result of her torture, into his house and bed. Later, he makes an arduous journey across the desert to restore her to her people. The army arrives to fight the barbarians in his absence, and he is imprisoned for treason and tortured on his return. But the army finally abandons the village to its fate and releases the magistrate. Once again under his leadership, the few remaining villagers wait for the barbarian hordes to descend upon them.

Published at the height of controversy over the treatment of detainees, *Waiting for the Barbarians* contains several echoes of the recent events in South Africa. The jargon employed by Coetzee's Security Police resembles similar euphemistic phrases used in South Africa: Colonel Joll "is here under the emergency powers" (1), he has "set procedures" for interrogation (4), the prisoners must be held "incommunicado" (18). When the first prisoner dies mysteriously after an interrogation session, the official report of his death given to the magistrate is reminiscent of the explanations of Stephen Biko's death: "During the course of the interrogation contradictions became apparent in the prisoner's testimony. Confronted with these contradictions, the prisoner became enraged and attacked the investigating officer. A scuffle ensued during which the prisoner fell heavily against the wall. Efforts to revive him were unsuccessful" (6). The stilted syntax in which the only active subject is "the prisoner" obscures the actions of the Security Police and hides their responsibility for the death. But when the magistrate examines the corpse, he finds crushed lips, broken teeth, and one empty bloody eye-socket. The testimony of the body belies the testimony of the word as given in the official record.

The magistrate's own treatment at the hands of the Security Police is equally brutal. He is kept naked and not allowed to bathe. After months of torture and humiliation at the hands of Warrant Officer Mandel, he is abruptly ordered to leave. He claims that he is a prisoner and demands a trial, but is told, "How can you be a prisoner when we have no record of you? Do you think we don't keep records? We have no record of you.

So you must be a free man" (125). He has only been detained, and as is the case with many detainees in South Africa, there are no official records of his existence or treatment. Coetzee thus suggests the power of the written record to obscure the origins of oppression. These particular echoes of South African practices not only direct the novel's critique to the specific historical situation but also reveal the role that discourse has played in that situation.

Even the titles and structures of authority in the Empire remind us of South Africa. The Third Bureau of the Empire, like the South African Security Forces, is a special branch of law enforcement with "contempt for the regular police and for due process of law" (77). The magistrate's ill-treatment is meted out by a Warrant Officer holding the same rank and title as several men involved in Biko's death. The particular title and responsibilities of the magistrate are another link between the world of the novel and contemporary South Africa. Coetzee calls special attention to the protagonist's official capacity by referring to him only as the magistrate, never giving his name. His position appears, particularly to the American reader, to include a strange blend of administrative and judicial responsibilities: "I collect the tithes and taxes, administer the communal lands, see that the garrison is provided for, supervise the junior officers who are the only officers we have here, keep an eye on trade, preside over the law-court twice a week" (8). These are the responsibilities of a South African magistrate. Appointed by the Minister of Justice, magistrates have both judicial and administrative powers; in most country districts they are the local representative of many State departments and perform such duties as granting and paying pensions, collecting revenue, and providing relief programs for farmers and children. Magistrates preside over both criminal and civil cases, and have jurisdiction over all offenses except treason and murder (*South Africa 1983* 292–95). They had come under particular criticism in South Africa for their reluctance to investigate even the most blatant cases of mistreatment of prisoners and detainees. In these particular echoes of South African practices and structures, Coetzee directs the novel's critique of torture to his own country.

Waiting for the Barbarians is, according to its author, "about the impact of the torture chamber on the life of a man of conscience" ("Into" 13). One such man of conscience who must come to an understanding of responsibility and guilt is the magistrate. A second may be the writer who produces a novel about torture. Several years after writing *Waiting for the Barbarians,* Coetzee described two moral dilemmas faced by the writer who depicts "the dark chamber" ("Into" 13). First, he or she must find a middle way between ignoring the obscenities performed by the state, on the one hand, and producing representations of those obscenities, on the other. Coetzee believes that realistic depictions of torture in fiction assist the state in terrorizing and paralyzing people by showing its oppressive methods in detail. Excessive realism may be merely a gratuitous submission to the fascination of the forbidden chamber. Yet these acts must not be hidden either. The author has an ethical responsibility not only to refuse complicity with those in authority who practice torture but also to recognize the fact that torture is a sign, a word, that desperately needs the exposing light of interpretation. The challenge thus faced by the author "is how not to play the game by the rules of the state, how to establish one's own authority, how to imagine torture and death on one's own terms" (13).

The second problem, which is both moral and aesthetic, concerns how to represent the person of the torturer. Coetzee thinks many authors resort to cliches: the figure of satanic evil, the tragically divided man, the faceless functionary. Other writers—he identifies Mongane Serote and Alex La Guma among them—present the world of torture "with a false portentousness, a questionable dark lyricism" (35). Again, the author needs to find a middle course, between trivializing and glamorizing the figure responsible for inflicting pain.

Waiting for the Barbarians embodies Coetzee's fictional solutions to these two dilemmas. His combination of allegory, traditionally a more precise technique, with a text emphasizing gaps and uncertainties represents in part his solution to the moral issue of how a novelist should treat torture in fiction. Rather than speaking with the authoritative voice of the omniscient narrator or through a strong protagonist, Coetzee narrates this novel in the persona of a weak and wondering man who continually finds that words fail him. As the magistrate tells his story, he repeatedly invokes images of impotence. Both pen and penis are unable to perform. The old bureaucrat draws a parallel between his flagging interest in sex and his struggles to articulate his story: "It seems appropriate that a man who does not know what to do with the woman in his bed should not know what to write" (58). The metaphor works both ways: "there were unsettling occasions when in the middle of the sexual act I felt myself losing my way like a storyteller losing the thread of his story" (45). Even after he consummates his sexual relationship with the barbarian woman, he is unable to establish its meaning: "No thought that I think, no articulation, however antonymic, of the origin of my desire seems to upset me. 'I must be tired,' I think. 'Or perhaps whatever can be articulated is falsely put.' My lips move, silently composing and recomposing the words. 'Or perhaps it is the case that only that which has not been articulated has to be lived through.' I stare at this last proposition without detecting any answering movement in myself toward assent or dissent. The words grow more and more opaque before me; soon they have lost all meaning" (64–65). With his combination of sexual and authorial images, his antonymic articulations, and his failure to discover meaning in words, the magistrate seems to be wandering in the wilderness of deconstructive criticism. His statement that "whatever can be articulated is falsely put" is in itself an articulation and so, as Derrida puts it, "endlessly constructs its own destruction" ("White" 71). The process of the magistrate's thought in this passage resembles Derrida's comment that a metaphor "always has its own death within it" (74). Articulation causes falsehoods to emerge.

The magistrate's sexual and linguistic failures demonstrate his lack of authority. He can neither read the text of his world nor create a text that precisely conveys his experiences. Throughout the novel, when the magistrate searches for meaning, he confronts blankness. When he tries to remember the barbarian woman as a prisoner, he sees only "a space, a blankness" (47). After the woman leaves, he tries in vain to remember her face. His recurring dream of trudging across an endless snow-covered plain ends when he looks into the "blank, featureless" face of a hooded child (37). His inconclusive dreams demonstrate that the magistrate cannot even read the text of his own identity: "I try to look into myself but see only a vortex and at the heart of the vortex oblivion" (47). His attempts to locate fixed meanings inevitably fail. Lois Zamora suggests, "If the resistance of the magistrate's dreams to interpretation and translation is due in part to their indeterminacy, it is also due to the magistrate's own blindness." The magistrate "is denied the consolation of allegory," but the reader is not, for we see the "blankness as full of meaning" ("Allegories" 8).

The echoes of contemporary literary theory suggest the authorial impotence of the novelist who attempts to write about torture, oppression, and—in Coetzee's particular case—South Africa. The novelist must struggle to articulate torture without falsifying it, to understand and to depict oppression without unconsciously aiding the oppressor, to find texts transparent enough to carry meaning. Coetzee may also be addressing the paradox of the contemporary critic who believes in the radical indeterminacy of the text yet is still politically and socially committed, for despite the magistrate's doubts about articulation and truth, he does narrate the story, he does give us a text, provisional though it may be.

Another incident in the novel points even more blatantly to contemporary critical theories about language and meaning. In his amateur archeological diggings in the desert, the magistrate has discovered hundreds of white wooden tiles containing mysterious inscriptions. Colonel Joll orders him to decipher these inscriptions, but the magistrate does not know what they say:

> In the long evenings I spent poring over my collection I isolated over four hundred different characters in the script, perhaps as many as four hundred and fifty. I have no idea what they stand for. Does each stand for a single thing, a circle for the sun, a triangle for a woman, a wave for a lake; or does a circle merely stand for "circle", a triangle for "triangle", a wave for "wave"? Does each sign represent a different state of the tongue, the lips, the throat, the lungs, as they combine in the uttering of some multifarious unimaginable extinct barbarian language? (110)

The magistrate's musings point to the difficulty of ascertaining the connection between the signifiers and the signifieds, the text and the meaning. Lance Olsen comments, "As Derrida would have it, those wood slips form an absence which may be supplemented in an endless number of ways, cut off from responsibility, from authority, an emblem of orphaned language" (53). However, when importuned by Joll, the magistrate picks up a tile and "reads" story after story that reveals the Empire's cruelty to the barbarians, thus giving the language a temporary father-interpreter and employing the language responsibly.[5]

This incident again suggests the ambiguous nature of texts and the freedom of the reader to interpret such texts, but in the magistrate's "translation" of the tiles lies the hope that through storytelling—impotent, opaque, and uncertain as it might be—oppression may be unveiled. Olsen sees the multiplicity of meaning generated by the tiles as negating the possibility of a correct reading. He argues that the magistrate is a complete deconstructionist: "The magistrate believes in the metaphysics of absence, in the idea that 'meaning' and 'truth' must be allowed to float free" (53). But the magistrate's own reading of the tiles is in a sense a correct reading, for it points to the Empire's barbarism. The fact that the slips do not hold a single and unambiguous meaning does not mean that they are without meaning, just as Coetzee's multifaceted allegory can reveal truth. Perhaps in this incident, in his actions as a storyteller, the magistrate begins to dispel his own blindness.

Olsen denies that the magistrate comes to any kind of moral recognition: "We have arrived, as we often do in postmodern fiction, at a giving up, a frustration, a despair before the arbitrariness of language and its essential defectiveness for depicting the world. We have circled around again to the notion that language is a game, that the game is futile, that linguistic zero is ever-present" (55). Such a reading suggests that Coetzee is politically irresponsible.[6] But although Coetzee recognizes the problems of ambiguity and authority that plague the creator of a text, neither he nor the magistrate gives up using this uncertain medium to advance moral truths. The very fact that he has referred to the "moral dilemmas" of the author indicates Coetzee's own concerns and priorities. In fact, Coetzee's affirmation of the tentative qualities of language, his recognition of multiple interpretations, multiple voices, multiple languages, is an embrace of Others and a rejection of rigid authoritarianism.

Barbara Eckstein provides another rebuttal of Olsen's argument that also sees a moral and political dimension in the novel's depiction of language. She examines the connections between the body in pain and language and concludes that the magistrate learns that knowledge from pain is more certain than knowledge from language. The magistrate's hesitant language exists "because his awareness of his complicity as authority and voice leave him without moral language . . . because torture of his body leaves him without any voice outside the boundaries of his body." Eckstein concludes: "The political implications in Coetzee's analysis of body and voice are clear. Coetzee indicts colonial barbarity, indeed, all interpretation of 'barbarians' by barbarous authority and its ideology of otherness" (193). Although the narrative structure of *Waiting for the Barbarians* is far more coherent and tightly woven than either of Coetzee's previous books, the magistrate's narrative voice again is "feminine" in its focus on the language of the body and its inclusion of uncertainty and blankness.

The magistrate's storytelling thus suggests Coetzee's own solution to the first moral dilemma of the author writing about torture. The narrator comments on the specific technique to be employed when the magistrate tells Joll that the tiles "form an allegory. They can be read in many orders.

Further, each single slip can be read in many ways. Together they can be read as a domestic journal, or they can be read as a plan of war, or they can be turned on their sides and read as a history of the last years of the Empire—the old Empire, I mean" (112). As storyteller and prophet, the magistrate turns to an imprecise allegory that can be interpreted in a number of different ways. Coetzee's own technique is similar. By setting his novel in an unnamed country at an unnamed time, by terming the two parties the Empire and the barbarians, and by simplifying the technology and weapons of the people, Coetzee creates an allegorical landscape that loosely suggests the Roman Empire on the verge of collapse but undoubtedly points to South Africa today.

Not all readers have been pleased with the vague setting. Nadine Gordimer criticizes its "revulsion" from history ("The Idea" 3), and Peter Lewis concludes, "this kind of fiction as a whole, peopled as it is mainly by stereotypes, is often in danger of moving so far away from the familiar in its determination to establish universals that it defeats its own purpose." Irving Howe similarly states: "One possible loss is the bite and pain, the urgency that a specified historical place and time may provide. . . . such invocations of universal evil can deflect attention from the particular and at least partly remediable social wrongs Mr. Coetzee portrays" (36). But despite its ambiguities of time and place, the setting of *Waiting for the Barbarians* is given in concrete sensual detail, resulting in an unusual movement between historical suggestiveness and fictional reality.[7] Paul Ableman notes that as soon as the reader examines the novel "for clues as to a possible historical model the book's meaning sways towards the allegorical. Conversely, if you look for specific allegorical components the vivid, concrete qualities reassert themselves. The frontier town is real and its inhabitants are as plausible and as inconsistent as living people" (21). Although the effect of Coetzee's technique is to reveal truths about any oppressive society that employs torture as a technique, *Waiting for the Barbarians* also is inescapably tied to South Africa not only by its echoes of contemporary events but also by its historical production as a novel written by a South African in 1979.

By using this kind of setting, Coetzee solves his first moral dilemma. He does not ignore the obscene acts performed by his government under the guise of national security, yet neither does he produce representational depictions of these acts. Instead, he insists on his own authority, tentative as it might be, and imagines death and torture on his own terms. Eschewing a moral voyeurism, he does not identify particular atrocities performed by the South African Security Police in Vorster Square (as André Brink and Alex La Guma do). Nonetheless, the maiming of the barbarian woman and the torture of the magistrate ineluctably point to the treatment of political prisoners in South Africa. In suggesting universal truths about torture and oppression, Coetzee also specifically condemns his own country, as most readers readily perceive.

Dismantling the Myth of Others

Rejecting both the state's authority to define torture and the language of the one authoritarian voice, Coetzee chooses to employ the equivocal voice of the storyteller who recognizes his own complicity and failings. This metafictional technique has political and ethical dimensions. The solution he posits to his second moral dilemma—how to depict the person of the torturer—rests on the deconstruction of dichotomous thinking and the recognition of the common elements of humanity that extend across cultural differences. The first such deconstruction occurs in the magistrate's view of what it means to be a torturer. Initially, he seems unable to comprehend the existence of such people. He speculates about Colonel Joll: "I wonder how he felt the very first time: did he, invited as an apprentice to twist the pincers or turn the screw or whatever it is they do, shudder even a little to know that at that instant he was trespassing into the forbidden? I find myself wondering too whether he has a private ritual of purification, carried out behind closed doors, to enable him to return and break bread with other men. Does he wash his hands very carefully, perhaps, or change all his clothes; or has the Bureau created new men who can pass without disquiet between the unclean and the clean?" (12). He asks Mandel, the man who tortures him, "Do you find it easy to take food afterwards? I have imagined that one would want to wash one's hands. But no ordinary washing would be enough, one would require priestly intervention, a ceremonial of cleansing, don't you think?" (126). The magistrate sees both Joll and Mandel as types of Pilate, who must somehow absolve themselves of the responsibility for their dreadful acts.

Both men represent some kind of moral vacuum, an absence that is reflected in their eyes.[8] Colonel Joll wears dark glasses, in what might appear to be one of the cliches of the torturer, except that the "two little discs of glass suspended in front of his eyes in loops of wire" are a new phenomenon to the frontier people, a modern curiosity of civilization (1).

"Is he blind?" the magistrate wonders in the opening lines of the novel. The eyes of Mandel are uncovered, but as hidden as Joll's: "I look into his clear blue eyes, as clear as if there were crystal lenses slipped over his eyeballs. He looks back at me. I have no idea what he sees. Thinking of him, I have said the words *torture . . . torturer* to myself, but they are strange words, and the more I repeat them the more strange they grow, till they lie like stones on my tongue" (118). Again, words fail the magistrate and are inadequate to depict the physical reality of torture. Like Wendy Woods at Stephen Biko's inquest and many white South Africans in the 1970s, the magistrate attempts to comprehend the existence of a man who tortures other human beings. Questioning Mandel, the magistrate claims that he is neither blaming nor accusing his torturer: "I am only trying to understand. I am trying to understand the zone in which you live. I am trying to imagine how you breathe and eat and live from day to day. But I cannot!" (126). Perhaps the magistrate's failure represents the author's own failure, for by centering his novel in the narration of the magistrate, Coetzee avoids having to depict the zone of the torturer. So, in one sense, Coetzee solves this dilemma by posing it: how can the mind of a torturer even exist?

Yet in another sense Coetzee does enter the zone of the torturer, the oppressor, in his rendition of the magistrate himself. When the magistrate takes in the barbarian woman after the Security Police have left, he acts like an obsessed man. He continually asks her about her experience of being tortured, probing for every last detail. He stands in the room in which the torture took place and tries to imagine the act. But most perversely, he nightly strips the woman and in his own ritual of purification, washes her, always beginning with her maimed feet. In his physical exploration of the woman, Rosemary Jolly says, "he treats her body as a surface, a map of a surface, a text" (72). But he also seems to be trying to absolve himself of the guilt he feels for having allowed the torture to take place, and trying to penetrate her secret being, to find her deepest and most hidden feelings. In frustration at his inability to enter her either psychologically or physically, he wonders, "What do I have to do to move you?" (44). But this is the question of the torturer, as the eye imagery again indicates: "with a shift of horror I behold the answer that has been waiting all the time offer itself to me in the image of a face masked by two black glassy insect eyes from which there comes no reciprocal gaze but only my doubled image cast back at me." The magistrate immediately denies this recognition: "*No! No! No!* I cry to myself. . . . There is nothing to link me with torturers, people who sit waiting like beetles in dark cellars. . . . I must assert my distance from Colonel Joll! I will not suffer for his crimes!" (44).

Coetzee resolves his dilemma of how to depict the torturer by exposing the false dichotomy between "them" and "us"; those who torture and those who do not. The magistrate participates in the acts of the torturer first by his passive acceptance of the actions of Colonel Joll and later in his objectification of the woman as the site of torture. Through the figure of the magistrate, Coetzee identifies the common tendency of those "civilized" people who are not Security Police to acquiesce, to be complicit, to wait for the barbarians to act and to wait on the acts of the barbarians. And in the magistrate's desire to "know" the woman—to know what happened in the torture chamber, to uncover her deepest and most hidden feelings, to engrave himself on her—Coetzee suggests the voyeuristic aspect of discourse on torture. The international discussion that thrives on delving into and exposing the crimes against humanity committed in South Africa also paradoxically thrives on the agony of the tortured. Our moral outrage, scholarly writing, and fashionable political activity are inescapably fueled by the mysterious figure of the tortured.

In dismantling the myth of the torturer, Coetzee exposes one way oppression is sustained in South Africa. However, just as the division between those who torture and those who do not quickly becomes blurred, so too does the division between barbarian and Empire that legitimates the existence of torture. The fact of torture in the modern world is a horrifying sign of humanity's tendency to achieve self-definition and power by denominating and thus distancing certain people as Others. The most common rationale given for torture is that those who are tortured are not human beings like ourselves. Amnesty International points out "the refusal or inability of the torturer to recognise himself in the agony of his victim" (*Report on Torture* 65). Similarly, Eckstein suggests, "Beneath the rationalization of interrogation, what may well allow the torturer to tolerate or even ignore the prisoner's pain . . . is an indoctrination in otherness, an atmosphere of otherness" (184). Social or cultural difference frequently becomes the means by which Otherness is established. Amnesty's *Report on Torture* concludes, "if our education systems, newspapers, and politics teach us from earliest days that members of one race, or religion, or political belief are not to be regarded as humans like ourselves, then it will be normal if we treat them inhumanly" (64). One example appears in the testimony of a

Vietnam veteran: "It wasn't like they were humans. . . . when you shot someone you didn't think you were shooting at a human. They were a Gook or a Commie and it was okay" (65). It is this conception of Otherness that the magistrate's account begins to undo.

Modern South African society is founded on the notion of Otherness. In a similar way, the dichotomy between the Empire and the barbarians is marked by physical and social differences. In the common conjunction of blackness and Otherness that has characterized Western thought, the woman the magistrate takes in "has the straight black eyebrows, the glossy black hair of the barbarians" (25).[9] The barbarians are nomads rather than farmers; they wear wool and hides rather than cotton; they eat meat and milk instead of grains and fruit. Their significantly different way of life evokes a "litany of prejudice" from the settlers of the Empire: "barbarians are lazy, immoral, filthy, stupid" (38). As we have seen, the early settlers of the southern tip of Africa stereotyped the natives in a similar fashion: "One of the commonplaces of the Discourse of the Cape is that the Hottentots are idle," Coetzee states in *White Writing* (16). He continues, "Idleness, indolence, sloth, laziness, torpor—these terms are meant both to define a Hottentot vice and to distance the writer from it" (18).

Waiting for the Barbarians calls into question the Otherness of the Other. Throughout the course of the narrative, the differences between barbarian and settler are deconstructed. The novel's exposure of the barbarity of the civilized Empire is most vivid in the scenes of torture, but we also find the stereotypes of idleness and slovenliness questioned. Despite his liberal leanings and outrage at Joll's behavior, the magistrate initially repeats the litany of prejudice, trapped within the Empire's categories of discourse: "Do I really look forward to the triumph of the barbarian way: intellectual torpor, slovenliness, tolerance of disease and death?" (52). But his narrative suggests in many ways that it is the people of the Empire who are idle, slovenly, and dissolute. With his food, wine, hobbies, and favorite prostitute, the magistrate is happy to live out his "days on this lazy frontier, waiting to retire" (8). Similarly, the hardy and disciplined barbarians survive the rigors of the desert with ease, while the soldiers of the Empire are destroyed by their physical and mental weakness. Although the magistrate accuses the barbarians of tolerating disease and death, it is his soldier whose foot becomes infected during the journey into the desert because he has not followed the sanitary precautions established by the magistrate.

The magistrate begins to understand that these dichotomies are false only after he fulfills the conditions of his dream, struggling across the vast desert to return the woman to the barbarians, and consequently is imprisoned and tortured into a "barbarian state" by the security forces. When he leaves the barbarian woman with her people, he realizes that he could have better spent his long evenings with her learning her language rather than attempting to decipher her body. By focusing on the body, and the differences created by her torture, he has perpetuated the Otherness and put himself into the position of Colonel Joll. Only when he reaches the abyss of his own torture does he express the language of common humanity. Dangling from a tree with his arms cruelly wrenched behind his back in a parodic crucifixion, the magistrate begins to bellow uncontrollably: "I bellow again and again, there is nothing I can do to stop it, the noise comes out of a body that knows itself damaged perhaps beyond repair and roars its fright." "He is calling his barbarian friends," says a witness. "That is barbarian language you hear" (121). Like Benjy Compson's bellow, "the grave hopeless sound of all voiceless misery under the sun" (Faulkner 395), the magistrate's cries affirm his oneness with those who suffer. Even though his torture and imprisonment have physically reduced him to the level of an animal, these experiences also have elevated his moral awareness.[10] He no longer views the barbarians as Others, for he has spoken their language and lived in their environment. Their forms of civility are only different ways of working out their relations to each other and to the natural world.

Paradoxically, the magistrate's unity with the barbarians also allows him to perceive his complicity in the acts of the Empire. Only after his experience of suffering does he realize that he has used the woman and has wanted to engrave himself as deeply on her as Colonel Joll: "From the moment my steps paused and I stood before her at the barracks gate she must have felt a miasma of deceit closing about her: envy, pity, cruelty all masquerading as desire." He sees his acts of kindness as "futile gestures of expiation" as he attempted to erase the guilt of his passive acceptance of the state's atrocities. He finally can admit:

> I was not, as I liked to think, the indulgent pleasure-loving opposite of the cold rigid Colonel. I was the lie that Empire tells itself when times are easy, he the truth that Empire tells when harsh winds blow. Two sides of imperial rule, no more, no less. But I temporized, I looked around this obscure frontier . . . and I said to myself, "Be patient, one of these days he will go away, one of these days quiet will return. . . ." Thus I seduced

myself, taking one of the many wrong turnings I have taken on a road that looks true but has delivered me into the heart of a labyrinth. (135–136)

Although the magistrate ends his narrative "feeling stupid, like a man who lost his way long ago but presses on along a road that may lead nowhere" (156), his moment of self-recognition and the changes in his behavior suggest that he may have found the right road after all. When the army brings back a new set of barbarian prisoners, he escapes from his prison to denounce publicly their cruel treatment. Deliberately answering the rhetoric of Otherness, he protests: "You would not use a hammer on a beast, not on a beast!" Reconstituting the biblical rhetoric of the Afrikaners, he cites the Psalms: "We are the great miracle of creation! . . . Look at these men! . . . *Men!*" (107). Colonel Joll then accuses the magistrate of wanting to make a name for himself as "the One Just Man, the man who is prepared to sacrifice his freedom to his principles" (113–14).

But in his struggle to take on Christ-like attributes, the magistrate must guard against the barbarism in his own heart; he must not merely change sides but reformulate the rules of human relationships to resist the creation of Otherness. At the scene of public torture, he resolves, "what has become important above all is that I should neither be contaminated by the atrocity that is about to be committed nor poison myself with impotent hatred of its perpetrators" (104). And when Colonel Joll huddles in his carriage as he flees the town, the magistrate must again restrain his own propensity for evil and torture: "I shiver from the cold, but also from the tension of suppressed anger. An urge runs through me to smash the glass, to reach in and drag the man out through the jagged hole, to feel his flesh catch and tear on the edges, to hurl him to the ground and kick his body to pulp" (146). The lesson he has learned, he tells Joll, is "The crime that is latent in us we must inflict on ourselves. . . . Not on others" (146).

In *Waiting for the Barbarians,* Coetzee thus suggests that all human beings have a latent capacity for crime, an inner corruption that prompts the creation of Others. Everyone is guilty; everyone is in need of a ceremony of purification like Pilate's ritual cleansing. Turning from the examination of the loss of transcendence in his earlier novels, Coetzee now exposes the barbaric heart inherent in all of us. Webster Schott says, "The intelligence Coetzee brings us in *Waiting for the Barbarians* comes straight from Scripture and Dostoevsky: We possess the devil. We are all barbarians" (12). The need to project this evil onto some Other and the political consequences of such an act are suggested in the poem "Waiting for the Barbarians" (1904) by the Alexandrian Greek poet Constantine Cavafy, from which Coetzee takes the title of his novel. The poem begins:

> What are we waiting for, assembled in the forum?
> The barbarians are due here today.
> Why isn't anything going on in the senate?
> Why are the senators still sitting there without legislating?
> Because the barbarians are coming today.

The decadent Roman rulers assemble in expectation of the barbarian arrival, donning embroidered scarlet togas, amethyst bracelets, and emerald rings, and carrying elegant silver and gold canes. The extensive preparations lead to nothing, however:

> Why this sudden bewilderment, this confusion?
> . . . . .
> Because night has fallen and the barbarians haven't come.
> And some of our men just in from the border say
> There are no barbarians any longer.
> Now what's going to happen to us without barbarians?
> They were, those people, a kind of solution.   (27, 31–35)

By positing an enemy, one achieves strength, unity, and identity. Throughout *Waiting for the Barbarians,* we are never convinced that the barbarians actually pose any kind of military threat to the Empire. Instead, they provide a solution, a legitimate scapegoat on which to cast one's own barbarity. The brutal actions of the Security Police vividly render the false dichotomy established in the words *barbarian* and *Empire,* for those who act barbarously throughout the novel are the forces of "civilization." Confronting Colonel Joll, the magistrate asserts, "*You* are the enemy, *you* have made the war, and *you* have given them all the martyrs they need—starting not now but a year ago when you committed your first filthy barbarities here! History will bear me out!" (114).

As the magistrate grows in understanding, his recurring dream takes on new dimensions. He now sees that the face of the child is that of the barbarian woman, and in one dream she gives him a piece of bread in an apparent peace offering. The final affirmation of hope for the future lies in the closing scene of the novel, in which the magistrate's dream appears to become reality. Winter is coming, and he crosses the square and comes upon a group of children building a snowman. The children work together in their play:

> They have completed the great round body, now they are rolling a ball for the head.
>
> "Someone fetch things for the mouth and nose and eyes," says the child who is their leader.
>
> It strikes me that the snowman will need arms too, but I do not want to interfere.
>
> They settle the head on the shoulders and fill it out with pebbles for eyes, ears, nose and mouth. One of them crowns it with his cap.
>
> It is not a bad snowman. (155–56)

In his previous dreams, the children having been building objects in the snow—a castle or a town—that suggest social structures and hierarchies. Now they work together to build the figure of a human being. The magistrate does not interfere, does not give in to the impulse to tell them the figure needs arms (with its negative connotation of weapons). Instead, he feels "inexplicably joyful" as he watches their work. The sense of hope associated with the next generation is further suggested by Coetzee's dedication of the novel to Nicolas and Gisela, his own children.

The final myth of Otherness that *Waiting for the Barbarians* rejects is that created in Afrikaner historiography. Rather than depicting the Empire as a unique and chosen people, this novel suggests a circular history in which Empire and barbarian are continually opposing each other. One can see this circularity even within one lifetime. The magistrate observes that "once in every generation, without fail, there is an episode of hysteria about the barbarians" (8). His archeological digs reveal that an ancient unknown civilization once occupied what is now a frontier village. While implicitly rebutting the claim that both whites and blacks settled South Africa in the seventeenth century, the findings of the magistrate also prompt him to envision history as a series of similar struggles. Standing in the ruins of an ancient fort, he thinks, "Perhaps in my digging I have only scratched the surface. Perhaps ten feet below the floor lie the ruins of another fort, razed by the barbarians, peopled with the bones of folk who thought they would find safety behind high walls. Perhaps when I stand on the floor of the courthouse, if that is what it is, I stand over the head of a magistrate like myself, another grey-haired servant of Empire who fell in the arena of his authority, face to face at last with the barbarian" (15–16). Coetzee's narrative choice of allusive allegory, which serves to connect the modern South African regime with other oppressive societies, further discounts the Afrikaner typological version of history. Instead of the unique Chosen People heading for the Promised Land, the novel invokes a new pattern: one of oppressor and oppressed continually struggling throughout history, building fort upon fort, one false civilization after another.

Coetzee does not rule out the possibility of entering a Promised Land, but he does construct that vision more in New Testament terms than in the usual Afrikaner typology. As we have seen, *Waiting for the Barbarians* contains several biblical references, not to the Pentateuch story of the Chosen People but to the New Testament story of the suffering servant, Christ. Coetzee thus again posits an alternative story to the one that usually dominates South African discourse. Also, near the end of his essay about the novelist and torture, Coetzee speaks of his desire for a world where "humanity will be restored across the face of society," a world where all human acts "will be returned to the ambit of moral judgment" ("Into" 35). A world that rejects the notions of Otherness would allow for clearer moral judgments: "In such a society it will once again be *meaningful* for the gaze of the author, the gaze of authority and authoritative judgment, to be turned upon scenes of torture" (35). In a world without a moral center, in a world where barbarity hides behind all the faces of society, the author can only struggle to provide authority and meaning. Coetzee's fiction is full of absences and uncertainties, yet he nonetheless suggests that temporary presences, especially the presence of the storyteller, can at least approximate a moral and linguistic center. In *Waiting for the Barbarians* Coetzee demonstrates that the final impact of the dark chamber upon people of conscience is paradoxical: they realize the need to write and proclaim the truth about this kind of oppression, but they also realize their own inability to do so completely and effectively.

With *Waiting for the Barbarians*, Coetzee achieved his first major international success. The time was right. World interest in and outrage over South Africa's social conditions had grown. In the 1980s, American publishers began publishing more fictional and nonfictional works about South Africa. Writing in the *New York Times* in December 1981, Edwin McDowell noted that despite the censorship rules in their own country, South African writers continued to write, and "American publishers continue to be attracted to books by South African writers and about the nation itself" (26). McDowell then surveys a number of books by South Africans that had been or were about to be published in the United States, including *Waiting for the Barbarians,* which came out in 1982. First published in 1980 by Secker and Warburg in Great Britain to critical acclaim, *Waiting for the Barbarians* became the first fiction paperback original initiated by Penguin in the United States (literary fiction typically first appears in a hardcover edition). That same year, Penguin reissued *In the Heart of the Country,* which had first been published with limited success in the United States in 1977 under the title *From the Heart of the Country,* by Harper & Row. The Penguin reissue went back to the book's original title and featured a cover proclaiming, "By the Author of *Waiting for the Barbarians.*" Coetzee's new success also resulted in his British publishers' issuing his first novel, *Dusklands,* in 1982, which had previously appeared only in South Africa.

The increasing availability of Coetzee's work was accompanied by critical acclaim and additional literary honors. Coetzee had won the premier South African literary award, the CNA Prize, for the first time in 1977 for *In the Heart of the Country.* With *Waiting for the Barbarians,* he was awarded his second CNA Prize in 1980, as well as the Geoffrey Faber Memorial Prize and the James Tait Black Memorial Prize, both awarded in Great Britain. When *Waiting for the Barbarians* was chosen as one of the Best Books of 1982 by the *New York Times,* Coetzee took a major step in achieving recognition beyond South Africa. In so doing, he allowed the voice of the Other to be heard internationally. Despite some critics' wish that he were more specific in his fictional condemnations of South Africa, Coetzee's third novel contributed a powerful and moving voice to the international discourse on torture in the eighties.

· 6 ·

Apocalypse:
Life & Times of Michael K

As South Africa moved into the 1980s, the social and political situation grew increasingly unstable. Engaged in armed conflicts both within and without its national borders, subject to continued criticism and isolation from the world community, undermined economically by repeated strikes and threats of sanctions, disrupted by school boycotts and political protests, South Africa seemed mired in an ever deepening crisis. Speaking at the New York Institute of the Humanities in 1982, Nadine Gordimer described the turbulant atmosphere of Johannesburg: "I live at 6,000 feet in a society whirling, stamping, swaying with the force of revolutionary change" (*Essential* 262). Impending change and dislocation characterized the national consciousness as public discourse became increasingly obsessed with the ideas and images of a cataclysmic apocalypse.

Life & Times of Michael K, first published in Great Britain in 1983 and in the United States in 1984, reflects and participates in this national unease about the future direction of South Africa, this pessimism about the collective future of the country. However, Coetzee's fourth novel also suggests the other side of apocalypse, the millennial vision of a new heaven and a new earth. Within the structure of the novel, these oppositions of apocalypse are not conclusively resolved; the camp and the garden, cataclysmic history and millennial shalom, continue to war against each other. Without a clarifying catastrophe, lacking a final "revelation," *Life & Times of Michael K* is apocalyptic in the most profound biblical sense, obscurely pointing toward ineffable realities transcending discursive definition.[1] Coetzee's fourth novel also continues his exploration of the difficulties inherent in being a South African novelist and giving voice to the Other.

War is the Father of All

The epigraph of the novel comes from Heraclitus:

> War is the father of all and king of all.
> Some he shows as gods, others as men.
> Some he makes slaves, and others free.

The condition of war that introduces and overshadows the novel reflects and perhaps encouraged the growing belief in the late 1970s and early 1980s that South Africa was entering a new phase of racial conflict, a phase of armed resistance. After the events of the Soweto uprising in 1976–1978, the level of violence in South Africa increased dramatically. The large numbers of those killed and injured at the hands of the police, and the growing awareness of the brutal treatment of those in detention, prompted many blacks to turn to more violent means of protest. The Rockefeller Study Commission on U.S. Policy toward Southern Africa reported in 1982: "The combination of anger and fear stirred in the youths [by Soweto and its aftermath] is suggested by the fact that two years afterward, according to the head of the security police, 4,000 of those who had fled were in guerrilla training camps outside the country" (Study Commission 183). Responding to what it termed the "total on-slaught" against South Africa, the government issued a Defence White Paper in 1979 which claimed that the military threat against South Africa was growing at an alarming rate and argued for a "total strategy" involving both internal politics and international relations (*Survey 1979* 75). Guerrilla warfare was perceived to be the major threat, and subsequent events of 1980 and 1981 suggested that this fear was not misplaced.

More frequent guerrilla attacks and sabotage conducted by black nationalist groups set the entire country on edge. From 1977 to 1982, bombings by underground liberation movements caused damage estimated at $635 million (Lelyveld). A history of the African National Congress notes that official governmental reports are often "designed to boost confidence in the government's capacity to contain insurgency," but "even security police statistics . . . trace an outline of growing warfare." In 1976 these reports listed an average of two guerrilla attacks every six months; in 1986, the number had grown to an average of more than five bombings, raids, or assassinations every week (Davis 145). Reported incidents of political violence and sabotage rose from 59 in 1980 to 114 in 1981, 230 in 1982, and 395 in 1983 (*Survey 1983* 568).

Beginning in 1980, there was increased speculation about the possibility of war. In January three black nationalists armed with rifles took twenty-five people hostage in a suburban Pretoria bank and were subsequently killed, along with two hostages, in a police shootout. The proximity of the attack to the life of the average citizen caused the *Rand Daily Mail,* one of the more outspoken English-language papers, to appeal in a front-page editorial to the government to institute racial change before the country faced "terrorist war" ("Raid"). In June even more shocking events occurred when ANC guerrillas overcame a sophisticated alarm system to set off a series of explosions causing $8 million in damage to three of South Africa's most closely guarded oil processing facilities. The spectacular glow from the burning SASOL plants could be seen fifty-five miles away in Johannesburg. South Africa has entered "a state of revolutionary war," the *Rand Daily Mail* declared (Burns, "South African"). With guerrilla activity intensifying, peaceful protest spread to a new segment of the South African population. The Soweto protests had occurred primarily in the black areas, but the growing waves of strikes and student boycotts in 1980 took place, for the first time, among the coloured population. The police continued to respond to these mass gatherings with tear gas and bullets. In June, at least eight people died and fifty were hurt as the police moved in on demonstrations in the mixed-race areas near Cape Town. The Cape Flats mixed-race area was "in a state of siege," reported the *New York Times* on June 18, as skirmishes developed into a night of looting, stoning, and burning, and the road to the airport was blocked by demonstrators (Burns, "At Least").

Guerrilla attacks continued to multiply in 1981. General M. Malan, the Minister of Defence, reported a 200 percent increase in terrorist operations in the first six months of 1981 compared to the last six months of 1980. By October, the ANC had conducted more than forty attacks in urban areas alone: "It appeared the ANC was transforming its campaign of sporadic, scattered attacks into a sustained, low intensity guerrilla war" (*Survey 1981* 77). Police stations, electrical power stations, industrial facilities, and railway lines were the favored targets, as the ANC attempted to avoid civilian casualties and inflict economic and psychological damage.[2]

Besieged from within, the South African white minority also was conducting a virtual war on the national borders. The newly won independence of Mozambique, Angola, and Zimbabwe raised the specter of black border countries harboring ANC guerrillas, and the South

African Defence Forces (SADF) did not hesitate to carry their operations into these neighboring countries. Their frequent cross-border attacks and alleged support of revolutionary groups opposed to the ruling black governments in these countries constituted a large-scale military "destabilization campaign" (Price 20). In 1980, for example, Mozambique accused South Africa of massing a large number of troops along its border and of supplying the National Resistance Movement with arms and ammunition; Zambia claimed that South Africa sent two battalions of troops into its Western Province and assisted in a coup attempt against the government of President Kaunda. At a Frontline summit meeting in Maputo in 1982, delegates declared that South Africa was "waging a non-declared war against the free and independent states of the region" (*Survey 1982* 193). The militarization of South Africa was becoming more and more apparent even to ordinary citizens as a result of the introduction at the beginning of 1978 of compulsory military service for white men and subsequent controversies over the refusal of the government to grant those opposed to apartheid but not members of "peace churches" the status of conscientious objector.[3] According to the University of the Witwatersrand researcher David Shandler in 1989, nearly 4,500 university graduates, one fourth of the total number of graduates, were leaving South Africa each year primarily because of compulsory national service ("The Month" 6).

Most of those called up for service found themselves in Namibia. Although the United Nations General Assembly declared in 1973 that SWAPO, the South West Africa People's Organization, was the sole authentic representative of the people of Namibia, South Africa continued to try to install a white-dominated government in Namibia and to wage a virtual war against SWAPO guerrillas and their Angolan and Cuban military supporters. Robert Price reports, "Frequent incursions into Angola by the South African military began in 1977 and grew in size and scope, so that by 1981 they involved air strikes, sizeable ground forces, penetrations of as much as 200 miles inside Angolan territory, and the actual occupation of parts of southern Angola" (18). A report issued by a fact-finding mission from the European Economic Community (EEC) and the African, Caribbean and Pacific Countries (ACP) stated that South Africa maintained a constant military presence in south Angola throughout 1981. The South African Air Force made at least 1,617 reconnaissance flights and conducted 100 bombardments (*Survey 1981* 453). Despite numerous United Nations attempts to mediate a settlement, the escalation of war between SWAPO and SADF continued throughout 1983.[4]

Given the extensive military and guerrilla activity in the early eighties, it is not surprising that discourse in South Africa at this time became increasingly concerned with war, revolution, and apocalypse. The end of modern South African society as the whites knew it seemed close at hand. Military planning and budgeting, a steady increase in the length of required military duty, and the reports of the nightly news all suggested that South Africa had reached a breaking point. The prediction of terrorist war made by the *Rand Daily Mail* echoed almost every Afrikaner's deepest fear. During the time he spent living in South Africa, the anthropologist Vincent Crapanzano noted "the constant talk of change, of imminent bloodbath, of takeover and revolution." The South African people, he concludes, are "caught in a deadened time of waiting," most whites in fear, most blacks in hope (xxii).

Another American who spent time in conversation with South Africans in the early 1980s is Richard John Neuhaus, Director of the Rockford Center on Religion and Society. In his report of these conversations, *Dispensations: The Future of South Africa as South Africans See It,* he notes the constant feeling of South Africans that the end is near. Although Neuhaus believes there is little probability of an imminent revolution, he found both whites and blacks frequently talking about the possibility. One journalist told him how the government constantly warns "about total onslaught and the threat of South Africa being wrecked by apocalyptic violence" (276). Nthato Motlana, a prominent member of the antigovernment "Committee of Ten" in Soweto, told Neuhaus that the Afrikaners are terrified: "There is a great depopulation along the borders. Whites are leaving. North of here there are vast farms that have been abandoned. They try to hide it, but they are suffering, and most of all they are suffering a loss of confidence. That uncertainty, that insecurity, is going to increase" (267). In 1982 Gordimer saw South Africa as "living in the interregnum," the time between the dying of the old and the birth of the new: "The sun that never set over one or other of the nineteenth-century colonial empires of the world is going down finally in South Africa."[5]

One vision of impending doom that may have functioned to displace fears of a political apocalypse is shared by those South African whites who embrace a charismatic Christianity characterized by speaking in tongues, miraculous healings, world-wide conspiracy theories, and detailed interpretation of prophetic books of the Bible. The Renewal, or Reborn Christian Movement, is an interdenominational phenomenon, including Anglicans, Catholics, Baptists, Assemblies of God followers, and even younger members of the Dutch Reformed Church. Mary De Haas notes that in addition to spreading charismatic renewal to the mainline churches, the Renewal gave birth to several new independent churches, such as the Rheme Bible Church, founded in 1979, and the Christian Centre, operating in Durban since 1979 (38). The Cape Renewal Conference held in 1981 had over six thousand registered participants from several different denominations (Crapanzano 210). During his stay in Wyndal, Crapanzano noted the growing involvement in the Renewal in that Cape town, and he attended a Renewal meeting held one night in a packing shed during which a visiting dominee (minister) outlined the coming apocalypse in which the Illuminati—a band of leaders including Carter, Mao, Brezhnev, Rockefeller, Oppenheimer, the Rothschilds, Waldheim, and Thatcher—would take over the world. Crapanzano sees the growing appeal of the Renewal to the younger members of the middle class within the context of the increasing uncertainties of South African life: "They were there, at home, worried, threatened, overwhelmed even, when they thought of their own personal future and the future of their children and grandchildren—thoughts that they preferred not to harbor, I believe, and that they deflected, as they could, in transcending dramas of apocalypse and salvation" (287). Similarly, De Haas concludes that the politically conservative Renewal, with its lack of interest in social justice, "offer[s] a home to people who have become painfully aware that their very future is at stake" (40). The rhetoric of the Antichrist, the seven vials, and the great dragon with seven heads and ten horns coupled with jumbled accusations of the conspiratorial collusion of the Trilateral Commission, the National Council of Churches, Elton John, and Charles Manson (among others) represents one expression of the apocalyptic mentality of South African society.

The imagery and ideas of war, turmoil, and apocalypse are also apparent in critical and fictional writing of this time. André Brink entitled his book of criticism published in 1983 *Writing in a State of Siege,* while Jack Cope chose *The Adversary Within* to describe his analysis of dissident Afrikaans writers, which appeared in 1982. South African fiction of the 1980s, particularly those works written by white authors, embodies the state of turmoil both directly and indirectly. Thesen

Hjalmar's *A Deadly Presence* (1982) evokes a sense of an uncertain threat in its eery tale of a wounded leopard roaming and terrorizing the Cape, and anticipates Nadine Gordimer's similar novella, *Something Out There* (1984), in which a fierce baboon and the threat of terrorists combine to create fear in a town. Less allegorical and more terrifyingly realistic is Elsa Joubert's *Die Laaste Sondag* (1983), which depicts government troops fighting a group of terrorists who are bombing white-owned farms. Other novels are more overtly apocalyptic, projecting a fearsome end of the world and new future: Karel Schoeman's *Promised Land* (1978), Nadine Gordimer's *July's People* (1981), Christopher Hope's *Kruger's Alp* (1984).

Schoeman's novel describes the fortunes of a group of Afrikaners after the revolution, now dominated by an unidentified group termed "they." A young expatriate who has left the country "before the troubles" returns to his family farm, only to find it and most of the surrounding farms abandoned and neglected. The remaining Afrikaners live in poverty, fear, and covert rebellion. The role reversal Schoeman explores appears also in *July's People,* as a white family struggles to survive in their servant's "homeland" village while the revolution is fought in the cities. *Kruger's Alp,* a strange and bitter satire about the future of South Africa, uses the discourse of the Renewal in its account of how both the Afrikaner government and various revolutionaries are swept up in massive conspiracy of greed and hypocrisy, while a renegade priest and a few of his followers search for a legendary Boer utopia in Switzerland. Both Schoeman and Hope take the typological rhetoric of the Afrikaners and turn it on end in their ironic depictions of the "promised land."

In the introduction to *A Land Apart,* an anthology of contemporary South African writing, Brink and Coetzee point out that "an intimation of violence and death" underlies almost all contemporary Afrikaans literature. "In one form it emerges as a series of relentless explorations of war, conscription, border skirmishes, incursions into neighbouring territories, the invasion of privacy. . . . More generally, it is expressed as an intimation of apocalypse, which implies not just the death of the individual or the end of his hopes, but the destruction of the entire known world or a way of life" (13).[6] The intimations of violence and death, the premonitions and predictions of radical revolution, found voice in numerous works of fiction that explore both the fear and the hope that apocalypse brings.

The Times of Michael K

As the title indicates, *Life & Times of Michael K* not only focuses on the life of Michael but also depicts his "times," the end times of South Africa. The "time" represented by the novel, however, exists in multiple dimensions. Lois Zamora explains about apocalyptic writers, "The apocalyptist stands outside of time, recounting the past, present and future from an atemporal point of view beyond the end of time. In Revelation, St. John responds to God's urgent command, 'Write the things which thou has seen, the things which are, and the things which shall be hereafter'" (*Apocalyptic Vision* 3). In traditional apocalyptic texts the future is narrated as if it were past. In modern political apocalypses, the past tense obliquely suggests that the new order has succeeded the old. Brink points out the past tense employed in George Orwell's *1984*: "The narrator is writing about Winston Smith from a vantage point much further into the future than '1984,' looking back at events already concluded—something he could conceivably do only if Big Brother's regime has become extinct in the meantime" ("Writing" 189–90). As an apocalyptic parable, *Life & Times of Michael K* is set in a future South Africa but contains Coetzee's first fictional use of the past tense, in its primary narrative. In its different layers of context and allusion, the novel recounts past, present, and future. It sketches the impending chaotic dissolution of white-ruled South Africa much as Gordimer's *July's People* or Schoeman's *Promised Land* does, imagining an unspecified future during which South Africa is wracked by civil war. The narrator's use of the past tense, however, may suggest that he is writing about Michael from a vantage point beyond the war, from a historical position in which oppression has been overcome.

However, the particulars of Michael's life not only are prophecies as to what will become of someone like him when the fabric of South African life begins to unravel under the pressure of war but also are a tragically accurate depiction of the way that blacks in South Africa have been and are still being treated. Gordimer views the novel primarily in this way, as an expression of current events in South Africa: "If it is set ahead in time at all, then this is done as a way of looking, as if it had come to the surface, at what lies under the surface of the present. The harried homelessness of Michael K and his mother is the experience, in 1984, of hundreds of thousands of black people in South African squatter towns and 'resettlement' camps" ("The Idea" 3). Simultaneously projecting the future and reflecting the present, *Life & Times of Michael K* also rewrites the past, presenting in Michael's story a revision of several enduring Afrikaner myths.

The novel follows the life of Michael K, the harelipped son of a Cape Town cleaning woman and officially classified as "CM"—coloured male (70). After growing up in an institution for handicapped children, Michael works as a gardener in the Parks and Gardens department of Cape Town, and we begin to follow his fortunes in his thirty-first year as law and order break down in Cape Town and his mother's health degenerates. Against the backdrop of civil war, Michael embarks upon a quixotic mission to bring his mother back to the Karoo farm where she spent an idyllically remembered childhood. Although she dies enroute, Michael brings her cremated ashes to the farm and takes up a life as a gardener on the abandoned homestead. When an army deserter arrives, Michael flees to the mountains, where he lives in a stupor until he realizes that he is starving to death. He creeps down to the town and is placed in Jakkalsdrif, a resettlement camp for the unemployed and homeless. After a few weeks, he escapes, returning to the farm and again gardening, planting pumpkins and melons. Digging a burrow in the earth to hide from the deserter and the guerrilla fighters who occasionally visit the farm, Michael is content for a time. However, his sparse diet and inadequate shelter again weaken his body, and crawling out of his burrow, he is discovered by a group of soldiers who suspect him of aiding the guerrillas by running a supply station. Once again he is committed to an institution, a rehabilitation camp for rebels, located at the old Kenilworth racecourse in Cape Town. Here he refuses to eat and eventually escapes to the seaside suburb from which he began his long journey. In the final pages of the novel, Michael lies in his mother's old abandoned room, dreaming of returning to the farm. With the exception of the interlude in the rehabilitation camp, which is narrated by the camp medical officer and employs the present tense, the novel is written in the third-person past tense but is centered in Michael's consciousness.

Like *The Narrative of Jacobus Coetzee, Life & Times of Michael K* is firmly rooted in South African geography. Avoiding what he terms the "immense labor" of inventing a world out of place and time, as he did in *Waiting for the Barbarians,* Coetzee chose to set his fourth novel in a readily identifiable South Africa in the not too distant future. Brushing off a question about the geographical accuracy of the novel, Coetzee said,

"I don't have much interest in, or can't seriously engage myself with, the kind of realism that takes pride in copying the 'real' world" ("Two" 455). Nonetheless, he grounds the novel in South Africa to the extent of employing specific street names, a detail that could easily have been omitted. The realistic geography carries some significance. The shape of Michael's journey, particularly in light of Afrikaner history, has mythic resonances, moving steadily toward the heart of South Africa, the Karoo, and then returning to the chaos and corruption of the city.

Although these details of place are significant, even more central in the depiction of Michael's surroundings is the specter of war. As the epigraph reminds us, "War is the father of all," and whether viewed as a prophecy of the final conflict to come, a reflection of the historical reality of South Africa in the early eighties, or an ironic echo of the great Anglo-Boer War, Michael's times are times of war. The constant and apparently random movement of troops throughout the novel and the incidents of sabotage, such as the spectacular explosion and fire in Prince Albert reminiscent of the SASOL attack, give Michael's times a nightmare quality of senseless violence. The novel never explains the war— who is fighting, the progression of battles, the victories and defeats. Rather, we see the war from Michael's perspective, as a disruptive and meaningless event with institutions and structures that allow the strong to triumph over the weak. When a solitary soldier with an automatic rifle robs Michael of the money his mother left at her death, Michael asks, "What do you think the war is for . . . for taking other people's money?" (37). Even the medical officer at Kenilworth fails to understand the larger purpose of the war and of his job. "Can you remind me why we are fighting this war?" he asks his superior. "I was told once, but that was long ago and I seem to have forgotten" (157).

This lack of focus on the war has provoked criticism. Gordimer, while praising Coetzee's depiction of the oppression currently rampant in South Africa, is disappointed with the "revulsion against all political and revolutionary solutions [that] rises with the insistence of the song of cicadas to the climax of this novel" ("The Idea" 6). However, Coetzee does allow the radical point of view both voice and validity in the character of Robert, the man who befriends Michael in the relocation camp and explains how what appears to be charity is actually a means of supplying cheap labor and of preventing the able-bodied men from joining the guerrilla forces in the mountains. "You're a baby," Robert tells Michael. "You've been asleep all your life. It's time to wake up" (88). Michael wonders, "Is this my education? . . . Am I at last learning about life here in a camp?" (89), and in a later meditation on the oppression of the authorities realizes that he has come to think like Robert (95). He even considers joining the guerrillas when they come to the farm, dreaming of feeding them pumpkins and prickly pears and "drinking in their words" (109). If Michael were to choose between the soldiers and the guerrillas, he clearly has the most sympathy with the guerrillas. Although the specific politics of the revolutionary struggle are not the primary focus of Coetzee's story and the central character of Michael does not actively embrace a revolutionary solution, Coetzee does not reject such a solution. He just has other concerns to address.

Rather than focusing on the political or military struggle, Coetzee concentrates on the institutional violence of South Africa. One of the great strengths of *Life & Times of Michael K* is its ability to depict this kind of war, the war of the bureaucracy against the individual. Gordimer praises how the novel "leaves nothing unsaid . . . about what human beings do to fellow human beings in South Africa" ("The Idea" 6), but fails to note how Coetzee goes beyond moral condemnation of corrupt individuals to condemn and expose corrupt structures. While *Waiting for the Barbarians* examines the existence of evil in individuals and the unbelievable reality of the world of the torturer Colonel Joll, *Life & Times of Michael K* concentrates more on exposing the evils of the system. In so doing, Coetzee acknowledges the kind of demands made in *The Kairos Document,* a statement issued by more than 150 theologians and church leaders in South Africa: "The general idea appears to be that one must simply appeal to the conscience and the goodwill of those who are responsible for injustice in our land. . . . At the heart of this approach is the reliance upon 'individual conversions' in response to 'moralising demands' to change the structures of a society. It has not worked and it never will work. . . . The problem that we are dealing with here in South Africa is not merely a problem of personal guilt, it is a problem of structural injustice" (29).

Coetzee highlights the structural injustice of South Africa in a number of ways. For example, until we reach the section narrated by the medical officer, none of Michael's oppressors have proper names.[7] They are all identified by their institutional roles: the railway clerk, the policewoman at the desk, the nurse, the soldier, the shopkeeper, the Free Corps man. Even the deserter Michael encounters at the farm names himself by means of relationships of authority and power: "I am boss Visagie's grandson" (60). The cruel farmer in khaki who calls Michael a "monkey" and demands that he work more efficiently is identified by Robert as "the brother-in-law of the captain of police, Oosthuizen" (87). In Michael K's times, individual identity is far less important than one's social role and place in the power structure. Ironically, the various institutions in which Michael is incarcerated are all identified by proper names, as if they were human beings: Huis Norenius, Jakkalsdrif, Kenilworth. The protagonist's own name suggests the way he straddles the worlds of individual identity—Michael—and faceless functionary—K.[8] The system's inability to recognize the individual is revealed by the way Michael is inscribed as "Michaels" in official documents and in the medical officer's memoirs. Michael's own understanding of himself as a person rather than a social role is demonstrated in the narrative's significant omission of any direct references to race, except for the racial category abbreviated on his charge sheet. Since the third-person narration is centered in Michael's consciousness, this silence reveals his refusal to capitulate to society's labels.

Many of the structures of the social system depicted in the novel directly reflect the reality of life in South Africa. Michael has no father; his mother works as a domestic, living in a cramped room intended for air-conditioning equipment while he resides in an impersonal hostel. When his mother becomes old and disabled, her employers cut her salary by a third but allow her to remain in her room. "She lived in dread of the end of the Buhrmanns' charity" (6). Hospitalized for severe dropsy, Anna K is ignored and neglected:

> She had spent five days lying in a corridor among scores of victims of stabbings and beatings and gunshot wounds who kept her awake with their noise, neglected by nurses who had no time to spend cheering up an old woman when there were young men dying spectacular deaths all about. . . . When she wanted a bedpan, however, there was seldom anyone to bring it. She had no dressing-gown. Once, feeling her way along the wall to the lavatory, she had been stopped by an old man in grey pyjamas who spoke filth and exposed himself. . . . The tears she wept on the sixth day were thus largely tears of relief that she was escaping this purgatory. (5)

Michael is refused a wheelchair for his mother, but somehow helps her to the bus stop. "There was a long queue. The timetable pasted on the pole promised a bus every fifteen minutes. They waited for an hour while the shadows lengthened and the wind grew chilly. . . . When the bus came there were no seats. Michael held on to a rail and embraced his mother to keep her from lurching" (5–6). In a few pages of stark prose, Coetzee has rendered the inadaquate systems of employment, housing, old age pensions, public health, and transportation that marginalize and oppress the majority population of South Africa. The vividly rendered riot at Sea Point, the bureaucratic maze that Michael must run in an attempt to obtain permits to travel legally to Prince Albert, and the constant demands for green cards, or passes, are even more familiar elements in the apartheid system.[9] In its depiction of structural injustice, *Life & Times of Michael K* captures the mind-numbing effects of a social and economic system that destroys every element of human dignity.

Coetzee's emphasis on the system of oppression and the anomie it creates is skillfully rendered through his style. In his grammatical and syntactic constructions, disembodied voices speak, hands hold out green cards, sentences repeatedly begin in Hemingwayesque fashion: "It was." *Life & Times of Michael K* makes especially effective use of passive sentence structures, particularly those linguists term "short passives," in which the agent is never (grammatically) present. As a linguist, Coetzee has shown a special interest in the rhetorical effect of passive constructions, writing at least three essays on the topic.[10] He notes that most modern discussions of short passives have seen them as a means of evading attribution of agency. However, his analysis of Swift's and Gibbon's short passives reveals how these constructions evoke irony: "In their rhetorical/grammatical scheme, the agent is, so to speak, blocked out; but matters can be arranged so that it will be inferred (recovered) with fair accuracy. Thus they make of the short passive a vehicle for ironic understatement" ("Rhetoric" 217). Coetzee's own passives function in such a manner. The reader is never at a loss to identify the agent in the following sentences; the unnamed actor is always some representative of "the system":

> At midnight, when the operation *was about to be declared concluded,* a rioter with a bullet through his lung *was discovered* huddled in an unlit angle of a passageway in a block further down the road and *taken* away. (12)
> But the plaster statue of St Joseph with his beard and his staff was gone, the bronze plate *had been removed* from the gatepost, the windows *were shuttered.* (13)
> In the hospital he sat supporting her till it was her turn *to be taken away.*

When next he saw her she was lying on a trolley amid a sea of trolleys with a tube up her nose, unconscious. Not knowing what to do, he loitered in the corridor till he *was sent away.* (27)

Half-dressed, some wailing, some praying, some stunned with fear, men, women and children *were herded* on to the open terrain before the huts and *ordered* to sit down. (90)

They *were made* to line up at the gate and file out one by one. Everything they had with them they *were forced* to leave behind, even the blankets some of them wore wrapped over their nightclothes. (91)

He *was hit* a terrific blow in the pit of the stomach and fainted. (122)

As a form "in which the agent is first known, then omitted for rhetorical reasons, then recovered by the complicitous reader," Coetzee's short passives embody the anonymous quality of those in authority, suggest the ponderous inevitability of the lives of the oppressed, and finally involve the reader in the naming of the oppressor ("Agentless Sentence" 33).

That Coetzee's story emphasizes the structural injustice of South African life is most evident in the way that Michael's life progresses through and is governed by a series of institutions, or camps, as Michael thinks of them. Many of the camps are formal structures established to bestow "charity" on the needy, although Robert's political deconstruction of South African charity reveals its inherent oppresssion. His country has camps for everything, Michael thinks, "camps for children whose parents run away, camps for people who kick and foam at the mouth, camps for people with big heads and people with little heads, camps for people with no visible means of support . . ." (182). Throughout the novel, Michael's memories and dreams are haunted by his first camp, the school at Huis Norenius, where he went hungry, was kept from his own thoughts by a constantly blaring radio, and learned to withdraw into his own mental world when the pupils were made to sit with their hands on their heads, their lips sealed, and their eyes closed. He finds similar systems of dehumanization at both the resettlement camp and the army rehabilitation camp. Allowed to leave the camp only as members of a work party to provide cheap labor for the railways and the farmers, the inmates are stripped of volition. Although they are provided with (minimal) food and shelter, their lack of self-determination and privacy strips them of human dignity. Michael's story is a stern rebuttal to the common justification of the white majority that blacks in South Africa are much better off in a material sense than those in the black-ruled nations of Africa.

The denial of human freedom and identity that characterizes many of the institutions of South Africa appears in the attitude of the Jakkalsdrif guard, who asks Michael,

> "Why do you want to run away? You've got a home here, you've got food, you've got a bed. You've got a job. People are having a hard time out there in the world, you've seen it, I don't need to tell you. For what do you want to join them?"
>
> "I don't want to be in a camp, that's all," said K. "Let me climb the fence and go. Turn your back. Nobody will notice I'm gone. You don't even know how many people you've got here."
>
> "You climb the fence and I'll shoot you dead, mister. No hard feelings. I'm just telling you." (85)

A similar rigidity characterizes Sergeant Albrechts at Kenilworth. Despite his weak physical condition, Michael is made to do squats and "star-jumps" (jumping jacks) when he refuses to participate in the prescribed activity of singing. "How can you punish him with physical exercise?" the medical officer complains. "He's as weak as a baby, you can see that." "It's in the book," the sergeant replies (145). Within these institutions, people are marks in a book, objects in a system.

Even their relationship to the transcendent, their human need for religious meaning and ritual, is codified and imposed upon them. The children at Huis Norenius are dressed identically and "marched two abreast to the church on Papegaai Street to be forgiven" (105). Similarly, a pastor conducts a service at Jakkalsdrif, covertly preaching while he prays, "Let peace enter our hearts again, O Lord, and grant it to us to return to our homes cherishing bitterness against no man, resolved to live together in fellowship in Thy name, obeying Thy commandments" (83). The medical officer recognizes the empty nature of these rituals: "For their souls they have a choir and a pastor (there is no shortage of pastors), for their bodies a medical officer. Thus they lack for nothing. In a few weeks they will pass out certified pure of heart and willing of hand, and there will be six hundred bright new faces coming in" (143).

While in the rehabilitation camp, Michael refuses to eat or to receive intravenous feeding. "It's not that he wants to die," explains the medical officer. "He just doesn't like the food here. Profoundly does not like it. He won't even take babyfood. Maybe he only eats the bread of freedom" (146). The officer's analysis has an element of truth, but is simplistic in ascribing Michael's lack of freedom solely to his incarceration. When

Michael is first brought into the rehabilitation camp, his body already exhibits the signs of prolonged malnutrition. Throughout the course of his journey, he has frequently endured hunger and avoided food. Alternatively, while living in the relocation camp, he actively searches for food, begging from the ACVV women; on his return to Sea Point, he is tempted by the tinkle of the ice cream truck until he remembers he has no money. Michael's complex and erratic behavior with respect to food is that of an anorexic; as psychologists have demonstrated, anorectics often unconsciously rebel against their restricted lives by starving and feeding themselves as their only means of exerting control. Besides embodying his social powerlessness, however, Michael's failure to eat also symbolizes his inability to attain personal and spiritual freedom. Although he occasionally enjoys a eucharistic meal—eating a chicken pie in the hospital that "was so delicious that tears came to his eyes" (30), revelling in the soft and juicy flesh of a pumpkin—for the most part Michael shows little interest in food, preferring instead to withdraw to an inner world. His increasing detachment from reality is one way in which he resists the structural injustice and dehumanization that surrounds him and characterizes his "times."

Afrikaner Myth and Michael K

In the various stories of warfare and violence in *Life & Times of Michael K,* we see both the future and the present of South Africa in the 1980s. However, Michael's times also are suggestive of South Africa's past and some of the central myths of Afrikaner identity. Whether or not Coetzee consciously constructed it to do so, Michael's story in certain ways revises Afrikaner myth, and the parallels of his life and the Afrikaner past demonstrate the inherent irony of South African history. Within the cultural discourse of South Africa, the extension of these myths to Michael's life is revolutionary in both fictional technique and social implications. At least three different Afrikaner myths are retold in Michael's story: the Afrikaner's heroic independence and alienation from modernity, the tragic suffering endured in the concentration camps of the Anglo-Boer War, and the pastoral return to the land.

The myth of the Afrikaner's heroic independence finds its origins in the events of the Great Trek, that "stupidly daring" pilgrimage inland and away from the British Cape rule (Villet 72). That myth continues in the so-called laager mentality that characterizes many Afrikaners today. Convinced that they are misunderstood by the rest of the world, many Afrikaners almost glory in their international isolation as a mark of their special destiny. A letter written by an American to *Focus on South Africa,* a monthly newspaper distributed as a public-relations tool of the South African government, epitomizes this myth: "The refusal of South Africans to be intimidated by hostile economic measures, foreign financed subversion and terrorism, and ferocious threats aimed at them from many directions has aroused the admiration of people everywhere who admire independence and patriotism and courage and fortitude" (Bledsoe). In an essay written for a popular American periodical Coetzee remarked that the Afrikaner's history has "largely been a history of stubborn rejection: rejection of foreign control, of foreign ways of thinking. It is a history of holding tight to the past rather than planning toward the future" ("White Tribe" 544). But this is a negative representation of the myth. As manifested in most South African discourse, such independence and isolation are heroic qualities, venerated in the monuments to the Great Trek that dot the South African landscape "like stations of the cross" (Neuhaus 23), elevated in ritual celebration of the Day of the Covenant, idolized in the paintings of the Voortrekkers that grace Afrikaner living rooms like household shrines.

That quality of heroic independence is also inscribed in many classics of South African literature. One well-known South African short story, "The Pain" by Pauline Smith, participates in that myth and provides some intriguing parallels to part of Michael's story. "The Pain" is one of a series of stories that make up *The Little Karoo* (1925), a volume that enjoyed widespread success in Great Britain and the United States throughout the twenties and thirties. Beginning in the 1960s, increased critical attention was paid to Smith's writing in South Africa, culminating in extensive celebrations of the centenary of her birth in 1982, with a new edition of her fiction, a museum exhibition, and a series of public lectures. Smith, an English-speaking South African, wrote lyrical stories of rural Afrikaners in which she implicitly supported and extended many of the myths of Afrikaner identity.[11] "The Pain" relates the trek of an elderly rural Afrikaner couple, Juriaan and Deltje van Royen, in search of an antidote to the pain that is gripping Deltje's side and slowly killing her. Hearing of the wonders of the new hospital in Platkops, Juriaan improvises a sheltered nest for his ill wife in his ox-cart and spans his oxen for the three day journey to the hospital. While Deltje lies in a hospital bed receiving treatment, Juriaan camps in his cart by night and visits his wife twice every day. The ways of the hospital are incomprehensible to them, and the "brisk, bright, personal interference" of the efficient nurse who manages their lives "bewildered them as nothing else in the hospital." Unable to understand the course of treatment she is receiving and deeply pained over her separation from Juriaan, Deltje dreams of returning to their farm to drink from "the brown bubbling mountain stream which for fifty years had quenched her thirst" (222). As the pain grows in both of their hearts, Juriaan resolves to act and secretly removes Deltje from the hospital one night to bring her home. They drive slowly toward the farm, and Deltje thinks, "Up in the mountains sitting by the stream and drinking of its clear brown water she would have no pain. . . . Lying through the night by Juriaan's side she would have no pain. . . . She lay back among the pillows, a gentle, dying woman, her heart overflowing with its quiet content" (224). "The Pain" suggests that the simple love and faith of the old couple are far superior to the modern efficiency of the fancy new hospital. The van Royens' stubborn independence is heroic, and their trek is as inspiring as that of their Afrikaner ancestors. Feeling alienated from God when they are in town, they once again feel His presence on their way back to the farm and its streams of living water. Their simplicity is lovingly rendered without the slightest hint of condescension.

Consider reading *Life & Times of Michael K* within the context of "The Pain." Anna K also has a pain. After the purgatory of her hospital stay, she begins to dream of leaving the city and returning to the countryside of her youth: "Lying in bed in her airless room through the winter afternoons with rain dripping from the steps outside, she dreamed of escaping from the careless violence, the packed buses, the food queues, arrogant shopkeepers, thieves and beggars, sirens in the night, the curfew, the cold and wet, and returning to a countryside where, if she was going to die, she would at least die under blue skies" (8). Her son laboriously builds a cart out of two bicycle wheels and a box, and, offering himself as the ox to be inspanned, begins their trek to the farm. But when her health worsens, Anna finds herself again in an impersonal hospital, with Michael sleeping in an alley and wandering the cold streets at night until he is allowed to visit her. One morning he enters the ward to discover a strange woman in his mother's bed; she has died during the night.

Several elements of the two stories are similar: an old woman's mysterious internal pain, her wistful longing to return to the idyllic farm, the faithful husband/son who manages the practical details of the trek, the sterile and alienating hospital, and the naivete and simplicity of the protagonist. These echoes suggest Michael's quiet heroism and the fundamental mythic similarity of black and white, both of whom have deep ties to the land and are alienated by modern bureaucracy. The differences between the stories, though, ironically underscore the differences of historical circumstances. Anna dies alone and confused in a hospital bed; Deltje will die under the blue sky. Michael's clumsy human-cart reveals not only his sacrificial spirit but also his bleak material poverty. Perhaps most striking, however, is the different kind of relationship embodied in each story. The van Royens' love and devotion to each other never wavers; the pain that each feels includes the pain of their first separation in fifty years. Michael and his mother do not share a similar bond. Separated since Michael's childhood by her fear of his disfigurement, by his institutionalization, by her life as a domestic servant, Anna and Michael are united by little more than blood. Coetzee does not romanticize their bond; rather, he paints with realistic strokes what apartheid does to family relations, as he also subtly shades in Michael's steady devotion and instinctive love: "He found the sight of his mother's swollen legs disturbing and turned his eyes away when he had to help her out of bed. Her thighs and arms were covered with scratch marks. . . . But he did not shirk any aspect of what he saw as his duty. The problem that had exercised him years ago behind the bicycle shed at Huis Norenius, namely why he had been brought into the world, had received its answer: he had been brought into the world to look after his mother" (7). Michael wears a black band on his sleeve after her death, "but he did not miss her, he found, except insofar as he had missed her all his life" (34). Her hair flaming, the cremated Anna K haunts Michael's dreams, the ultimate manifestation of the lack of human love in Michael's life, the dark underside of heroic independence created by a social and economic system that destroys the possibility of family relationships.

The myth of Afrikaner suffering is even more clearly recast in the depiction of the relocation camp at Jakkalsdrif (jackals' ford). Not only a reflection of the hundreds of relocation camps into which black Africans are placed following their eviction from white areas and the prison camps that supply Afrikaner farmers with cheap labor, Jakkalsdrif also ironically resembles the notorious British-run concentration camps of the Anglo-Boer War. Its thirty tents and seven iron-roofed unpainted buildings surrounded by a fence topped with barbed wire recall the camps at Bloemfontein, Kimberley, and Mafeking, among others. Like those often cited camps, Jakkalsdrif houses primarily women and children, most of the men having disappeared into the mountains to join the guerrillas. South African history has come full circle as the apocalyptic guerrilla war of Coetzee's novel repeats the apocalyptic guerrilla war of the Afrikaner's struggle for freedom from British rule. In both conflicts, an insidious campaign of negligence adds to the suffering. Robert's story about the initial sanitary conditions at Jakkalsdrif recalls the reactions of the British humanitarian Emily Hobhouse on first encountering the Boer camps: "Not a month after they opened the gates everyone was sick. Dysentery, then measles, then 'flu, one on top of the other. From being shut up like animals in a cage. The district nurse came in, and you know what she did? Ask anyone who was here, they will tell you. She stood in the middle of the camp where everyone could see, and she cried. She looked at children with the bones sticking out of their bodies and she didn't know what to do, she just stood and cried" (88). After visiting Bloemfontein on January 24, 1901, Hobhouse wrote home: "The authorities are at their wits' end—and have no more idea how to cope with the . . . difficulty of providing clothes for the people than the man in the moon. Crass male ignorance, stupidity, helplessness and muddling. I rub as much salt into the sore places of their minds as I possibly can, because it is good for them; but I can't help melting a little when they are very humble and confess that the whole thing is a grievous mistake and gigantic blunder and presents an almost insoluble problem and they don't known *how* to face it" (Pakenham 537). Hobhouse's disclosures about the appalling conditions of the camps resulted in the War Office dispatching a committee of women, led by Millicent Garrett Fawcett, to investigate. The changes recommended by the Fawcett Commission, particularly the need to follow the most basic rules of sanitation, resulted in a significant drop in the death rate in the camps. Similarly, after the district nurse's visit, "they started dropping pellets in the water and digging latrines and spraying for flies and bringing buckets of soup" (88). The ACVV, the Afrikaner women's organization founded to perpetuate the work of the women's committees who ministered to the concentration camps, visits Jakkalsdrif three times a week to supply the children with food.[12] "The Vrouevereniging ladies" take pity on Michael and allow him to clean out the remnants of the soup bucket, even though the charity is supposed to be for children only (84).

The implication of this part of Michael's K's story is practically blasphemous to the Afrikaner mind. The suffering of the homeless and abandoned at Jakkalsdrif is equated with the holy suffering of the Boer women and children at the hands of the cruel British administrators. This juxtaposition not only highlights the ironic turn of events in South African history but also elevates the suffering of the black majority to its own mythic level. As Totius's poetry helped to form a new national consciousness through its invocation of communal sorrow, so the lyrical commemoration of a people's suffering in *Life & Times of Michael K* may assist in the construction of a new myth for South African history.

Michael embarks upon his own Great Trek and endures the infamy of the camps in order to return to the patch of garden surrounding the water pump at the abandoned farm in the Karoo. In so doing, he participates in yet another enduring South African myth: the pastoral return to the land.[13] In a manner similar to both the English farm novel and the Afrikaans *plaasroman,* Michael's story depicts the rejection of the corrupt town and embrace of rural life. But it does not affirm the conservative ideology of the Afrikaner myth nor does it resort to an idyllic retreat from social and political responsibility, as some critics have alleged. As Lawrence Buell has ably demonstrated about the American tradition of the return to the land, "the ideological valence of pastoral writing cannot be determined without putting the text in a contextual frame" (19). Michael's story, as we have already seen, is not ahistorical. The Visagie homestead resembles both those farms being deserted on the western border of South Africa in the 1980s and the future crumbling ruins of white farms left following the revolution, such as those depicted in Schoeman's *Promised Land.*[14] Within this historical context, and the context established by the South African literary tradition, Michael's return to the land offers a strategy for the future rather than a mystification of the past. Published during a time when South Africans and the world were wondering if the end was at hand, Life & Times of Michael K proposes the garden as a millennial alternative to the cataclysm of the camps. Michael's story rejects several common South African versions of pastoral to explore an alternative way that human beings might live in relationship to the land and to each other.

Michael's pastoral affirms neither patriarchy nor property rights. The Visagie grandson would write that pastoral in the manner of the *plaasroman,* following a program of "a renewal of the peasant order based on the myth of the return to the earth" (Coetzee, *White* 79). When he arrives at the farm, having deserted the army because he can see that the end is coming, the grandson immediately attempts to reinstate the peasant order, giving Michael orders and trying to "turn him into a body-servant" (65). Michael rejects this program, fleeing the farm, just as he also rejects the material and linear consciousness represented by the Visagies and typical of the Afrikaner myth: "He was wary of conveying the Visagies' rubbish to his home in the earth and setting himself on a trail that might lead to the re-enactment of their misfortunes. The worst mistake, he told himself, would be to try to found a new house, a rival line, on his small beginnings out at the dam. Even his tools should be of wood and leather and gut, materials the insects would eat when one day he no longer needed them" (104). This rejection of property rights and lineage, however, does not result in a purely savage or primitive relationship to the land. When Michael first arrives on the farm, he realizes, as did Robinson Crusoe under similar circumstances, that he no longer has any need for the money remaining in his pocket. Without the capitalistic mechanisms of production and consumption, he thinks at first that the only way he can survive is by killing the wild goats roaming the farm. He spends the entire day hunting: "At such moments, closing stealthily in on them, K felt his whole body begin to tremble. It was hard to believe that he had become this savage with the bared knife" (52). "I must be hard," he resolves in the midst of slaughtering a goat, "I must press through to the end, I must not relent" (53). Repulsed by the goat's carcass, nauseated by the act of cleaning the animal, he eventually eats the meat without pleasure. Unlike Robinson Crusoe, Michael does not efficiently tame the goats and begin to create a domestic structure. Rejecting savagery, capitalism, and the peasant order, Michael returns to the earth as a gardener.

When he worked for the municipal services of the City of Cape Town, Michael was classified as "Gardener, grade 1" (4). However, he does not discover his calling as a gardener nor the significance of the occupation until he has escaped the civil institution and reached the apparent freedom of the rural setting. "I am a gardener," he thinks during his first stay on the farm, "that is my nature" (59). Tempted to follow the guerrillas into the mountains, Michael remains hidden, "because enough men had gone off to war saying the time for gardening was when the war was over; whereas there must be men to stay behind and keep gardening alive, or at least the idea of gardening; because once that cord was broken, the earth would grow hard and forget her children" (109). Tossing on his cardboard bed when he returns to Sea Point, Michael continues to affirm his vocation: "It excited him, he found, to say, recklessly, *the truth, the truth about me.* '*I am a gardener,*' he said again, aloud" (181–82).

Michael calls himself a gardener, not a farmer, and the difference between the farm and the garden is an important one, for the former suggests a social order, with (South African) implications of hierarchy, while the latter evokes a personal and religious order. As a gardener, Michael finds what he has been denied all of his life: maternal love, self-determination, and transcendence. Kelly Hewson writes, "Michael K's retreat from History to cultivate his own garden can thus be understood as a creative, radical attempt to maintain innocence and to assert his own history" (66). He associates the land with a maternal deity. The childhood home of his mother, the tomb for her ashes, and the womb in which he engenders life, the land provides both the maternal love and the transcendent meaning missing from Michael's life. His relationship to the earth is primarily personal and instinctive, not part of a larger social structure. When he returns his mother's ashes to the earth, he discovers that he is a cultivator: "The impulse to plant had been re-awoken in him; now, in a matter of weeks, he found his waking life bound tightly to the patch of earth he had begun to cultivate and the seeds he had planted there" (59). His deepest delight, much like Deltje's, is in the miraculous flow of the underground stream that provides the water for his garden. During his second sojourn on the land, once again growing melons and pumpkins, Michael feels "a deep joy in his physical being" as he tenderly cares for his "poor second children" (102, 101). In his attachment to the maternal earth, nurturing the children who have grown out of the ashes of his mother, Michael discovers family love.

Michael's return to the land also includes responsibility and ritual. His belief that some must tend the garden while the guerrillas work to establish political and social freedom is based upon his recognition that human beings must live in harmony with the land and with other human beings. Michael's fear that "the earth would grow hard and forget her children" hints at the spiritual deprivation of humans dispossessed from the land, as black South Africans repeatedly have been, as well as the ecological destruction that unchecked warfare and prolonged neglect would bring.[15] As Coetzee remarks in his interview with Tony Morphet, "the question remains: who is going to feed the glorious opposing armies?" (Coetzee, "Two" 459). The tender care that Michael offers the earth produces both physical and spiritual fulfillment. When the first pumpkin is ripe, Michael ritually makes it a burnt offering:

> The fragrance of the burning flesh rose into the sky. Speaking the words he had been taught, directing them no longer upward but to the earth on which he knelt, he prayed: "For what we are about to receive make us truly thankful." With two wire skewers he turned the strips, and in mid-act felt his heart suddenly flow over with thankfulness. It was exactly as they had described it, like a gush of warm water. Now it is completed, he said to himself. All that remains is to live here quietly for the rest of my life, eating the food that my own labour has made the earth to yield.   (113)

Michael's celebration of the feast of the first fruits embodies all of the millennial aspects of his sojourn in the garden.

However, this Edenic idyll cannot last, as Michael knows only too well. When he thinks ahead, he momentarily exults at the apocalyptic possibility of "making this deserted farm bloom," but then quickly experiences "a sense of pain that was obscurely connected with the future" (59). As long as he can remain outside of social history, Michael is content to live in natural history: "He lived by the rising and setting of the sun, in a pocket outside time. Cape Town and the war and his passage to the farm slipped further and further into forgetfulness" (60). But the arrival of the Visagie grandson prompts Michael to realize that he cannot live outside of history: "I let myself believe that this was one of those islands without an owner. Now I am learning the truth. Now I am learning my lesson" (61). Commenting on his novel, Coetzee says, "Nor, I think, should one forget how terribly transitory that garden life of K's is: he can't hope to keep the garden because, finally, the whole surface of South Africa has been surveyed and mapped and disposed of" ("Two" 456).

When Michael returns to the garden for the second time, after his retreat to the mountains and his incarceration at Jakkalsdrif, he resolves, "I want to live here forever, where my mother and my grandmother lived" (99). However, to achieve that goal, he must hide from the world around him: "What a pity that to live in times like these a man must be ready to live like a beast. A man who wants to live cannot live in a house with lights in the windows. He must live in a hole and hide by day. A man must live so that he leaves no trace of his living. That is what it has come to" (99). Michael's earthen burrow, then, is not the ultimate symbol of his penetration of and union with the earth but rather demonstrates his inescapable historical situation. Living in fear of the return of the Visagies or the arrival of the police to send him into another camp, Michael tends his crop by night and camouflages the growing vines with cut grass. He chooses this beast-like existence over becoming entrapped in oppressive social structures again. He fears "hefty men who would hold their sides laughing at my pathetic tricks, my pumpkins hidden in the grass, my burrow disguised with mud, and kick my backside and tell me to pull myself together and turn me into a servant to cut wood and carry water for them and chase the goats towards their guns so that they could eat grilled chops while I squatted behind a bush with my plate of offal. Would it not be better to hide day and night, would it not be better to bury myself in the bowels of the earth than become a creature of theirs?" (106). Michael's pastoral is not pure idyll. It represents a stubborn and difficult compromise with the realities of his historical situation. And it cannot last, as Michael himself realizes when his body weakens, he finds he does not know how to store the ripening pumpkins, and his burrow is flooded. In a dream an old man grips his shoulder and warns, "You must get off the land. . . . You will get into trouble" (118, 119). Even before the soldiers discover him, Michael has left his burrow and resolved, "One cannot live like this" (120). Wandering around his beloved land, he discovers that the field, the river, and even his pumpkin progenies seem unreal. The pressures of history are too much for the millennial vision.

Coetzee's recasting of the myth of the return to the land, then, reveals both the oppressive patriarchy at the heart of the Afrikaner myth as well as the historical conditionality of Michael's Edenic myth. Although it sounds the thundering chords of oppression and cataclysm, it also speaks in a still small voice of an alternative world of freedom and peace. The failure of Michael's history does not necessarily imply its impossibility. Instead, his story provides a prophetic guideline for the new order that will emerge from the ravages of the war. In keeping alive "the idea of gardening," Michael posits a new history for his land.

In the final pages of the novel we find a moving intimation of the new heaven and new earth that could result from a South African apocalypse. Michael's last dream vision is of a return to the country with a companion, an elderly father-figure with whom he will share the bounty of the earth. He will plant many different kinds of seeds and scatter them across miles of the veld. The novel closes with an image of cleansing and communion, as the old man looks at the pump that the soldiers have blown up and wonders what they are to drink. Michael will cope: "He would clear the rubble from the mouth of the shaft, he would bend the handle of the teaspoon in a loop and tie the string to it, he would lower it down the shaft deep into the earth, and when he brought it up there would be water in the bowl of the spoon; and in that way, he would say, one can live" (184). Hewson says, "The conditional tense of the final line of the novel points to a possibility. One of the possibilities is that through creative, cooperative enterprise, a community can be founded. It need not posit a rural utopia, this idea of tending the earth, but suggests a means of achieving some personal power, independence and interdependence against a backdrop which denies individual integrity and privacy" (68). As in *Waiting for the Barbarians,* Coetzee closes this novel in a spirit of tentative hope and affirmation.

Silence and Stories

Michael's life reveals many truths about the oppressive systems of South African life in its evocations of future, present, and past. One of the most striking and revealing aspects of Michael's character, however, is his silence. Physically, Michael's harelip causes his speech to be distorted and alienates him. In situation after situation, Michael stumbles over his words, whispers a response from a dry throat, or simply does not answer a question. "You don't talk," says a man working with him to clear the railway tracks. "I thought you must be sick" (43). Michael's silences frustrate the medical officer, who is himself an effusive talker. "I am not clever with words," Michael tells him (139). The narrative perpetuates Michael's silences in its point of view and use of passive sentence constructions. Unlike the central characters in Coetzee's previous novels, who all are obsessive talkers, endlessly chronicling their lives in their first-person accounts, Michael does not tell his own story. In using a third-person limited point of view, Coetzee gives us access to Michael's mind but preserves Michael's silence. Even Michael's thoughts are strangely muted by Coetzee's grammar. For example, one passage reads "It did not seem to him that he had been a coward. Nevertheless, a little further on it struck him . . ." (38), rather than "He thought he had not been a coward. Nevertheless, a little further on he realized"; or "I must be hard, the thought came to him" (53). Such constructions emphasize Michael's passivity and silence.

Michael's verbal clumsiness and reticence cause those around him, and perhaps even the reader, to conclude that he is simple-minded and slow, although he demonstrates craftiness, persistence, and ingenuity. Most of Michael's silences occur when he is confronted by a person who wishes to exercise authority over him, which evokes a feeling of stupidity within him. After reveling in the freedom of the garden, Michael feels "the old hopeless stupidity invading him" when the Visagie grandson appears and claims his position as master (60). In the last section of the novel, Michael thinks, "at least I have not been clever, and come back to Sea Point full of stories of how they beat me in the camps till I was thin as a rake and simple in the head. I was mute and stupid in the beginning, I will be mute and stupid at the end" (182). The camps have not made Michael mute; he has been silenced throughout his entire life. When he is young, his mother takes him to work with her because the smiles and whispers of the other children bother her: "Year after year Michael K sat on a blanket watching his mother polish other people's floors, learning to be quiet" (3–4). At Huis Norenius, not only did he learn to sit in the classroom with his "lips pressed tightly together" (68), but the first rule posted on the dormitory door was "there will be silence in dormitories at all times" (105). Those rules were "his father," he says. Michael has been born to and raised for silence.

Michael's inarticulate and simple personality has prompted some criticism of Coetzee's racial and historical bias. After all, his previous protagonists, all white, are articulate and intelligent, even though often paralyzingly self-conscious.[16] However, if we view Michael's limited and distorted speech within the context established both by the novel and by South African history, we see how his disability points to the epidemic of silence that has poisoned South Africa. Gordimer says, "the split lip and strangled speech [are] the distortion of personality that South African race laws have effected, one way or another, in all of us who live there, black and white" ("Idea" 3). More specifically, given the context of Michael's race and position with respect to institutions in the novel, his silences testify to the history of the silencing of Others in South Africa. Seen in the context of the impersonal forces that control and shape his life, Michael's passivity suggests the hopelessness that such a system breeds. As a physically handicapped, coloured, apparently simple-minded gardener who works for the Council and lives in a hostel, Michael epitomizes those at the margins of power and authority who have been repeatedly silenced in South Africa.

As one who has been silenced, Michael is unable to tell his own story, neither in the construction of the narrative nor in his encounters with people. Other characters in *Life & Times of Michael K* tell many stories. Michael's mother tells the nostalgic story of her pastoral childhood; the Visagie grandson relays the events of his desertion and his memories of Christmas on the farm; Robert narrates his family's story with a political interpretation; the pimp and the prostitutes Michael meets at the beach explain their urban survival skills. Michael thinks with longing about the stories of the guerrillas: "The stories they tell will be different from the stories I heard in the camp, because the camp was for those left behind . . . people who have nothing to tell but stories of how they have endured. Whereas these young men have had adventures, victories and defeats and escapes. They will have stories to tell long after the war is over, stories for a lifetime, stories for their grandchildren to listen to open-mouthed" (109).

Throughout Michael's adventures, people continually attempt to get him to become a storyteller. The officials at the hospital where his mother dies, the Visagie grandson, the police in Prince Albert: all are curious about Michael's story. The medical officer is the most insistent, becoming obsessed with Michael's silences. "What is it to this man if I live or die?" Michael wonders about the doctor's concern that he eat. In a letter addressed to "Michaels," the doctor responds: "The answer is: Because I want to know your story" (149). Earlier he had urged, "Give yourself some substance, man, otherwise you are going to slide through life absolutely unnoticed. . . . Well then, *talk*, make your voice heard, tell your story!" (140). But Michael feels inadequate as a storyteller. When he watches the guerrillas leave the farm without him, he struggles to articulate why he has chosen to stay. Although he attempts to define himself as a gardener, he remains unsatisfied with this story: "Always, when he tried to explain himself to himself, there remained a gap, a hole, a darkness before which his understanding baulked, into which it was useless to pour words. The words were eaten up, the gap remained. His was always a story with a hole in it: a wrong story, always wrong" (110). He experiences a similar inadequacy when he attempts to tell his story to the pimp and the prostitutes. Much like the magistrate in *Waiting for the Barbarians,* Michael recognizes the incompleteness and silences that fill his story, even when he occasionally struggles to articulate it.

But if Michael is unwilling to tell his story, others have no hesitation. The official papers about Michael portray him as an arsonist who "was running a flourishing garden on an abandoned farm and feeding the local guerrilla population when he was captured" (131). In his eagerness to understand the significance of Michael's life, the medical officer readily composes stories *for* Michael. When he refuses to answer questions about the guerrilla operations in Prince Albert, the medical officer makes up a story to satisfy the police, telling Michael "by my eloquence I saved you" (142). And even though he is stymied in his attempts to learn Michael's story, within his narrative the medical officer supplies a final story for Michael. Envisioning him as a new Adam who lives outside history, the medical officer understands his "persistent *No*" (164), his resistence to the life and food of the camp, as bearing an ultimate significance. "You are a great escape artist, one of the great escapees," he tells Michael in his journal. "Your stay in the camp was merely an allegory . . . of how scandalously, how outrageously a meaning can take up residence in a system without becoming a term in it" (166). Not content that Michael die without a story or without a meaning, the medical officer creates one for him.

The medical officer's section of the novel has frequently been criticized as ineffective and disruptive. Cynthia Ozick writes, "the doctor's commentary is superfluous; he thickens the clear tongue of the novel by naming its 'message' and thumping out ironies. For one thing, he spells out what we have long ago taken in with the immediacy of intuition and possession" (26). Similarly, Christopher Lehmann-Haupt complains, "The problem here is that this meaning the doctor detects is evident without his pointing it out." Dick Penner believes "This segment is perhaps best viewed as an aesthetic choice which did not work as well as it might have, one which is a consquence of Coetzee's feeling a necessity to include a point of view other than Michael K's" (110). In assigning meaning to Michael, in telling his story for him, the medical officer both belabors the obvious and strips Michael of his humanity. His obsessive desire to comprehend Michael ironically robs him of the very complexity and independence that constitute his being. Similarly, the medical officer's explication of Michael is, as James Lasdun writes, "a series of pat formulae grabbed at in an effort to turn this wretched man who refuses his help into a symbol he can accommodate."[17]

However, the interpolation of the medical officer's narrative, with its pat formulae and insistent message, warns us of the dangers of assigning meaning to and of composing stories for the Other. Thinking that we can provide salvation through our eloquence, we often are patronizing and simplistic. Although some critics have suggested that *Life & Times of Michael K* is the first Coetzee novel that does not address issues of self-referentiality and interpretation, Coetzee actually highlights these issues by means of the medical officer's section.[18] The abrupt shift in the point of view highlights self-consciously the pitfalls of writing about Others, about being a South African novelist. Michael sees the demeaning side of the medical officer's insistence that he tell a story. "Everywhere I go," he thinks, "they want me to open my heart and tell them the story of a life lived in cages. They want to hear about all the cages I have lived in, as if I were a budgie or a white mouse or a monkey" (181). Similarly, our dissatisfaction with the officer's interpretation of Michael demonstrates the inadequacy of turning human flesh and blood into abstract intellectual meaning. The medical officer's philosophizing over-inscribes Michael and robs him of his human mystery. In writing *Life & Times of Michael K,* Coetzee commits himself to a similar failure. As apocalypse, Michael's story resists complete explication even as it unveils the truth.

Writing for the Other:
Foe

With the publication of *Life & Times of Michael K,* Coetzee's international success continued. His fourth novel not only was awarded a CNA Prize in South Africa (his third) but also went on to win two prestigious international awards: Britain's Booker-McConnell Prize in 1983 and France's Prix Femina Étranger in 1985. Coetzee became a more visible presence in the Anglo-American literary world as he conducted writing workshops and gave public readings in the United States during 1984; was awarded an honorary doctorate from the University of Strathclyde, Scotland, in 1985; and was one of the fifty foreign guests of honor at the 48th International PEN Congress held in New York in January 1986. At home, he was appointed a Life Fellow at the University of Cape Town in 1983 and was promoted to professor of general literature in 1984.

Along with these awards and honors, Coetzee began to participate in a form of public discourse in the United States that further enhanced his position as a South African novelist. Throughout his career, Coetzee had written numerous essays for journals both inside and outside South Africa, but before this point these essays had appeared primarily in academic and specialist publications, such as *University of Cape Town Studies in English, Journal of Literary Semantics,* and *Modern Language Notes.* However, starting in 1984, Coetzee began writing reviews and essays regularly for three of the most visible intellectual periodicals in the United States aimed at a general audience: the *New Republic,* the *New York Times Book Review,* and the *New York Review of Books.* These articles, with only one or two exceptions, concerned South African books, people, and issues. In 1985, Coetzee joined forces with André Brink to compile and edit an anthology of South African literature for the general reader. *A Land Apart: A Contemporary South African Reader* was first published by Faber and Faber in Great Britain in 1986 and appeared in the United States in 1987 in simultaneous hardcover and paperback editions from Viking Penguin. Coetzee's fifth novel, *Foe,* appeared at the same time as *A Land Apart,* published in London by Secker and Warburg and in New York again by Viking Penguin. In the three years between *Life & Times of Michael K* and *Foe,* Coetzee had assumed a new role as a promoter of South African literature for an international audience.

Despite taking on this role as a reviewer and editor, Coetzee became increasingly unwilling to comment on his position as a South African novelist. Nonetheless, his critical and popular success, coupled with the growing international concern over events in South Africa throughout the eighties, resulted in a certain canonization of Coetzee, along with Nadine Gordimer, as a literary spokesperson for South Africa. In numerous international forums, Coetzee found himself cast as a representative South African voice, as an authority on his country, his people, and their politics. For example, an interview printed in 1985 in *Le Nouvel Observateur* begins with several questions about Coetzee's views of recent political events in South Africa: the abolition of the Immorality Act and the establishment of a new multiracial parliament incorporating Indian and mixed-race parties (Wauthier). In interviews earlier in his career, conducted primarily for a South African audience, Coetzee showed little reluctance to discuss how being a South African had influenced his writing. When Stephen Watson asked him in 1978 if he believed that South African writers should see themselves as having any definite responsibilities, Coetzee responded fairly straightforwardly, "I guess so. Let's say that in a way it's easier and more difficult being a writer in South Africa than in West European countries; because there are such gigantic subjects of such unassailable importance facing a writer in South Africa" (Coetzee, "Speaking" 22).

Later interviews reveal a certain cageyness and refusal to speak as a South African novelist. Reporting in the *Washington Post* in 1983, Allister Sparks noted Coetzee's "extraordinarily reticent manner." According to his close friend Ian Glenn, Coetzee is "in something of a quandary" about his success. "I think he's uneasy about the role of being a public figure who pronounces on public issues and signs manifestos and things like that" (Sparks C8). Similarly, writing in *Le Monde* in 1985, Bernard Géniès noted about an interview with Coetzee: "even as he hints at his principles, Coetzee would rather sidestep the slippery path of politics. He is irritated by critics who want to confine him to that domain. 'Why should one automatically try to interpret my thinking in political terms?'

he asks. 'It is not necessary to know my ideas to understand my novels'" (60). Coetzee's comments on the career of Alan Paton are particularly revealing. Reviewing a collection of essays by Paton published posthumously, he notes how "Paton was turned, not wholly unwillingly, into a sage and oracle, the guide for editors and interviewers in search of wisdom on South Africa" ("Too Late" 39). Paton, he says, was "trapped" in this role for the rest of his life: "The effects can be seen not only in the increasingly ex cathedra tone of his pronouncements, and in his tendency to think, speak, and write in brief, easy-to-chew paragraphs, but in his failure to break new ground and to develop as a writer" (39). In an interview conducted in 1983, Coetzee speaks almost disparagingly of "that vast and wholly ideological superstructure constituted by publishing, reviewing and criticism that is forcing on me the fate of being a 'South African novelist'" (Coetzee, "Two" 460). Coetzee's ambivalence about that fate is apparent in the contrast between his public explication of his country in his reviews and essays and his equivocal statements in interviews.

As readers, interviewers, editors, and prize committees grew more interested in hearing what Coetzee had to say about South Africa, his country became increasingly effaced from international discourse. The "new dispensation" granted in South Africa in November 1983, with white voters approving limited participation in the political process by Indian and Coloured races, did little to quell the turbulence of the beginning of the decade. Instead, violent protests, massive detentions, and iron-fisted law enforcement continued throughout 1984 and 1985. However, with the state of emergency instituted in 1985, the world saw less and less of South Africa in newspapers and magazines, on the nightly news, or in debates of politicians and social activists. The silencing of dissent in South Africa reached perhaps its greatest effectiveness in 1984 and 1985—during the same period in which Coetzee ironically achieved his greatest international voice. As his land and its oppressed people were immersed in silence, Coetzee found himself asked increasingly to speak for that land and people. This is the historical position Coetzee occupied as he compiled *A Land Apart* and wrote *Foe*.

Although its subject matter appears radically removed from contemporary South African life, *Foe*'s focus on the nature of narrative and imagination and on the question of who will write and who will remain silent are thoughtful responses to the questions of silencing and speech confronting Coetzee in his new role as a prominent South African novelist. Coetzee told Tony Morphet in 1987, "*Foe* is a retreat from the South African situation, but only from that situation in a narrow temporal perspective. It is not a retreat from the subject of colonialism or from questions of power. What you call 'the nature and processes of fiction' may also be called the question of *who writes?* Who takes up the position of power, pen in hand?" (Coetzee, "Two" 462). Written at a time when black South Africans were not permitted to write their own lives—either politically, socially, or fictionally—*Foe* speaks to the realities of that silencing in its revision of the legendary story of *Robinson Crusoe,* a story with particular relevance to both the South African social situation and Coetzee's own literary situation.

The Other Story of Robinson Crusoe

Daniel Defoe's *Robinson Crusoe,* first published in 1719, has become a cultural myth. Regardless of whether they have read the novel or not, most people know the amazing story of the man cast away on a desert island for twenty-eight years who not only survives but conquers his harsh environment, building shelters and fashioning clothing, setting up plantations and cattle herds, and even crafting that ultimate symbol of civilization: an umbrella. Reading the Bible he has rescued from the wrecked ship and examining his life in his journal, Robinson Crusoe passes through a crisis of faith and becomes reconciled to his life on the island. He rescues Friday from certain death at the hands of cannibals and remakes him into a Christian manservant. Robinson Crusoe is a "master": he controls his physical and social environment. In traditional Defoe scholarship, Robinson Crusoe's story has been seen as an eighteenth-century testament to the superiority of rational civilization over nature and savagery, a dramatization of the Puritan spiritual autobiography, and a celebration of the value of hard work and faith. Ian Watt says, "Crusoe lives in the imagination mainly as a triumph of human achievement and enterprise," and James Sutherland claims, "his life history is at least a progress from the careless self-indulgence of the natural man, without forethought or reflection, to a life of reason and introspection and ultimately of faith."[1]

In recent years, our understanding of *Robinson Crusoe* has taken on new dimensions as various readers have demonstrated its delineation of the imperialistic attitudes informing the colonization of the Third World.[2] Within the context of South African literary criticism particularly, *Robinson Crusoe* has been exposed by one of the leading black South African novelists and critics, Lewis Nkosi, as a central cultural text extolling a myth of civilization based on oppression. Nkosi claims, "Englishmen, on the whole, cannot read *Robinson Crusoe* properly, just as they cannot read *The Tempest* for what it is, because they cannot read themselves into the book"—at least from his perspective as "a member of the subject races" (*Home* 154). In self-imposed exile from South Africa since 1960, Nkosi reads the novel with sensitivity to its depiction of black-white relationships. His essay "Robinson Crusoe: Call Me Master" reveals the hidden oppression of *Robinson Crusoe* in a manner similar to Chinua Achebe's well-known revisionary reading of Conrad's *Heart of Darkness,* "An Image of Africa."

After praising Defoe's apparently artless realistic style, Nkosi moves into the heart of his argument by quoting James Joyce's comments on the novel: "The true symbol of the British conquest is Robinson Crusoe, who cast away on a desert island, in his pocket a knife and a pipe, becomes an architect, a carpenter, a knife grinder, an astronomer, a baker, a shipwright, a potter, a saddler, a farmer, a tailor, an umbrella-maker, and a clergyman. He is the true prototype of the British colonist, as Friday (the trusty savage who arrives on an unlucky day) is the symbol of the subject races" (153–154). Nkosi continues, "In *Robinson Crusoe* the element of myth regarding the painstaking industry of building a civilization from nothing, *ex nihilo,* is inseparable from the story of colonisation, of subjugation, exploitation, and finally christianisation" (154). Examining Crusoe's capitalistic investments in the early part of the story, Nkosi points out Crusoe's moral lapses in selling the Moorish boy with whom he escaped from the Turkish pirates for sixty pieces of silver and in concocting a scheme in Brazil to round up more Africans to be sold into slavery. "He has become a slave-runner. This new development, and the form the enterprise takes, does not disturb Crusoe unduly." He adds dryly, "The descendants of those 'subject races' may be forgiven if they see in Crusoe's shipwreck the dispensation of natural justice" (155).

On the island Crusoe is concerned to subjugate all of nature—including Friday—to build a civilization based on law and order. Initiating Friday into the rites of the English language, Crusoe "made him know his Name should be *Friday,* which was the Day I sav'd his Life," and then, "I likewise taught him to say *Master,* and then let him know, that was to be my Name" (Defoe 161). Employing the gun, the Bible, and the pen, Crusoe proves his superiority, assuming "a new mantle of power" in his appellation of "Master" (*Home* 156). As his focus on the significance of the names indicates, Nkosi pays special attention to the power of discourse in Crusoe's rule: "We must remember also the importance of 'naming' and classification in building up a civilization. It is significant that not only does Robinson Crusoe have ink and parchment for keeping a diary, he also calculates time by cutting notches on the tree in order to differentiate time in an island in which time and the seasons are amorphous. Tabulation, classification: they are at the very heart of civilization" (155). As one of Friday's race who himself has been tabulated and classified, Nkosi demonstrates the potency of the myth of *Robinson Crusoe* for the South African situation. His reading suggests Friday's perspective on the triumphant story of Robinson Crusoe and how Defoe's eighteenth-century colonialist ideology has filled and guided his transformation of the story of Alexander Selkirk, the historical prototype for the novel.

Coetzee's re-vision of *Robinson Crusoe* works like Nkosi's to uncover the silence and oppression at the heart of the classic story and to suggest the power of discourse. *Foe* pays particular attention to the role of the storyteller played by Daniel Defoe in constructing *Robinson Crusoe* and potentially by J. M. Coetzee in constructing stories about South Africa. Without presuming to speak for Friday or for the oppressed races of South Africa, Coetzee nonetheless explores their silencing and his own struggle to speak on their behalf. To do so from a position that eschews power and authority, he once again takes on the persona of a woman. "How can one question power ('success') from a position of power?" he asks Morphet. "One ought to question it from its antagonist position, namely, the position of weakness" ("Two" 462). Nkosi looked at *Robinson Crusoe* from Friday's perspective; Coetzee tells us the story again, from the perspective of a character who has been omitted from and silenced by Defoe's account: Susan Barton, an Englishwoman who is marooned for a year on the island with Cruso (Coetzee's spelling) and Friday. Historically, "Foe" is the birth name of Daniel Defoe, who added the prefix "De" to his name in 1695, but the denotation of "enemy" also reveals the author's adversarial stance to Susan.[3]

In the first chapter, Susan relates her story, beginning her epic *in medias res*: "At last I could row no further. My hands were blistered, my back was burned, my body ached. With a sigh, making barely a splash, I slipped overboard. With slow strokes, my long hair floating about me, like a flower of the sea, like an anemone, like a jellyfish of the kind you see in the waters of Brazil, I swam towards the strange island" (1). We later learn of the events leading up to her arrival on the island. In search of her daughter, who has been abducted by an English slave-runner, Susan leaves England and journeys to Brazil. After two fruitless years of searching, she boards a ship to Lisbon and becomes the captain's mistress. The crew mutinies, kills the captain, and sets her adrift with the corpse, a spike sticking out of his eye. When she abandons the boat and swims to the island, she finds Cruso, a strange, moody castaway. Cruso's life is barren; he has few tools, no gun, no Bible, no writing utensils, no records. Friday is equally silent, though not out of choice. His tongue has been cut out (by Cruso? by slavers? we never know). While Susan watches the horizon and wanders the wind-swept island longing to be rescued, Cruso labors every day constructing gigantic terraces walled by stone, which stand empty and barren for he has no seed. "The planting is reserved for those who come after us and have the foresight to bring seed," he tells Susan. "I only clear the ground for them. Clearing ground and piling stones is little enough, but it is better than sitting in idleness" (33). In his years on the island, he has built twelve levels of terraces, carried a hundred thousand or more stones to erect these meaningless walls. Cruso's barren life is epitomized by his lack of sexual desire for Susan, with whom he couples only once, following a hallucinatory fever.

When the castaways are rescued, Cruso dies on board the ship to England, and Susan lands in London penniless with Friday. She resolves to sell their story to Daniel Foe, the famous writer who will recount their adventures and make them wealthy. Chapter II consists of her letters describing life on the island and attempting to persuade Foe to write a book about the island sojourn. But Foe is much more interested in the story of Susan's lost daughter, so when a strange girl appears claiming to be that daughter, Susan suspects that she has been sent by Foe. When Foe goes into hiding in order to avoid being imprisoned for debt, Susan and Friday move into his abandoned house, and she continues to plead with him to compose their story. In Chapter III, Susan and Friday visit Foe in his hiding place, and Susan has a long talk with him about his difficulty in writing the story. She then sleeps with him. At Foe's suggestion, the next morning Susan attempts to teach Friday to write. The novel ends in a brief chapter containing a dream vision of an unnamed speaker who visits their room as they sleep and imaginatively descends into the sea.

Susan, Stories, and Silence

The contrast between Defoe's account and Susan's is marked. Her story of the sullen Cruso, the desolate island, and the deformed Friday shatters the optimistic myth of *Robinson Crusoe*. The meaningless construction of the terraces lays bare the hollowness at the core of empire-building. The simplicity of life on Cruso's island makes his autocratic rule of both Friday and Susan more visible. As Hanjo Beressem points out, Coetzee invades and deconstructs "the economic utopia of Crusoe's island" (222). Stripped of "metaphysical legitimation" (the providential seeds, the Bible, the island's natural resources), Cruso's adherence to the work ethic, says Beressem, is exposed as a "ludicrous spectacle" (225). In addition, by shifting the emphasis from the ostensibly unmediated narrative of Crusoe to the informing intelligence of the author, Foe, Coetzee highlights the way that discourse enables and informs oppression. Coetzee's revision examines the power of the pen that Nkosi noted from the perspective of one who does not have a pen or does not know how to wield it effectively, the woman. In its consideration of storytelling and the act of writing, *Foe* brings to the surface a hidden subtext in Defoe's account.

Perhaps one of the most notable things about Susan, in Coetzee's account, is her interest in stories. Her narration of the novel is only one of a number of times that she acts as a storyteller. "Let me tell you my story," she says to Cruso without prompting after her arrival on the island (10). Similarly, when she was rescued by the crew of the *Hobart,* she sat with Captain Smith drinking Madeira "and told him my story, as I have told it to you, which he heard with great attention" (40). After she returns to England, the ruling passion in her life is to have her story told. In her letters to Foe, she continually pleads with him to use his art and imagination to write her story. Unable to rest, she pursues Foe (and her story) until she finds his hiding place, and one of the first questions she asks him is "The history of ourselves and the island—how does it progress? Is it written?" (114).

One of the greatest frustrations Susan experiences on the island is Cruso's lack of interest in stories. He chronicles his history in so many different and contradictory accounts that Susan suspects that age and isolation have clouded his memory. He has no stories to tell of his life as a planter before the shipwreck, and he is not interested in Susan's stories about Bahia. He is equally uninterested in the future; while Susan is eager to imagine their rescue and subsequent life, he will not indulge in these stories, either. "It was as though he wished his story to begin with his arrival on the island, and mine to begin with my arrival, and the story of us together to end on the island too," Susan complains (34). Cruso's wish to confine the story parallels his attempts to confine Susan: "While you live under my roof you will do as I instruct!" he rages when she goes out exploring despite his orders to remain in the encampment (20). His attempts to exert patriarchal control over both the story and Susan foreshadow Foe's similar attempts.

What prompts Susan's desire to tell stories? Why does she persist in telling her story to everyone she meets and in urging Foe to put that story in writing? One reason is that stories help us to remember. Amazed that Cruso keeps no journal and has not kept track of the number of years he has spent on the island, she asks, "Would you not regret it that you could not bring back with you some record of your years of ship-wreck, so that what you have passed through shall not die from memory? And if we are never saved, but perish one by one, as may happen, would you not wish for a memorial to be left behind, so that the next voyagers to make landfall here, whoever they may be, may read and learn about us, and perhaps shed a tear?" (17). Memories grow uncertain, she tells Cruso; only by committing their experiences to paper and ink, or wood, or stone, can their story survive. A written story grants eternal life, constitutes a never-fading memorial, provides edification for the fol-lowing generations. Stories also appear to have some commodity value for Susan, as is suggested when she claims one as her inheritance: "it is I who have disposal of all that Cruso leaves behind, which is the story of his island" (45). Her persistence in having Foe write the story seems to be materially motivated. She tells Friday, "all these particulars Mr Foe is weaving into a story which will make us famous throughout the land, and rich too" (58). Importuning Foe in a letter, she pleads, "Can you not press on with your writing, Mr Foe, so that Friday can speedily be returned to Africa and I liberated from this drab existence I lead?" (63). Once she is commemorated as the subject of a successful book by a renowned writer, Susan believes that she will achieve fame and fortune.

However, the production of her story offers Susan more than material benefits. Figuratively, the wealth and freedom that she could achieve represent the ability to live a full, rich, independent, and meaningful life, because she will have achieved an identity and a wholeness from the writing of her story. Several of Susan's comments suggest the wider significance of wealth and freedom. For example, she expresses her hope that by making "the air around him thick with words," she may awaken Friday's memories of a life before Cruso's story-less island: "Though his ears Friday may yet take in the wealth stored in stories and so learn that the world is not, as the island seemed to teach him, a barren and a silent place (is that the secret meaning of the word story, do you think: a storing-place of memories?)" (59). Memories provide a kind of wealth, even as meaning provides a kind of freedom. Until her story is written, Susan feels as though she lacks substance. "Will you not bear it in mind," she reminds Foe, "that my life is drearily suspended till your writing is done?" (63). Without her story, Susan feels insubstantial, suspended, incomplete, trapped in a world of things and events without order or meaning. The philosopher Alasdair MacIntyre claims that human beings, in their actions and practices, as well as their fictions, are essentially storytelling animals. "Deprive children of stories and you leave them unscripted, anxious stutterers in their actions as in their words" (216). Susan needs her story to be told in order to take shape as a human being.

But that story cannot take just any form. MacIntyre says that human beings are tellers of "stories that aspire to truth" (216), and Susan steadfastly demands that her story be true. Her narrative demonstrates that she is well aware of the ways that people falsify stories. She is scornful of the disparities in Cruso's stories and frustrated by her inability to discern "what was truth, what was lies, and what was mere rambling" (12). She contrasts her truthful account to the more fantastical "travellers' tales" and to "the old mariner by the fireside spinning yarns of sea-monsters and mermaids" (7, 18). When Captain Smith suggests that the booksellers will hire an author to "put in a dash of colour" in her story, she is indignant. "I would rather be the author of my own story than have lies told about me," she declares. "If I cannot come forward, as author, and swear to the truth of my tale, what will be the worth of it? I might as well have dreamed it in a snug bed in Chichester" (40). The value of a story lies in its truth, its ability to record reality but also its ability to reveal meaning. Susan knows the events of her life's story, but she longs to find out their larger significance: "The waves picked me up and cast me ashore on an island, and a year later the same waves brought a ship to rescue me, and of the true story of that year, the story as it should be seen in God's great scheme of things, I remain as ignorant as a newborn babe" (126).

Susan's belief that she is unable to perceive the true story of her year on the island is part of the lack of confidence which prompts her to ask Foe to write her story. That she is a good storyteller we can attest from the evidence of the first chapter. So captivated is Captain Smith by her tale that he urges her to set it down in writing and offer it to the booksellers. But Susan fears that she lacks the art to transform the story into writing, that the liveliness and charm of the oral rendition will be missing. Terming her written account "a sorry, limping affair," she writes to Foe, "though my story gives the truth, it does not give the substance of the truth" (47, 51). Anticipating Virginia Woolf by some two hundred years, she continues, "To tell the truth in all its substance you must have quiet, and a comfortable chair away from all distraction, and a window to stare through; and then the knack of seeing waves when there are fields before your eyes, and of feeling the tropic sun when it is cold; and at your fingertips the words with which to capture the vision before it fades. I have none of these, while you have all" (51–52). Lacking a room of her own, an imaginative vision, and an appropriate vocabulary, Susan claims that she cannot write an effective story. This presumed inability to write is associated with her gender, as Captain Smith indicates, assuring her that "the booksellers will hire a man to set your story to rights" (40). Susan's description of the writing process clearly demonstrates that she conceives of the author as male: "The Muse is a woman, a goddess, who visits poets in the night and begets stories upon them. In the accounts they give afterwards, the poets say that she comes in the hour of their deepest despair and touches them with sacred fire, after which their pens, that have been dry, flow. When I wrote my memoir for you, and saw how like the island it was, under my pen, dull and vacant and without life, I wished that there were such a being as a man-Muse, a youthful god who visited authoresses in the night and made their pens flow" (126). The association of sexual effectiveness and the ability to write appears also in Cruso's absence of desire for either sex or authorship.

Susan's lack of literary confidence represents the condition of many eighteenth-century women—raised in a patriarchal society, denied the social and educational opportunities given to men, ridiculed as unnatural if they dared usurp the pen. Fictional and historical eighteenth-century women testify to this literary anxiety. Defoe's Moll Flanders writes about her conversion: "those impressions are not to be explained by words, or if they are, I am not mistress of words enough to explain them" (270).

Anne Finch's ironic lament in "The Introduction" demonstrates the origins of such insecurity in the common cultural assumptions about gender:

> Did I my lines intend for public view,
> How many censures would their faults pursue,
> Some would, because such words they do affect,
> Cry they're insipid, empty, uncorrect.
> . . . . .
> True judges might condemn their want of wit,
> And all might say they're by a woman writ.
> Alas! a woman that attempts the pen
> Such an intruder on the rights of men,
> Such a presumptuous creature is esteemed,
> The fault can by no virtue be redeemed. (1–4; 7–12)

The assumption that authorship is a male domain is not confined to the eighteenth century, however. Throughout Western culture, Sandra Gilbert and Susan Gubar point out, "the text's author is a father, a progenitor, a procreator, an aesthetic patriarch whose pen is an instrument of generative power like his penis" (6). Susan's silencing thus evokes a widespread historical and cultural phenomenon. Condemned by her gender to silence, Susan must turn to the more adequately equipped male in order to see her story brought into the world.

As Foe works on the story, however, he soon manifests his desire to control and direct it. Reading his questions and claims through the medium of Susan's epistolary replies, we perceive that Foe is more interested in what will sell than in the truth of the story. "It would have been better," he suggests, if Cruso would have saved a musket and ammunition from the wreck, and perhaps a carpenter's chest (55). Foe finds the story lacking in exotic circumstances; he wants to put some excitement into the account, such as a threat of cannibals landing on the island. Susan persists: "What I saw, I wrote. I saw no cannibals; and if they came after nightfall and fled before the dawn, they left no footprint behind" (54). Of course, the story that Foe prefers is the story as it appears in *Robinson Crusoe,* complete with the now-famous dramatic footprint. Susan's deepest fear, that Foe will decide the story would be better if it included only Cruso and Friday, "better without the woman," is fulfilled in Defoe's account, which writes the woman out (72). Tiring of the dull details of life on the island, Foe begins to press Susan for additional information about her life in Brazil and her search for her daughter. He seems to be interested in writing a different story. When the strange girl appears claiming to be her long-lost daughter, Susan knows she has been sent by Foe. The story the girl tells is a composite of events from Defoe's *Moll Flanders* and *Roxana*. Her childish desire to grow up to be a gentlewoman and her sojourn with the gypsies resemble similar parts of Moll Flanders' story; her search for her mother with the assistance of her maidservant Amy recalls the quest of Roxana's daughter Susan. Foe has written the woman out of *Robinson Crusoe* only to insert her in two of his other fictions. The woman has no place in the political and religious story Foe constructs for the island; instead, her place is within the psychological drama of mother-daughter relationships.

In writing *for* Susan, attempting to determine her story, to write the significance and meaning of her life, Foe assumes that authorship and authority are equivalent. Susan comments on his God-like control when she sarcastically remarks to Friday about the strange girl's appearance by echoing John 14: "It is only a poor mad girl come to join us. In Mr Foe's house there are many mansions" (77). The powerful author as God is a common eighteenth-century metaphor, appearing most notably in Fielding's prefatory chapters in *Tom Jones,* and again associates writing with male generation. As Edward Said has shown, the idea that the writer "fathers" a text in the same way God "fathers" the world is built into the very word *author* (*Beginnings* 83). Such "masculine" writing consists of a certain logical hierarchy: "the unity, or integrity, of the text is maintained by a series of genealogical connections: author-text, beginning-middle-end, text-meaning, reader-interpretation, and so on. Underneath all these is the imagery of succession, of paternity, or hierarchy" (162). Foe constructs Susan's story in such a tidy hierarchical manner: "We therefore have five parts in all: the loss of the daughter; the quest for the daughter in Brazil; abandonment of the quest, and the adventure of the island; assumption of the quest by the daughter; and reunion of the daughter with her mother. It is thus that we make up a book: loss, then quest, then recovery; beginning, then middle, then end" (117). The story that Susan prefers to tell, as she fully realizes, is deficient in its genealogical connections: "it is a narrative with a beginning and an end, and with pleasing digressions too, lacking only a substantial and varied middle" (121). The silence at the heart of the story arises because of the silence of Friday.

Throughout much of *Foe* Susan resists Foe's authority and insists on telling her own story. Enacting the myth of the babes in the wood, she abandons the strange girl in the forest and tells her, "what you know of your parentage comes to you in the form of stories, and the stories have but a single source. . . . You are father-born. You have no mother" (91). Nonetheless, Foe again confronts Susan with the girl and her servant when Susan finds him in his hiding place. Susan embraces the girl in an attempt to judge her substantiality, but she still feels that the girl is not her daughter, pointing out that "ghosts can converse with us, and embrace and kiss us too" (134).[4] Although earlier she had declared, "I am not a story, Mr Foe" (131), his continued insistence that the mysterious girl is her daughter prompts her to feel that Foe is creating her very identity: "now all my life grows to be story and there is nothing of my own left to me. I thought I was myself and this girl a creature from another order speaking words you made up for her. But now I am full of doubt. Nothing is left to me but doubt. I am doubt itself. Who is speaking me? Am I a phantom too? To what order do I belong? And you: who are you?" (133). If stories give us our identities and if we are written by others, Susan wonders, do we exist for ourselves?

Hanjo Beressem suggests that in this scene Susan learns to accept her intersubjectivity (and intertextuality, since her daughter comes from the pages of *Roxana*): "It is the relation to her daughter that will make Susan realize how everyone's existence is implicated by others" (232). However, it seems to me that Susan fully recognizes this truth already; her concern is that her story explore the way in which her existence is implicated by Cruso and Friday, not by the imaginary daughter of Foe's mind. Perhaps the greater significance of the scene lies in its dramatization of the power of the pen. Susan's existential dilemma is prompted by an author who asserts omnipotent authority, by a man who attempts to determine, to write, the story of a woman's life. If understanding ourselves within the context of a story is indeed a crucial part of our self-identity, those who dominate storytelling become capable of great oppression. The differing morals that Foe and Susan draw from the story of a woman who went on confessing and throwing her confession in doubt until she was hung suggest the different viewpoints of the one who speaks and the one who is silenced: Foe claims, "the moral of the story is that there comes a time when we must give reckoning of ourselves to the world, and then forever after be content to hold our peace" (124). Susan responds, "To me the moral is that he has the last word who disposes over the greatest force" (124). Foe focuses on the power of the individual to make a decision about his or her story; Susan demonstrates that social power can determine discourse, that in the politics of competing interpretations, the power given by gender, race, or class can determine what story is told.

Friday and the Word

The relationship of social power and discourse becomes even more manifest when we consider Friday: the silent slave. Cruso claims that the slavers cut Friday's tongue out—perhaps to eat it, perhaps because they were tired of his "wails of grief," perhaps "to prevent him from ever telling his story," perhaps as a punishment (23). Susan suspects that Cruso might have removed the tongue, and perceives that he keeps Friday in silence, teaching him only the few words necessary for the black to follow his commands; Friday understands the order *firewood,* but does not know the more generic term *wood.* Friday's duty to collect firewood is reminiscent of Caliban's assignment in *The Tempest,* and Cruso occasionally resembles Prospero in his evening reveries: "One evening, seeing him as he stood on the Bluff with the sun behind him all red and purple, staring out to sea, his staff in his hand and his great conical hat on his head, I thought: He is a truly kingly figure; he is the true king of his island" (37). Prospero and Miranda do teach Caliban the English language, to transform "a thing most brutish" into a man; nonetheless Caliban says, "You taught me language, and my profit on't / Is, I know how to curse" (I.ii. 357; 363–64). The scenario suggests again the symbiosis between discourse and power. As a silenced slave, Friday will never be a "master of English" (22).

In *The Tempest,* Caliban first learns language and then attempts to rape Miranda. Susan also associates verbal ability with sexual potency, fearing that Cruso might be using a metaphor when he says that the slavers cut out Friday's tongue, and wondering "whether the lost tongue might stand not only for itself but for a more atrocious mutilation; whether by a dumb slave I was to understand a slave unmanned" (119). Although later Friday reveals his nakedness as he spins around wearing Foe's red robe, Susan never clearly states what she sees: "What had been hidden from me was revealed. I saw; or, I should say, my eyes were open to what was present to them" (119). Although many readers have assumed that Friday has been castrated, the text is not clear on this point, and the description of the dance carries a strong sexual connotation: "The whirling robe was a scarlet bell settled upon Friday's shoulders and enclosing him; Friday was the dark pillar at its centre" (119). Commenting on this issue, Coetzee said, "Whether Friday is potent or not I don't know. What is more important, Susan doesn't know" ("Two" 463). Friday may be more potent, more capable of speech, than Susan suspects. Nonetheless, her association of the loss of Friday's tongue with castration suggests again the metaphoric connection of pen with penis and demonstrates that Friday's silencing confines him to the realm of the powerless feminine. Whether or not Friday has been physically castrated, he demonstrates no desire for Susan, in sharp contrast with Caliban, and so testifies to Foucault's conclusion that desire is dependent on language, and particularly on writing.

Friday's allegorical significance has caused a great deal of speculation. Coetzee's transformation of the light-skinned, European-featured native of *Robinson Crusoe* into a woolly-haired, thick-lipped, dark-complexioned Negro both reveals the true African hidden in Defoe's account and suggests Friday's kinship with the indigenous people of South Africa. Dick Penner says, "Friday's muteness can be read as a symbol of the inexpressible psychic damage absorbed by blacks under racist conditions" (124), while Robert Post points out how "South African whites have silenced the black majority as surely as Cruso, or, according to him, the slavers silenced Friday" ("Noise" 147).[5] Paul Williams argues that as the symbol of oppression and of the Other, Friday embodies the world of self-absorption without self-consciousness; without the Cartesian split of self and other, Friday has no desire and hence no stories (34–35). Friday's silence, however, is not so much an ontological state as it is a social condition, imposed upon him by those in power. As a symbol of oppression, Friday represents those who have been silenced because of race, gender, and class. Like the barbarian girl and Michael K, Friday's textual reality speaks eloquently of the silences imposed throughout South African history on Others.

Susan's desire to have her story told truthfully and the frustrations she encounters as she spars with Foe give her new insight into Friday's situation. Initially, she appears as a daughter of her time and class, unthinkingly repeating the prejudices of British society in a manner similar to Defoe's Crusoe. Despite her own daughter's abduction by a white slaver, Susan shows little concern for the victims of oppression, implying in her account of the mutiny that she had joined the captain in abusing the crew (10). In her first months on the island, she treats Friday with "little more attention than I would have given any house-slave in Brazil" (24). When Cruso tells her the story of Friday's lost tongue and enslavement, she moralizes, "Where is the justice in it?" but continues to regard the silenced black's life with "as little thought as I would have a dog's or any other dumb beast's" (23, 32). The fact of Friday's mutilation, however, fills her with such horror that she tries not to think about him at all and "flinches" when he comes near her (32). Whether unthinkingly accepting him as a slave or turning him into an object of sympathetic horror like the magistrate with the barbarian girl, Susan negates Friday's personhood and identity. It is only when witnessing Friday scattering white petals over the surface of the sea that Susan has her "first sign . . . that a spirit or soul—call it what you will—stirred beneath that dull and unpleasing exterior" (32). She notices no other expression of this soul on the island, and her moralistic paternalism emerges most vividly in her assumption that Friday must be taken away from the island: "I beseech you to send your men ashore again," she says to Captain Smith, "inasmuch as Friday is a slave and a child, it is our duty to care for him in all things, and not abandon him to a solitude worse than death" (39). In assuming the White Man's Burden, Susan begins to romanticize Friday, pleading that he be allowed to sleep near Cruso: "He would rather sleep on the floor at his master's feet than on the softest bed in Christendom" (41). The loyal servant that she depicts in this scenario suggests the humble and subservient Friday of Defoe's novel.

Once in England, Susan gradually comes to view herself as an oppressor. When she sees Friday jeered on the streets as a cannibal, growing fat and listless on oatmeal, learning to launder clothes, she now realizes that her paternalistic care has ruined him. His life with her "is a terrible fall . . . from the freedom of the island" (56). If Foe would only write their story, she idealistically thinks, she could return Friday to his life in Africa, "bearing fine gifts," to be reunited with his parents, "and marry at last and have children, sons and daughters" (58). But when Foe becomes caught up in the story of Susan's daughter, she resolves to give Friday his freedom in another way. Funding their journey by selling some of Foe's books, she travels to Bristol with Friday in a vain attempt to arrange his passage back to Africa. No reputable captain will take Friday on board, and she soon discerns that those who will take him are secretly planning to sell Friday back into slavery. Like the magistrate, who returns the barbarian girl to her people, Susan attempts to atone for the sins of the past. However, the errors of history in this case are not so easily repaired: Where in Africa will Friday go? Does he know his parents? How can he be brought there? Susan is trapped by her responsibility as an oppressor.

Her reaction to Friday's silence initially was horror and avoidance, but as Susan meditates on the power of stories, and experiences the frustrations of having her own story transformed by Foe, she becomes increasingly concerned about Friday's muteness. Like the magistrate when he learns to speak barbarian language, Susan finds that her own oppression allows her to see the powerlessness of others more clearly. Her quest to achieve freedom by having her story told is eventually matched by her desire to give both freedom and voice to Friday, to return him "to the world of words" (60). Herself a victim of Foe's discursive manipulation, Susan perceives how Friday's lack of words perpetuates his slavery:

> Friday has no command of words and therefore no defence against being re-shaped day by day in conformity with the desires of others. I say he is a cannibal and he becomes a cannibal; I say he is a laundryman and he becomes a laundryman. What is the truth of Friday? You will respond: he is neither cannibal nor laundryman, these are mere names, they do not touch his essence, he is a substantial body, he is himself, Friday is Friday. But that is not so. No matter what he is to himself (is he anything to himself?—how can he tell us?), what he is to the world is what I make of him. (121–22)

She tries various means of communication: talking at great length with him, attempting to soothe him by the tone of her voice, drawing pictures, playing music, even performing his wild whirling dance. All of these attempts fail.

Susan's efforts to bring Friday to the word accompany her effort to write their story herself as she sees Foe's interest in the project waning. Living in Foe's abandoned house, sitting at his desk, using his pen, she determines to be the author. But as she strives to write, she discovers the difficulty and the temptation of authority. Laboring with words as Cruso labored with stones, searching for incidents and words to flesh out her story, Susan understands for the first time the holes in the story and the temptation to invent "new and stranger circumstances" (67). The unanswered questions are many, but all of the mysteries can be summed up in the loss of Friday's tongue. The silence at the heart of Susan's story is the silence created by Friday. She tells Foe, "many stories can be told of Friday's tongue, but the true story is buried within Friday, who is mute. The true story will not be heard till by art we have found a means of giving voice to Friday" (118). Friday's voice will liberate not only himself but also Susan, for her story is dependent upon his meaning. As she writes, Susan also discovers the tendency of stories to evoke numerous associations: "Alas, my stories seem always to have more applications than I intend, so that I must go back and laboriously extract the right application and apologize for the wrong ones and efface them" (81). This multiplicity of meaning she attributes not to the nature of stories but to her own inadequacy: "Some people are born storytellers; I, it would seem, am not" (81). Susan's efforts to write reveal the disjunctures and ambiguities all authors face, but rather than covering up these difficulties with a smooth and coherent story, with an ordered beginning-middle-end, Susan highlights the mysteries and the silences.

It is only after Susan sleeps with Foe, descending upon him as his Muse, that Foe gives up his obsession with the story of her daughter and turns to the problem of Friday. Assuming the upper position in the sexual act, Susan claims the power of the Muse "to father her offspring" (140), envisioning the feminine role as powerful and creative. The gender reversal is complete when later Foe wonders if he serves as her whore, her mistress, or her wife, experiencing the role of powerlessness (152). Having impregnated Foe with the story of the island and the meaning of Friday, Susan then lies in bed with her new ally, and they speculate about the meaning of Friday's ceremony of the petals. Foe first suggests an archetypal male myth reminiscent of *Beowulf* or *Moby-Dick:* Friday paddles into a bed of seaweed and the hidden beast called the *kraken* extends a great arm and pulls him beneath the surface. Susan wryly comments, "What led Foe to talk of sea-monsters at such a time I could not guess, but I held my peace" (140). Foe then suggests that Friday was scattering the petals over the ruins of a slave ship, remembering his lost companions. The question of why Friday paddled out to the seaweed is the eye of the story, Foe claims, and they must descend into that eye or "sleep without dreaming, like babes" (141). Susan would call the un-known depths of the story a mouth: "It is for us to descend into the mouth (since we speak in figures). It is for us to open Friday's mouth and hear what it holds: silence, perhaps, or a roar, like the roar of a seashell held to the ear" (142). Foe, too, is now interested in Friday's silences: "We must make Friday's silence speak, as well as the silence surrounding Friday" (142). Although they are now agreed on the importance of Friday's silence, Susan still notes the practical difficulties: "It is easy enough to lie in bed and say what must be done, but who will dive into the wreck?" (142). Friday's silence defeats the possibility of hearing Friday's story.

The answer that Foe proposes is to teach Friday how to write. Susan says that "letters are the mirror of words," so without speech, Friday cannot write (142). However, Foe asserts the Derridian notion that "writing is not doomed to be the shadow of speech" (142). "We are accustomed to believe that our world was created by God speaking the Word; but I ask, may it not rather be that he wrote it, wrote a Word so long we have yet to come to the end of it?" (143). Foe's metaphor once again associates the role of the author with the role of God, but it also suggests that "writing" may take forms other than the physical inscription of ink on paper, including the physical ordering of reality. Foe claims, "Speech is but a means through which the word may be uttered, it is not the word itself. . . . The waterskater, that is an insect and dumb, traces the name of God on the surfaces of ponds, or so the Arabians say. None is so deprived that he cannot write" (143–44). Speech, as Derrida has shown, depends on presence and authority; writing, opening up endless displacements of meaning, paradoxically grants the oppressed—those without presence or authority—a voice. Susan's initial efforts to teach Friday culturally relative words such as *house, ship,* and *Africa* are not successful, and she despairs of ever conveying to Friday the meaning of words such as *freedom.* Foe explains that words are removed from reality but nonetheless function pragmatically: "Freedom is a word like any word. It is a puff of air, seven letters on a slate. It is but the name we give to the desire you speak of, the desire to be free. What concerns us is the desire, not the name. Because we cannot say in words what an apple is, it is not forbidden us to eat the apple. It is enough that we know the names of our needs and are able to use these names to satisfy them, as we use coins to buy food when we are hungry. It is no great task to teach Friday such language as will serve his needs. We are not asked to turn Friday into a philosopher" (149). Susan, in her newly found wisdom, continues to insist that "the urgings of Friday's heart" will include a desire for freedom: "There will always be a voice in him to whisper doubts, whether in words or nameless sounds or tunes or tones" (149). The uncertainties of words not withstanding, Friday is drawn to the child's slate and pencil, first inscribing rows of eyes upon feet and later filling a page of paper with the letter *o.* Chapter III ends on a note of hope: "It is a beginning," says Foe. "Tomorrow you must teach him *a*" (152).

The Word of the Silenced

Susan's and Friday's inability to tell their own stories demonstrates how the literary tradition has long silenced and marginalized those defined as Other. In one sense, Coetzee's *Foe* grants voice to the silenced through writing and the word: Susan Barton has been written out of *Robinson Crusoe* in the same way that women have been written out of literary history, but in Coetzee's fictional world she appears and relates her own story. *Foe* is a true re-vision, in Adrienne Rich's words "the act of looking back, of seeing with fresh eyes, of entering an old text from a new critical direction" ("When" 18). Susan's story fills the silence of *Robinson Crusoe,* uncovers the hidden colonialism and oppression. However, her story also ironically speaks of the process of silencing. Silenced intertextually by Daniel Defoe and textually by Foe, Susan nonetheless speaks to us, for we read her story, *as she wrote it.* Those readers who view *Foe* as pessimistic, expressing "a profound skepticism about the ability of speech and writing to tell the truth about the mute and thereby free them," overlook the significance of the narrative perspective.[6] Beressem elaborates on the paradox: Susan "has a story to tell, and, throughout the book, she attempts to tell and re-tell it. It is, however, exactly because she cannot find the proper words, and writes about the difficulty of writing that she finally succeeds in assembling it" (231). In revising *Robinson Crusoe, Foe* comments not only on the silences of colonialism but also on the silences of literary history. While Defoe is commonly seen as one of the "fathers" of the novel and *Robinson Crusoe* as marking the beginning of a new literary genre, Susan's story embodies the voice of the woman that has been silenced in traditional literary history. The four chapters of the novel represent four different narrative modes, which parallel the development of the novel and thereby suggest a new feminine literary history.[7]

Chapter I has an oral quality; it appears to be an unmediated record of a voice speaking in the first person. Suggesting both the origins of English literature in the oral tradition and the apparently artless renditions of Defoe's Moll Flanders and Robinson Crusoe, the first chapter relates the story of Susan's adventures on the island. Each paragraph opens (but does not close) with a quotation mark, indicating that Susan is speaking to someone. The oral quality of the narrative is further suggested by her metacommentary and address to the auditor. "I have

told you how Cruso was dressed; now let me tell you of his habitation";
"Within the fence, protected from the apes, grew a patch of wild bitter
lettuce. This lettuce, with fish and birds' eggs, formed our sole diet on
the island, as you shall hear" (9). Similarly, "I would gladly now recount
to you the history of this singular Cruso, as I heard it from his own lips"
(11).

Our impression that we are hearing Susan's story from her own lips
is further reinforced by her characterization as a storyteller, eager to tell
and retell her life history. When she relates her history to Cruso, she
gives us a tale within a tale. These paragraphs have two levels of
quotation marks:

> "'My name is Susan Barton, and I am a woman alone. My father was
> a Frenchman who fled to England to escape the persecutions in Flanders.
> His name was properly Berton, but, as happens, it became corrupted in
> the mouths of strangers. My mother was an Englishwoman.
>
> "'Two years ago my only daughter was abducted and conveyed to
> the New World by an Englishman, a factor and agent in the carrying
> trade. . . . (10)

The conclusion of this history—"at last I could row no further"—brings
us back to the opening of the novel. Throughout Chapter I, we receive
the impression that Susan is speaking directly to us, that we are the "you"
of her address, the audience for her speech. It is not until the second-to-
last sentence of this chapter that we are disabused of this notion, when
Susan identifies her auditor: "Do you think of me, Mr Foe, as Mrs Cruso
or as a bold adventuress?" (45). The chapter ends with a final closing
quotation mark indicating that the narrative is concluded.

In Chapter II, we move into the next stage of the history of the novel:
the epistolary narrative, with echoes of another "master" and "father" of
the novel, Samuel Richardson. In the opening of this chapter, we learn
that the previous chapter actually is Susan's written account of her
adventures which she is sending to Foe in order to give him the facts
from which to construct the story he is writing. Written in the present
tense, in the middle of her experience, the letters of Chapter II are made
up solely of Susan's side of her correspondence with Foe. By employing
Richardson's technique of writing "to the moment," the first two sections
of *Foe* ostensibly lack the controlling authoritative presence of the God-
like author preferred by Richardson's foe, Fielding. Susan's actions and
thoughts are in continual flux; she does not create a coherent plot out of
these fragments of her life. Like Pamela, Susan continues to write even

when she is unable to deliver her letters. "To whom am I writing?" she wonders. "I blot the pages and toss them out of the window. Let who will read them" (64). Similarly, Pamela perseveres: "Now I will tell you what has befallen me. And yet how shall you receive what I write? . . . I will every day, however, write my sad state; and some way, perhaps, may be opened to send the melancholy scribble to you" (130). Susan, like Pamela, seems compelled to write in an effort to control her life, to write her destiny, to assert her identity. Keeping the undelivered letters neatly stacked in a box (Pamela hides hers in her underwear), Susan contrives to write her own story despite Foe's efforts to take control.

By Chapter III, Susan has assumed more narrative control and no longer feels that it is necessary to remind us that she is writing the account. Much like a nineteenth-century novelist, she employs a first-person narrative written in the past tense. Chapter III has no apparent audience beyond the reader; no fictional character appears as its reader. Using dialogue, description, and commentary, she dramatizes her encounters and debates with Foe. She no longer employs quotation marks or the epistolary headings of date or address. Even as women writers came into their own in the nineteenth century, Susan now has fully established herself as a writer: her productions include the autobiographical narrative, the box full of letters, and her own attempt at popular fiction—"The Female Castaway. Being a True Account of a Year Spent on a Desert Island. With Many Strange Circumstances Never Hitherto Related." Yet, also like the nineteenth-century woman novelist, Susan remains trapped both economically in the house of Foe and artistically in the patriarchal house of fiction.[8] Hence, the "anxiety of authorship" that she manifests throughout chapters II and III.

In the puzzling final chapter of *Foe,* the narrative undergoes a Shakespearean "sea change." Climbing the staircase to Foe's room in the night, an unnamed "I" stumbles over the body of a woman, whose face is wrapped in an endless grey woolen scarf. The speaker then finds Susan and Foe in bed, illumined by moonlight; their skin, "dry as paper, is stretched tight over their bones" (153). They appear to be dead. Laid out in the alcove, Friday has a faint pulse, "as if his heart beat in a far-off place" (154). The speaker pries open Friday's mouth and lies next to him, with an ear at his mouth: "At first there is nothing. Then, if I can ignore the beating of my own heart, I begin to hear the faintest faraway roar: as she said, the roar of waves in a seashell. . . . From his mouth, without a breath, issue the sounds of the island" (154).

After the break the story is told again. This time it is a bright autumn day, and the speaker again stumbles over the body of a woman on the landing. The couple are in bed, and Friday, with a scar around his neck, lies in his alcove. On the table, the speaker finds Susan's manuscript and reads: "'Dear Mr Foe, At last I could row no further'" (155). The quotation marks close, and the speaker imaginatively enters Susan's story: "With a sigh, making barely a splash, I slip overboard" (155). Diving beneath the seaweed and Friday's petals, the speaker enters the wreck beneath the surface. Susan Barton and the dead captain float in the ship's cabin. Finding Friday hidden in the depths of the ship, the speaker attempts to ask, "What is this ship?" Within the medium of the sea, however, speech is not possible: "this is not a place of words. Each syllable, as it comes out, is caught and filled with water and diffused. This is a place where bodies are their own signs. It is the home of Friday" (157). Again opening Friday's mouth, the speaker releases a nonverbal communication: "From inside him comes a slow stream, without breath, without interruption. It flows up through his body and out upon me; it passes through the cabin, through the wreck; washing the cliffs and shores of the island, it runs northward and southward to the ends of the earth. Soft and cold, dark and unending, it beats against my eyelids, against the skin of my face" (157).

Despite varying interpretations of this elusive chapter, most readers agree that in the lyrical and dream-like conclusion of *Foe,* Friday's silence is broken. Denis Donoghue writes, "The end of the book is ambiguous: who is speaking, in the last few pages? I take it as the voice of the poetic imagination, its sympathies expanding beyond all systems to reach the defeated, the silenced" (27). Maureen Nicholson tentatively identifies the speaker more specifically: "it is tempting to conclude that the 'I' is Coetzee himself" (57), and Jane Gardam agrees, "Coetzee himself goes searching for the body of Friday, seeking it in the waters off the island in the wreckage of a slave ship" (49). Nina Auerbach, however, hears the voice as that of Susan. Viewing *Foe* as chronicling the separation of men's and women's plots, Auerbach writes, "Susan relinquishes her compulsion to narrate herself to Foe . . . and, in a dream vision, she returns to the island that has become her source and solution of all human enigmas. But she no longer sleeps on the shore: she dives into the wreck . . . to immerse herself in the mystic stream that issues from the mutilated mouth of a visionary Friday" (37).

Auerbach briefly notes the way the final chapter of *Foe* echoes Adrienne Rich's epic of female creativity, "Diving into the Wreck," and these parallels are worth exploring further. Armed with the alienating instruments of masculinity—a book of myths "in which / our names do not appear" (93–94), a camera, and a sharp knife—Rich's poetic persona descends into the sea. Here she finds a world governed by other rules:

> the sea is not a question of power
> I have to learn alone
> to turn my body without force
> in the deep element.
> . . . . .
> you breathe differently down here.   (41–44, 51)

Coming "to see the damage that was done / and the treasures that prevail," the diver explores the wreck of civilization (55–56). She wants to get beyond discourse: "the wreck and not the story of the wreck / the thing itself and not the myth" (62–63). Like Susan, her "dark hair / streams black" (72–73) as she circles the wreck and dives into the hold. Returning to primal beginnings, the origin of life, she discovers

> I am she: I am he
> whose drowned face sleeps with open eyes
> whose breasts still bear the stress
> whose silver, copper, vermeil cargo lies
> obscurely inside barrels
> half-wedged and left to rot
> we are the half-destroyed instruments
> that once held to a course . . .   (77–84)

The colon functions to indicate that everything that follows "I am she" is encompassed within that "she." Wendy Martin states, "In the depths of the sea, diving into the wreck, she completes the circle of life, resolving the tensions between mind and matter, male and female, subject and object" (185). The feminine imagination celebrated by Rich is able to make the silences of civilization speak, to rewrite the myths so that all of the names will appear.

In very similar terms, Chapter IV of *Foe* embodies the feminine imagination. The suggestion that the body—of Friday, of the wreck, of "the thing itself"—can write invokes a language beyond difference. As Beressem puts it, Friday's "mute language is the natural language of the island . . . a language in which referent and sign are short-circuited. This 'silent language' is the final perspective point of semiosis and the Symbolic and refers to the human as a body and a living organism, the smallest common denominator which ultimately defines the master as well as the slave, marking them as living beings. Apart from all cultural determinations it denotes their position within the realm of the Real" (233). This focus on the language of the body, the repetitive structure, and the obscurity and openness of the final chapter resemble again the *écriture féminine* that French feminists urge should replace male-dominated analytical discourse. Instead of being written in Foe's authoritative and ordered discourse, this chapter is spoken in a voice that is associative and lyrical. In a manner similar to *In the Heart of the Country*, the fourth chapter of *Foe* concludes the history of novelistic discourse by embodying twentieth-century experimental writing as a means of giving voice to the silenced.

Foe has received a mixed critical response. Many readers praise the lyrical style and appreciate the clever revision of *Robinson Crusoe*. The initial reviews contained many statements like that of Francis King: "That Susan's narrative should, despite its lack of drama, be so compelling, is due in some measure to the sharpness of its observation but in even larger measure to the beauty of the style—measured, limpid, euphonious—which Mr Coetzee has devised for it" (33). Similarly, Rhoda Koenig states, "I was not satisfied by the mystical and murky end of *Foe*, but until then I was held by the needle-sharp precision of Coetzee's mock-eighteenth-century prose, by turns flowery, formal, and stern, and by the voice of his heroine, crying out for her life, and calling into the wind" (91–92). But as both of these comments suggest, *Foe* has also been criticized for its slow narrative and extended passages about literary theory. Penner notes how Coetzee's concern with theories of narrative art contributes to a feeling of "stasis" (128), and Nicholson complains that it is "a laboriously articulated narrative marred by incessant contrivance and good intentions" (53). Comparing *Foe* to *Waiting for the Barbarians* and *Life & Times of Michael K,* critics have seen Coetzee's fifth novel as "literary," "emotionally distant," lacking intensity and urgency, avoiding his previous "excruciatingly direct representations of politics and pain."[9]

However, as a meditation on imagination, storytelling, writing, and silence, *Foe* addresses an aspect of oppression in South Africa different from the issues of torture, institutional violence, social injustice, and Afrikaner history and myths broached in his earlier novels. I have shown how the question of the silencing of the Other has been considered in other of Coetzee's works, but in *Foe,* written when Coetzee was increasingly seen in the international community as a literary spokesperson for South Africa, the issue of the authority of the storyteller has become his primary concern. Susan's frustrations as an author suggest the dilemma faced by Coetzee as a South African novelist in the 1980s. If the oppressed are unable to speak, how can we hear their silence? How can we speak for them without becoming an oppressor ourselves? Words can liberate, but they also can oppress, as Magda discovered. Similarly, Susan wonders about her own motivations: "I tell myself I talk to Friday to educate him out of darkness and silence. But is that the truth? There are times when benevolence deserts me and I use words only as the shortest way to subject him to my will" (60). Susan's struggles demonstrate the difficulty at the heart of the fictional process for South African writers. Nicholson says, "it seems to me that, in *Foe,* what we can read is the writing of a man who is now explicitly questioning his right to speak through his characters, who is engaging in a protracted examination of his own influences, ethics and power" (56–57).

Foe embodies a concern for the silenced Other along with an examination of the benefits and dangers of storytelling. Susan affirms the psychological and social value of storytelling, as Coetzee himself does, but she nonetheless struggles with the unreliability and corruptibility of the authority of the author, the uncertainty embodied in language itself, and the influence that power has on discourse. As Beressem says, the novel "stresses the importance for a culture to be able to create a reservoir of stories and discourses within a free discursive space, and takes up a position against any form of censorship" (234). Similarly, Geoff Dyer suggests that in "writing about the impossibility of writing," Coetzee prophetically speaks of the silences and "white spaces" of South African society, in which newspapers appear with blank spaces where stories have been censored (25). *Foe* speaks of conditions in South Africa as well as of Coetzee's own dilemma as a writer. Auerbach charges: "Uncharacteristically, Coetzee speaks here as a writer writing for other writers, rather than as an appalled representative of humanity" (37). But viewing *Foe* in the context of the development of Coetzee's career, we can see that Coetzee speaks as a writer who is an appalled representative of humanity, who hesitates to take upon himself the mantle of moral authority even as he tries to criticize injustice and promote freedom. *Foe* ultimately addresses the issue of how one can write for—in support of—the Other without presuming to write for—assuming power over—the Other.

· 8 ·

The Unquiet Dead:
Age of Iron

Having struggled with the demons plaguing the authoritative storyteller in *Foe,* Coetzee appears to have come to terms with himself as a South African novelist in *Age of Iron,* published simultaneously in the United States and Great Britain in the fall of 1990. While *Foe* left no doubt that Coetzee valued and would continue to pursue the act of writing, that novel also demonstrated his continued search for a form that facilitates truth-telling and presents an alternative to manipulations of history. In *Age of Iron* Coetzee turns to a novelistic form more realistic than any of his previous books, but still employing a figurative or allegorical narrative technique. Coetzee gives us another first-person narrator in an unusual position: she is dead. Her voice comes from the realm of Virgil's "unquiet dead."

Written as an extended letter, *Age of Iron* contains the final thoughts of Mrs. Curren, an elderly Cape Town resident. In an allusive, impressionistic monologue, the narrator relates the circumstances of her last days: her suffering from bone cancer, her encounters with South African injustice, and her struggle to redeem her soul. Her story reveals her personal odyssey but also suggests the hopeless situation of her country. Full of apocalyptic images of fire and references to other stories about death, *Age of Iron* is an elegy, mourning the end of South Africa even as it tells the story of the death of its narrator. A prominent theme in and controlling metaphor for its account of such destruction is the relationship of parents and children. The novel both suggests how the idea of childhood has been perverted in contemporary South Africa and implies that the hope for the future embodied in children has been obliterated.

Children and Death

Unlike any of Coetzee's previous novels, *Age of Iron* is directly linked to a particular historical moment in South Africa. This connection is made apparent by the dates recorded on its final page—1986–1989—which represent both the years during which Coetzee was writing the novel and the specific time in which it is set.[1] The novel's dedication reveals the personal significance of these years for Coetzee and suggests an additional autobiographical reason for its elegaic mode:

For

V.H.M.C. (1904–1985)

Z.C. (1912–1988)

N.G.C. (1966–1989)

These three sets of initials refer to Coetzee's mother, Vera; his father, Zacharias; and his son, Nicolas. The death of Coetzee's mother may have suggested his use of an elderly woman narrator, but the more poignant allusion lies in the reference to his son Nicolas, who was killed in an automobile accident in 1989, the same year in which Coetzee concluded this novel about death and the mysterious relationship between parents and children.

The social and political situation of South Africa during 1986–1989 in some crucial ways mirrors these same concerns, which lends a historical appropriateness to the allegorical suggestiveness of the story. These were years of unparalleled violence; as the crisis in the townships worsened, the number of those killed in incidents of black protest reached the thousands. The distortions of personal life wrought by the apartheid system became more widespread, and both parents and children found themselves unable to function in their traditional roles. In both the fight for freedom and the system of oppression, the very notion of childhood was being destroyed. Although students had been on the forefront of activism ever since the Soweto uprising of 1976, in 1985 student-led educational boycotts became one of the most important battlegrounds in black protest. Thousands of students stayed away from school for months, boycotted university entrance exams, and marched in the township streets, demanding the withdrawal of military and police units from campuses. The youth movement adopted slogans such as "Liberation now, education later" and "Liberation before education." Although the boycotts primarily affected black high schools, children as young as nine or ten also participated in the protests. Increasingly impatient with their lack of opportunities and the slow pace of change, black youth paid little attention to adult anti-apartheid leaders, many of whom viewed the school boycotts as educational suicide. Jakes Gerwel, the vice-chancellor of the University of Western Cape, commented in 1986, "the youth movement has developed a momentum of its own beyond the organized control of any adult movement—a development whose possible consequences become more profound in light of the increasingly violent nature of political protest" (8).

Amid the increasing press restrictions of 1986, the youth protest continued. Few South Africans were aware of the extent of the disruptions, while international coverage also diminished.[2] Nonetheless, the *New York Times* continued to report some of the children's activities: when the new school term began on July 14, 1986, thousands of students stayed away from classes; in August, the government estimated that 100,000 black students had not registered for school as required; by November seventy-one schools in the Eastern Cape and ten schools in Soweto had been closed by the government because of the boycotts (Cowell, "South African Schools" A1; "Zulu" A3; Cowell, "South Africans Close" A3). Francis Wilson and Mamphela Ramphele write in their Carnegie report: "By the mid–1980s the crisis in the classrooms had reached breaking-point. Boycotts by children, lock-outs by the authorities, lessons in the presence of armed police, saw the schools at the epicentre of the political storm raging in South Africa. In addition to their astonishing courage and their determination to put 'liberation before education,' what also became apparent was the children's vulnerability. . . . Yet despite this vulnerability these young teenagers shook the country" (176).

With a youth movement at the forefront of protest, it is not surprising that the vulnerable children also became a new target for state authorities. Although the Republic of South Africa had long mistreated non-white children by denying them not only basic human rights but also basic human necessities—such as decent food, shelter, clothing, and education—a cruel new development in official systems of oppression emerged in the years 1985 and 1986 as the government instituted new measures, dubbed by some human rights experts "the war against children." Thousands of children for the first time were included among the political detainees—held without charges and without trial—and consequently another new organization came into being, the Detainees Parents

Support Committee. In December 1986, with the government's acknowl-
edgment that 256 children between the ages of eleven and fifteen were
being detained, South African and international condemnation grew.
Anti-apartheid organizations claimed that up to 1800 children were being
detained (Cowell, "Pretoria" A3). In 1987, the government admitted that
it had jailed black children eleven years old or younger during the most
recent eight-month crackdown on protest ("South Africa Acknowledges"
A10).

The violence in the townships also took its toll on children. The New
York–based Lawyers' Committee for Human Rights issued a report in
1986 entitled *The War Against Children: South Africa's Youngest Victims,*
which "provides detailed and chilling evidence of state violence, largely
perpetrated by the police and the army against children" (Wilson and
Ramphele 149). The 184-page report, with an introduction by Bishop
Desmond Tutu, chronicles dozens of individual cases in which children
were killed or tortured by security forces. "A generation of children is
growing up in South Africa knowing nothing but the daily violence of
the white minority regime," the report stated (Gargan A4). According
to the government's statistics, the South African police killed at least 201
children during 1985 and 92 children during 1986 (Wilson and Ramphele
149; "Pretoria Says" A4). This war against children represents the final
outrage in the self-destruction of South Africa and is the context that
informs both the substance and the rhetoric of Coetzee's novel.

The primary story of *Age of Iron* concerns both children and death,
and is played out against the background of the school boycotts and
township violence of 1986. A retired classics professor, Mrs. Curren has
lived alone in her Cape Town house since her only daughter emigrated
to the United States in 1976 as a protest against her country's racial
policies. The day Mrs. Curren hears that medical science can do nothing
to defeat the cancer that is steadily eating away her bones, she encounters
a derelict sleeping next to her garage. At first repulsed by him, she later
befriends the man, named Mr. Vercueil, who becomes her unlikely
confidant. In a significant and deliberate omission, Mr. Vercueil's race is
never identified, although we can assume he is black or coloured. Mrs.
Curren asks Mr. Vercueil to mail her narrative to America after her
death. Fearful that the unreliable alcoholic might fail in his task, she
quotes several lines from Virgil on "the unquiet dead," explaining that
the Latin means, "if you don't mail the letter to my daughter I will have
a hundred years of misery" (192). The text she cites speaks of the restless

souls who wait for the boatman Charon to transport them across the Styx to the land of the dead. A fairly literal translation of the Latin given in her account reads, "Nor is it granted them to cross the frightful waves and noisey streams before their bones rest in their graves. A hundred years they wander and flit about these shores; then, admitted at last, they see again the fens they desire."[3] The reference to Virgil suggests the importance of her manuscript to Mrs. Curren; its delivery is equated with her bones resting in a grave, and her soul achieving a final resting place.

As Mrs. Curren's life ebbs away, she encounters an outer world that reflects her own inner reality. As the cancer gradually turns her into a hollow woman, so the cancer of violence and injustice crumbles South Africa from within as the country moves inexorably towards its death. Mrs. Curren's meditations on death are both interrupted and further stimulated by the violent events unfolding in the outlying townships of Cape Town and spilling over into the quiet harbor of her decaying house in the center of the colonial city. In an attempt to escape the chaos resulting from the school boycotts, Mrs. Curren's maid, Florence, brings her fourteen-year-old son Bheki back with her from the township of Guguletu. The police follow the boy, however, and Mrs. Curren witnesses them pushing Bheki and his friend John up against a parked van. When Bheki disappears back into Guguletu, Mrs. Curren accompanies Florence on an eery journey into the underworld of the violence-torn township. Led by a black Virgil through water and fire, Mrs. Curren, like Dante, enters hell, witnessing the burning of a squatter camp and finding Bheki's body with a neat bullet hole in the boy's forehead. Finally, she protests impotently as the police storm her servant's quarters and shoot John, who has hidden there following his release from the hospital.

In the last section of the novel, Florence and her daughters, Hope and Beauty, disappear back into the inferno of Guguletu, and Mrs. Curren moves closer to her own death. Increasingly reliant on pain-killing drugs, she inhabits a shadow world of dreams and hallucinations. Her relationship with the elusive Mr. Vercueil deepens, and he moves into the house to care for her, becoming the "shadow husband" who sleeps by her side and is the sole remaining object for her love (189). Her story concludes with a chilling account of her final embrace with death, represented by Mr. Vercueil: "I got back into bed, into the tunnel between the cold sheets. The curtains parted; he came in beside me. For the first time I smelled nothing. He took me in his arms and held me with mighty force, so that the breath went out of me in a rush. From that embrace there was no warmth to be had" (198).

Mrs. Curren's Odyssey

Facing death, Mrs. Curren, like many human beings, begins to explore ultimate issues, telling her daughter, "This was never meant to be the story of a body, but of the soul it houses" (185). Her deathbed confession reveals her changing attitudes toward her country and her conviction of her own historical responsibility. Her story records an attempt "to keep a soul alive in times not hospitable to the soul" (130). Coetzee locates the progress of the soul in the context of both the material and the historical, the body and the times. Speaking often of her "metamorphosis," Mrs. Curren witnesses to the terrible emotional and spiritual struggle of one facing death, attempting to give birth to "the soul, neophyte, wet, blind, ignorant" (186). In that struggle, *Age of Iron* traces the efforts of liberal white South Africans to find an ethical position in the paradoxes and contradictions of their history. As his diction and allusions suggest, Coetzee is not afraid to address these issues in transcendent as well as material terms.

An avowed liberal, Mrs. Curren frequently lashes out at the Afrikaner government and its tactics. One target of her scorn, reminiscent of Coetzee's earlier treatment in *Dusklands,* is the media. Well aware that the South Africa portrayed in the government-controlled media is a fiction, she complains, "Of trouble in the schools the radio says nothing, the television says nothing, the newspapers say nothing. In the world they project all the children of the land are sitting happily at their desks learning about the square on the hypotenuse and the parrots of the Amazonian jungle" (39). Only through Florence does she learn the truth of the school boycotts and the township violence. The South African media show only "a land of smiling neighbors" as the government struggles to maintain its master myth (54). But like the Americans held spellbound by the images of Vietnam, Mrs. Curren continues to consult her radio and television, despite knowing their distortions. White South Africans, she says, are obsessed with the ritual parade of Afrikaner politicians nightly appearing on the television screen: "We watch as birds watch snakes, fascinated by what is about to devour us. Fascination: the homage we pay to our death. Between the hours of eight and nine we assemble and they show themselves to us" (29).

As the reference to snakes suggests, the indirect or ironic condemnation of Afrikaner thought in Coetzee's earlier novels becomes, in *Age of Iron,* a scathing and bitter attack upon the Afrikaners themselves. Presenting them as a heavy, stupid, loutish people, Mrs. Curren claims that they have cast off both legitimacy and reason. In another remarkably vivid passage, she epitomizes their corruption in animalistic terms:

> a locust horde, a plague of black locusts infesting the country, munching without cease, devouring lives. . . . What absorbs them is power and the stupor of power. Eating and talking, munching lives, belching. Slow, heavy-bellied talk. Sitting in a circle, debating ponderously, issuing decrees like hammer blows: death, death, death. Untroubled by the stench. Heavy eyelids, piggish eyes, shrewd with the shrewdness of generations of peasants. Plotting against each other too: slow peasant plots that take decades to mature. The new Africans, pot-bellied, heavy-jowled men on their stools of office . . . Sluggish hearts, heavy as blood pudding. (28–29)

Playing on their self-appellation of Boers, Mrs. Curren views the Afrikaners as "boars that devour their offspring" (30). The policies that they have instituted and attitudes that they have instilled in the next generation can have only one result: extinction.

Mrs. Curren's opinions about her country are obviously politically correct in most Western eyes, yet her narrative reveals the limits and paradoxes of her liberalism. Fully aware of the corruptions of her country, she still is unable to show genuine concern, or charity, for those caught in its death throes. Initially she thinks more of her own death than of the boycotts, riots, and brutality that fill Florence and Bheki's world: "The country smolders, yet with the best will in the world I can only half-attend. My true attention is all inward, upon the thing, the word, the word for the thing inching through my body. An ignominious occupation, and in times like these ridiculous too, as a banker with his clothes on fire is a joke while a burning beggar is not. Yet I cannot help myself. 'Look at me!' I want to cry to Florence: 'I too am burning!'" (39). The references to fire suggest the apocalyptic fervor of the times as well as the stark reality of her own imminent return to dust and ashes. Despite her will, and her intellectual knowledge that the country's death is more important than her own, Mrs. Curren cannot help her emotional preoccupation with her own death.

Although she has long deplored the policies of apartheid, Mrs. Curren, like most of her peers, has seldom personally witnessed the human cost of such policies. Only once before has she considered the difficult life of the township family, when she gave Florence a ride to the place where her husband worked butchering chickens. But as her body weakens, she sees the realities of her country with a new clarity. Her journey to Guguletu, during which she encounters the brutal conditions of township life that are by now familiar to American and European observers, is for her a stunning revelation. Looking upon Bheki's body, neatly laid out with four other dead children, Mrs. Curren thinks, "This is the worst thing I have witnessed in my life. . . . Now my eyes are open and I can never close them again" (102–103). Throughout the narrative, her newly opened eyes look upon many aspects of South African life: the chaotic turbulance of the townships, the black-on-black violence, the tragic consequences of the children's movement, the corruption of the South African police, the inadequate medical treatment given a black child, the cruel and calculating attitude of the security forces patrolling the townships, and the numb despair of the homeless who sleep on the streets of Cape Town.

Mrs. Curren fully recognizes her own economic and historical complicity in the system that perpetuates such injustices. Some of the chickens that Florence's husband labors six days a week at a minuscule wage to kill probably end up in Mrs. Curren's kitchen, stuffed with bread crumbs and sage. "A crime was committed long ago," she writes. "So long ago that I was born into it. It is part of my inheritance. It is part of me. I am part of it" (164). The guilt resulting from being born a privileged white South African is not unlike the Calvinist notion of original sin: one cannot escape responsibility and must find atonement. Mrs. Curren acknowledges that her guilt lies not only in her social position but also in the consequent ease with which she can forget the injustices kept so well hidden by her government:

> Sitting here among all this beauty, or even sitting at home among my own things, it seems hardly possible to believe there is a zone of killing and degradation all around me. It seems like a bad dream. Something presses, nudges inside me. I try to take no notice, but it insists. I yield an inch; it presses harder. With relief I give in, and life is suddenly ordinary again. With relief I give myself back to the ordinary. I wallow in it. I lose my sense of shame, become shameless as a child. The shamefulness of that shamelessness: that is what I cannot forget, that is what I cannot bear afterward. That is why I must take hold of myself, point myself down the path. Otherwise I am lost. (119)

Consequently, Mrs. Curren fights to retain her sense of urgency about injustice, battling the distractions provided by her own relentless progress toward death and the blinders established by her social position. "I want to rage against the men who have created these times," she explains to Mr. Vercueil. "I want to sell myself, redeem myself, but am full of confusion about how to do it" (117). Attempting to save herself, in a moral sense, she explores numerous ways to make amends, all of which fail.

One option she briefly considers is a public display of her condemnation of both herself and her country: she plans to set herself on fire in her car as she drives down Government Avenue, in the public center of Cape Town. She gives up this plan, however, realizing that such public shows of expiation are seldom clearly understood, as the story of *The Scarlet Letter* demonstrates. Another more practical means of atonement is to practice charity, and she attempts to do so by rescuing Mr. Verceuil from the streets, by assisting Florence in finding Bheki, by criticizing the behavior of the police and security forces, and by attempting to force herself to love John. These attempts at contrition, however, continually fail. Mrs. Curren cannot earn her own salvation. Mr. Verceuil does not want to be rescued; Bheki is dead; government officials pay little attention to a "mad old do-gooder" (105); and John, ironically named after the apostle of love, is supremely unlovable.

Even as she acknowledges that she feels no love for this black child, she admits that she played a part in making him unlovable. This paradox, so typical of the dilemma of white South Africans, adds to her feelings of impotence and guilt. In what she terms her "confession" to her daughter, Mrs. Curren writes about her feelings toward John: "I do not want to die in the state I am in, in a state of ugliness. I want to be saved. How shall I be saved? By doing what I do not want to do. That is the first step: that I know. I must love, first of all, the unlovable. I must love, for instance, this child. Not bright little Bheki, but this one. He is here for a reason. He is part of my salvation. I must love him. But I do not love him. Nor do I want to love him enough to love him despite myself" (136). Again she is caught in an endless circle of will and volition, of intellect and feeling. Like the magistrate in *Waiting for the Barbarians,* she finds herself "wandering in a fog" convinced that "God cannot help me" (136, 137). Once again Coetzee has graphically rendered the plight of many white South Africans. As Mrs. Curren tells Mr. Vercueil: "The spirit of charity has perished in this country. Because those who accept charity despise it, while those who give give with a despairing heart" (22).

Yet Mrs. Curren still clings to her sense of shame as a means of salvation. Only after she leaves the comfort of her home and spends a night on the streets of Cape Town with Mr. Vercueil does she recognize the limits of such guilt. Earlier, she had argued that the black youth movement was ill-directed; the children should save themselves, not mouth grand slogans such as "freedom or death!" (163). But awakening on the ground next to Mr. Vercueil, she asks him, "*who am I* to have a voice at all? How can I honorably urge them to turn their back on that call? What am I entitled to do but sit in a corner with my mouth shut?" (164). Her former rages against "the men who did the dirty work" and against her own complicity were carried out to maintain her sense of honor: "I strove always for honor, for a private honor, using shame as my guide. As long as I was ashamed I knew I had not wandered into dishonor" (164, 165). Her final confession, she tells Mr. Vercueil, is that she has been a good person, but her goodness is not enough: "What I had not calculated on was that more might be called for than to be good. For there are plenty of good people in this country. We are two a penny, we good and nearly good. What the times call for is quite different from goodness. The times call for heroism" (165). Symbolic public demonstrations, individual acts of charity, a classical sense of honor and shame—in recognizing the limits of these attempts at atonement, Mrs. Curren undergoes the metamorphosis of her soul. She writes to her daughter, "This struggling with sickness, the gloom and self-loathing of these days, the vacillation, the rambling too . . . all part of the metamorphosis, part of shaking myself loose from the dying envelope" (129).

The Messenger

As she recognizes her own shortcomings and begins her metamorphosis, Mrs. Curren looks for assistance to Mr. Verceuil. He is, as she asserts several times, her messenger. A former sailor resembling "one of those half-mythical creatures that come out in photographs only as blurs" (193), he serves as her "angel of annunciation" (Plott A13), the messenger who must carry her story across the water. Not only is he entrusted to mail her last testimony to the United States, but she hopes that he can also show her the way across the Styx to a final resting place: "All the days you have known me . . . I have been standing on the riverbank awaiting my turn. I am waiting for someone to show me the way across. Every minute of every day I am here, waiting" (179). When she first meets the homeless man, she has been reading a story by Tolstoy about an angelic visitor, and she wonders if Mr. Vercueil was similarly sent. In Tolstoy's "What Men Live By," a destitute shoemaker takes a naked man into his home and shares his meager food with him. The mysterious stranger says little about his past, but quickly learns the shoemaker's trade and brings prosperity to the house. In the conclusion, the stranger is revealed to be an angel, sent to earth to learn the secret of what men live by. Tolstoy concludes the tale with the angel explaining the lessons he has learned to the shoemaker. The greatest truth, the angel asserts, is that "every man lives, not through care of himself, but by love" (Tolstoy 38).

The reference to Tolstoy not only underscores the novel's discussion of charity but also sheds further light on the ambiguous Mr. Vercueil. For the angel in "What Men Live By" is one who transports souls at death; sent by God to take the soul of a mother with two small children, the angel refuses to let her die and so is condemned to live as a human until he learns the lesson of what men live by. Mrs. Curren is hoping for a similar revelation from the derelict, for her home "to tremble, as in the story, with angelic chanting!" (14). Groping to understand her life, she tells the reticent man:

> I wondered whether you were not, if you will excuse the word, an angel come to show me the way. Of course you were not, are not, cannot be—I see that. But that is only half the story, isn't it? We half-perceive but we also half-create.
>
> So I have continued to tell myself stories in which you lead, I follow. And if you say not a word, that is, I tell myself, because the angel is wordless. The angel goes before, the woman follows. His eyes are open, he sees; hers are shut, she is still sunk in the sleep of worldliness. That is why I keep turning to you for guidance, for help.   (168)

Mr. Vercueil acts as a guide and messenger more in what he hides than in what he reveals. Playing with various forms of his name, Mrs. Curren wonders, "Vercueil, Verkuil, Verskuil. . . . I have never come across such a name before" (37). The Dutch stem *kuil* means "hole in the ground," suggesting Mr. Vercueil's affinity with Dostoevski's underground man, while *verskuil* means "to hide" in Afrikaans. In this postmodern version of Tolstoy's overtly didactic story, the angel does not speak, does not deliver a clear message or moral. Instead, the message is made manifest in his silences. As he listens, he prompts and facilitates the story. And while telling and writing that story, Mrs. Curren saves her soul.

With Mr. Vercueil's silent assistance, she learns that one cannot earn salvation, but one can accept grace. By giving her confession to Mr. Vercueil to deliver and by relying on his physical care in her final days, Mrs. Curren puts her life into the derelict's hands. Without understanding the paradoxes involved, she says, "I give my life to Vercueil to carry over. I trust Vercueil because I do not trust Vercueil. I love him because I do not love him. Because he is the weak reed I lean upon him" (131). In so doing, she is no longer the guilt-ridden liberal; rather, she is a child in need of care, just like Mr. Verceuil. "It is not he who fell under my care when he arrived, I now understand, nor I who fell under his: we fell under each other, and have tumbled and risen since then in the flights and swoops of that mutual election" (196). This implausible partnership between the dying woman and the decrepit man offers a glimpse of the harmony that might one day be possible in South Africa. Lawrence Thornton calls the two the "harbingers of the *caritas* that is slowly, even glacially returning to South Africa. . . . The process has begun with these two unlike avant-gardes" (7). Thornton's reading may be overly optimistic given the novel's primary focus on death and apocalyptic change, but in her naming of "mutual election," Mrs. Curren has found a final peace for her soul. She no longer fears "Dies irae, dies illa," the day of wrath which will reduce the age to ashes, as described in the traditional requiem mass. Instead, her death will bring release, and she envisions herself becoming ash and blowing away.

The Prospect of Extinction

Although Mrs. Curren faces personal extinction, she believes that she will continue to live through her daughter and her grandchildren. The letter that she writes will also provide a measure of immortality, allowing her voice to speak from beyond the grave. A classics teacher, she has spoken and taught "dead" languages, and she describes her profession as "giving voice to the dead" (192). In her final letter, she continues to give voice to the dead—not only herself but also her country. As a representative of white South Africa, Mrs. Curren prophetically and allegorically speaks of the future of the country. D. J. Taylor says, "The prospect of extinction—personal and national—hangs over *Age of Iron*" (5). Mrs.

Curren's body will crumble and turn to ash; similarly, the day of wrath for South Africa will usher in change with apocalyptic fire. An overtly allegorical passage from Mrs. Curren's letter uses the images of parent and child: "'Father can't you see I'm burning?' implored the child, standing at his father's bedside. But his father, sleeping on, dreaming, did not see" (110). The dreaming Afrikaners fail to recognize that the country is already self-destructing.

Mrs. Curren's use of parent/child imagery in this passage is typical of her entire account; writing to her daughter and meditating upon their relationship, she finds that everything reminds her of children. Embodying a physical continuation of their parents, children represent life and the future. Mrs. Curren speaks about the importance of children in a beautiful passage about her daughter: "How I longed to be able to go upstairs to you, to sit on your bed, run my fingers through your hair, whisper in your ear as I did on school mornings, 'Time to get up!' And then, when you turned over, your body blood-warm, your breath milky, to take you in my arms in what we called 'giving Mommy a big hug,' the secret meaning of which, the meaning never spoken, was that Mommy should not be sad, for she would not die but live on in you" (5–6). The maternal imagery is especially important: "I don't even know whether it is the same for a man," she writes. "But when you bear a child from your own body you give your life to that child. . . . That is why we do not really die: we simply pass on our life, the life that was for a while in us, and are left behind" (76). Children as the continuation of life—it is this understanding that has been destroyed in twentieth-century South Africa. While the appearance of children and the innocence of childhood had been a sign of hope in Coetzee's earlier novels, *Age of Iron* laments the death of South Africa by lamenting the death of the notion of childhood. Neither the roaming gangs of the townships nor the sheltered children of the suburbs offer the country a future: the gangs are "children scorning childhood, the time of wonder, the growing time of the soul. Their souls, their organs of wonder, stunted, petrified. And on the other side of the great divide their white cousins soul-stunted too, spinning themselves tighter and tighter into their sleepy cocoons" (7). Deeply encased in those cocoons, the sleeping white children may never undergo the necessary metamorphosis.

Instead of life, children now represent death. In her depiction of white South African oppressors, Mrs. Curren continually emphasizes their youth. Visiting Caledon Square in an attempt to lay charges against the police who injured Bheki and John, Mrs. Curren encounters "a young man, very neat and correct, one of the new breed of policeman" (85). A soldier in the security forces occupying the township is "a boy in an olive rain cape. . . . A boy with pimples playing [a] self-important, murderous game" (105). "You are all too young for this," she tells the officer summoned by the boy in the troop carrier (107). She describes a policeman who visits her home in terms of both his youth and his heritage: "A young man, solid, raw-boned. Son to someone, cousin to many. Many cousins, many aunts and uncles, great-aunts and great-uncles, standing about him, behind him, above him like a chorus, guiding, admonishing" (153). Unlike the magistrate in *Waiting for the Barbarians,* Mrs. Curren does not wonder how oppressors can exist; she recognizes only too well the impact of the parents upon the child: "Did we not have Voortrekkers, generation after generation of Voortrekkers, grim-faced, tight-lipped Afrikaner children, marching, singing their patriotic hymns, saluting their flag, vowing to die for their fatherland? . . . Are there not still white zealots preaching the old regime of discipline, work, obedience, self-sacrifice, a regime of death, to children some too young to tie their own shoelaces?" (51). The masculine imagery of this passage connecting children with death stands in marked contrast to the feminine imagery affirming children as life. The Afrikaner system has borne and bred oppressors, and thus the Boers devour their young, condemning them to self-destruction and a future apocalypse.

The childhood of black children has also been destroyed. Florence admits, "I cannot tell these children what to do. . . . It is all changed today. There are no more mothers and fathers" (39). Although Mrs. Curren insists, "There are always mothers and fathers," her story reveals how many black children have become "children of death," meting out their own bloody forms of retribution and justice (49). Whether the responsibility for such behavior lies in the black parents' failure to exercise their authority or in the cruel oppression by the whites (and Florence and Mrs. Curren debate this question), the careless attitude toward life, which serves the children well in the protest movement, will finally destroy them. The bloody history of the Greek city-states suggests to Mrs. Curren where such behavior will lead. "What kind of parents will they become who were taught that the time of parents is over?" she asks Florence. "Can parents be recreated once the idea of parents has been destroyed within us? They kick and beat a man because he drinks. They set people on fire and laugh while they burn to death. How will they treat their own children? What love will they be capable of? Their hearts are turning to stone before our eyes" (49–50). But Florence—"a Spartan matron, iron-hearted, bearing warrior sons for the nation"—insists, "These are good children, they are like iron, we are proud of them" (50). Living in a time "when childhood is despised," an age of iron, Mrs. Curren can only wonder, "How long, how long before the softer ages return in their cycle, the age of clay, the age of earth?" (50). But in the coming apocalypse, those made of iron will survive. White people like herself burn well, Mrs. Curren tells Mr. Vercueil, "whereas these people will not burn, Bheki and the other dead. It would be like trying to burn figures of pig iron or lead. They might lose their sharpness of contour, but when the flames subsided they would still be there, heavy as ever" (124). The "children of iron" may survive the apocalypse, but they are also in danger of losing their most vital human characteristic: their ability to love and nurture a future generation.

South Africa's mutilation of the parent/child bond is also starkly rendered in Mrs. Curren's own relationship with her absent daughter. Although her account testifies to her overwhelming love and longing for her child, Mrs. Curren refuses to tell her daughter about her terminal illness. "When I lie in bed at night and stare into the black hole into which I am falling," she tells Mr. Vercueil, "all that keeps me sane is the thought of her. I say to myself: I have brought a child into the world, I have seen her to womanhood, I have seen her safely to a new life" (72). She visualizes her daughter's daily routine, drawing a simple picture of her peeling onions in her kitchen. But most of all, she longs to touch her daughter, hoping to find comfort and salvation in the face of death from her child's love. Mr. Vercueil advises, "Phone her in America. Tell her you need her here," and when Mrs. Curren refuses, warns, "Then don't tell her afterward, when it is too late. She won't forgive you" (74). Once again South Africa has caused parents and children to act unnaturally. Mrs. Curren knows that her daughter will not come back until the political situation of South Africa has changed: "She is like iron. I am not going to ask her to go back on her vows" (75). "You are like iron too," Mr. Vercueil replies. The iron rigidity of political and social beliefs prevents mother and daughter from touching.

Mrs. Curren's inability to see or touch her child as she dies parallels her inability to see or grasp a future for her country. And instead of the life represented by her daughter, her new offspring brings death and destruction: "To have fallen pregnant with these growths, these cold, obscene swellings; to have carried and carried this brood beyond any natural term, unable to bear them, unable to sate their hunger: children inside me eating more every day, not growing but bloating, toothed, clawed, forever cold and ravenous. . . . My eggs, grown within me. *Me, mine:* words I shudder to write, yet true. My daughters death, sisters to you, my daughter life" (64). Unable to give birth to the cancer destroying her from within, Mrs. Curren sees herself as emblematic of her country, itself destroyed by the children of violence it harbors.

The broken connections between parents and children also are manifested in Mrs. Curren's reminiscences about her own mother. Throughout her life, she has clung to a story about her mother traveling to the seaside by ox-wagon as a girl. High atop Prince Alfred's Pass, the wagon stopped for the night, and her mother slept underneath it with the other children. Watching the stars through the spokes of the wagon, her mother began to wonder if the stars were moving or if the wheels were slowly moving and the wagon beginning to roll away. She spent the night in fear, and "her sleep was full of dreams of death," but she woke the next morning "into light and peace" (17). Mrs. Curren tells Mr. Vercueil: "If each of us has a story we tell to ourself about who we are and where we come from, then that is my story. That is the story I choose, or the story that has chosen me. It is there that I come from, it is there that I begin" (120). This story of origins reveals Mrs. Curren's close attachment to the land but an uncertainty and fear about her relationship to the changing world. Her attachment is associated with her mother and cast in feminine terms. Previously, she says, she could have instinctively found the spot where her mother slept under the wagon: "A desire, perhaps the deepest desire I am capable of, would have flowed from me toward that one spot of earth, guiding me. *This is my mother,* I would have said, kneeling there. *This is what gives life to me.*" That love for the life-affirming land has been destroyed, however, in another perversion of child/parent relationships: "that desire, which one may as well call love, is gone from me. I do not love this land anymore" (121).

The multiple depictions of what has happened to parents and children in South Africa paint a pessimistic picture. The disruption of Mrs. Curren's natural bonds with her daughter and her love for her country suggest the dead end of the liberalism she represents. Similarly, the older generation of non-whites, represented by Mr. Vercueil, will not provide a future for South Africa: "There is an air of childlessness about him.

Of having no children in the world but also of having no childhood in his past" (11). His own childhood made impossible by his social position, Mr. Vercueil will leave no progeny. He is an observer, not an actor; one who suffers but does not judge. His drinking, Mrs. Curren says, helps him to forgive: "He drinks and makes allowances. His life all allowances. He, Mr. V., to whom I speak. Speak and then write. Speak in order to write." Mr. Vercueil facilitates discourse and stands in marked contrast to the "rising generation" of Bheki and his peers: "The new puritans, holding to the rule, holding up the rule. Abhorring alcohol, which softens the rule, dissolves iron. Suspicious of all that is idle, yielding, roundabout. Suspicious of devious discourse, like this" (82). Since neither Mrs. Curren nor Mr. Vercueil will leave descendents in South Africa, the children of iron and the soul-dim, cocoon-encased Afrikaners—children of death both—are left to battle for the land. The offspring of the "marriage" between the ill woman and the alcoholic man in the final section of the novel is death.

The Child-Story

Yet this unlikely union produces one other progeny: the text that we read. Because Mrs. Curren can first speak to Mr. Vercueil, she then can write her account to her daughter. As she puts it, she must "speak in order to write" (82). Rehearsing her account to Mr. Vercueil during the day, she then inscribes it on paper at night. The final delivery of the text is also dependent upon Mr. Vercueil, who must mail the lengthy letter to America. Mrs. Curren speaks of her account as a child: her words "come from my heart, from my womb," and are living inside her (145). "Stirring inside you like life in the womb," her words are as real and as mysterious as human life (145). If children represent hope for the future, Mrs. Curren's child-story represents her last measure of hope and reaffirms Coetzee's belief in the value of storytelling, even in a place such as South Africa. But as in all of Coetzee's previous works, Mrs. Curren's account also includes a great deal of self-reflection on the limits and pitfalls of storytelling.

During the course of her narration, Mrs. Curren's ostensible reason for writing shifts. Originally struggling to relay her deepest thoughts and emotions to her child, she eventually realizes that the cancer eating away her country is a more important reason to record her account. The first pages of her letter concern Mr. Vercueil, but those descriptions have a selfish motivation: "When I write about him I write about myself. When I write about his dog I write about myself; when I write about the house I write about myself. Man, house, dog: no matter what the word, through it I stretch out a hand to you" (9). Yet after visiting Guguletu and gazing upon Bheki's body, Mrs. Curren writes with a new purpose: "I tell you this story," she says to her daughter, "not so that you will feel for me but so that you will learn how things are" (103). How things are in South Africa, however, includes her own complicity and suffering, and once again Mrs. Curren's story blends with that of her country. Verbally assailing the security forces patrolling the township in armored troop carriers, she wants "to make them see it with their own eyes: a scar, any scar, the scar of all this suffering, but in the end my scar, since our own scars are the only scars we can carry with us" (106). The witness she bears unavoidably includes her own self as it implicates herself. Her story cannot escape her self, but that self does not have to be its sole focus.

Mrs. Curren has a certain measure of authority in telling her tale—as a historical eyewitness, an educated and reflective person, a suffering and dying woman. David Plott writes, "Deathbed utterances, like suicide notes, are a powerful coinage, stamped by an awareness that words can outlive us" (A13). The narrative's sardonic humor, gentle lyricism, and moving renditions of a mother's love for her daughter also imbue it with authority. Plott claims, "What makes the novel so powerful is how skillfully Mr. Coetzee weaves the tale Mrs. Curren tells of South Africa with the old woman's tortured love of her own daughter" (A13).[4] However, as a feminine text, *Age of Iron* also makes clear the limits of its own authority and power. Mrs. Curren is careful not to claim too much.

A classicist, Mrs. Curren loves words. She ponders their etymology, crafts puns, and playfully manipulates their levels of meaning. She even dreams about particular words. But the various levels of possible reference increasingly make words an elaborate and ambiguous puzzle: "Borodino, Diconal: I stare at the words. Are they anagrams? They look like anagrams. But for what, and in what language?" (138). In the chaotic circumstances of South Africa, words no longer seem to have a place. Pleading with John to be "slow to judge," Mrs. Curren is not even sure herself what her words mean. They have even less authority for the black child: "My words fell off him like dead leaves the moment they were uttered. The words of a woman, therefore negligible; of an old woman, therefore doubly negligible, but above all of a white" (79). The novel shows how "the time for words has already passed," states Thornton.

"The historical process of revolution sweeps them aside in its indefatigable rush toward the future" (7). *Age of Iron* thus questions its own basis for existence.

The uncertainty of words also lies in the possibility that they may never even find an audience; they may remain dead leaves. Whether pleading with John, questioning the reticent Mr. Vercueil, or writing to her absent daughter, Mrs. Curren finds that her words enter a void. If Mr. Vercueil does not mail her letter, her words will not reach anyone: "These papers, these words that either you read *now* or else will never read. Will they reach you? Have they reached you? Two ways of asking the same question, a question to which I will never know the answer, never. To me this letter will forever be words committed to the waves: a message in a bottle" (32). Her voice is uncertain, doubtful of its reception and existence, as well as fully cognizant of its own failure to communicate accurately. For a story is always presented through its storyteller's eyes. The terrible realities of Guguletu can be recorded only as she sees them, never in complete objectivity, and the danger is that too much attention thus is paid to the teller of the tale: "the storyteller, from her office, claims the place of right. It is through my eyes that you see; the voice that speaks in your head is mine. Through me alone do you find yourself here on these desolate flats, smell the smoke in the air, see the bodies of the dead, hear the weeping, shiver in the rain" (103). "Draw back," Mrs. Curren advises her daughter, "attend to the writing, not to me. If lies and pleas and excuses weave among the words, listen for them. Do not pass them over, do not forgive them easily. Read all, even this adjuration, with a cold eye" (103, 104).

Mrs. Curren, like many of Coetzee's protagonists, recognizes the uncertain nature of language and the tendency of writers to insert their own prejudices and errors into their compositions. She also realizes the apparent dichotomy between words and action. Merely writing her story is not the act of heroism she knows is required of contemporary South Africans. She recognizes the justness of the radical's question: "What is the point of consuming yourself in shame and loathing? I don't want to listen to the story of how you feel, it is just another story, why don't you *do* something?" (145). She can only agree with such questions, yet she also insists that there are ambiguities between the clear distinctions of gratuitous stories and true action. Mrs. Curren answers this impatience with words and storytelling by speaking of her words as a child: "You do not believe in words. You think only blows are real, blows and bullets.

But listen to me: can't you hear that the words I speak are real? Listen! They may only be air but they come from my heart, from my womb. They are not Yes, they are not No. What is living inside me is something else, another word. And I am fighting for it, in my manner, fighting for it not to be stifled" (145). Alluding to the Chinese practice of smothering unwanted female children at birth, Mrs. Curren asks, "What is this thing called a daughter, that it must die?" (146). Why must her words be stifled as soon as they are born? Ambiguities are not allowed to be heard in an age of iron: "everything indefinite, everything that gives when you press it, is condemned unheard. I am arguing for that unheard" (146).

Mrs. Curren's frustration may mirror Coetzee's own experiences as a South African writer. His novels all map the uncertain terrain between rigid points of view. Like Mrs. Curren, he may say: "These are terrible sights. . . . They are to be condemned. But I cannot denounce them in other people's words. I must find my own words, from myself. Otherwise it is not the truth" (98–99). Faced with the unspeakable reality of Guguletu, Mrs. Curren says, "To speak of this . . . you would need the tongue of a god" (99). Neither she nor Coetzee would claim such a gift. *Age of Iron* falls short of such divine inspiration and authority, but it nonetheless powerfully renders the dissolution of South Africa as the final perversion of the relationship between parents and children. Published in a year of radical change in South African policies and politics, *Age of Iron* perhaps accurately predicts the end of an age.

Epilogue

Although the future of South Africa remains uncertain, with President F. W. de Klerk's proposal to dismantle the last remaining apartheid laws in 1991, a major historical period has come to an end. Within that period of banning, silencing, repression, and writing of the Other, J. M. Coetzee has emerged as a world author. The profound historical, ethical, and aesthetic achievements of his fiction lend credibility to the argument that he is not only the leading contemporary South African novelist but also a major international writer of the rank of Gabriel García Márquez, Milan Kundera, and Alexander Solzhenitsyn. As a South African novelist, Coetzee has responded to the dilemma posed by the relationship of art and commitment in radically new ways, ways that open up new possibilities for the novel as an ethical and historical action.

Over the past fifteen years, Coetzee has crafted a new kind of novel, a novel that arises out of history but also rivals history. Formal choices, as Coetzee insists overtly in his criticism and implicitly in his fiction, have social and ethical implications. In his own work Coetzee moves beyond realism to craft a self-aware fiction that arises within its historical context and yet also embodies alternatives to that context. While Coetzee would probably agree with the post-structuralist argument that realism is philosophically naive, he objects more strongly to the political and social implications of realism. An accurate and detailed reflection of contemporary atrocities may serve more to reinforce those atrocities, to support the oppression, than to open the eyes of the world. In Coetzee's metaphor, fondling the wound is gratuitous and does not bring healing. But by exploring the origins of the wound—the instruments of torture, the rhetoric of abuse, and the psychology of the one inflicting the pain—Coetzee's fiction encourages analysis and thought. The gaps and elisions that pervade his novels serve both to stimulate the reader and also to undermine the authority of the author. Eschewing the voice of the powerful, omniscient, God-like author, Coetzee acknowledges that the writer to a certain extent is limited by his or her time and place. Although one can revise or rewrite the discourses of the time, one is also always, to a certain extent, written by those discourses. Assertions can only be tentative; the writer can only see through a glass darkly.

Despite these limitations—imposed by historical context, limited understanding, and the construction of self revealed by Freud, Marx, and Foucault—Coetzee still insists on the ability of the writer to construct a story that is a rival to history, to redefine the rules of the game. In his own fiction, we see a gradual development toward and concern for giving voice to the Other so long silenced in South African history. This involves an act of the imagination, but a profoundly historical one. Coetzee's ethical imagination, rooted in the realities of his South African context, remains his greatest achievement. His haunting characters and narrative voices, the lyrical beauty of his landscapes, the intricate roadmaps of his narratives, the fertile intertextuality of his writing, his impressive command of the nuances of language—all of these aesthetic accomplishments are equally ethical accomplishments. Remaining true to the demands of both his art and his commitment, refusing to even acknowledge the possibility of a false schizophrenia, Coetzee's writing achieves a healing wholeness.

The novels of J. M. Coetzee, then, both arise out of history and transform history. The ethical and artistic attention that he pays to the unique problems of his troubled country provide a model for other twentieth-century writers with their own historical contexts and problems. The undeniably profound universal themes of the human capacity for evil, the human need for the transcendent, the oppression latent in power and authority, and the constructing power of discourse paradoxically arise only because Coetzee remains authentic to his cultural milieu. He speaks to all of us about ourselves because he speaks about himself and his country. As they enact the process of becoming self-critical and self-aware about power and discourse, Coetzee's novels reveal the possibilities and dangers of fiction in the twentieth century.

Notes

Works Cited

Acknowledgments

Index

Notes

1, History and the South African Writer

1. A full account of the lifting of the ban on *Burger's Daughter* appears in Gordimer, Dugard, and Smith, *What Happened to 'Burger's Daughter'* (1980). Also see Gordimer's "Censors and Unconfessed History," *Essential* 250–60.

2. Lukács 29. Clingman has traced Gordimer's increasing attraction to the work of Lukács (9–10).

3. Lukács himself admits as much, viewing the angst-ridden world of writers such as Kafka as the product of the reality of the capitalistic society and those writers' inability to see the solution offered by socialism: "Objective reality . . . is subjectivized and robbed of its historicity. Yet, while chaos and *angst* are the inevitable consequences of such subjectivization, their specific content, mood and ideological basis are determined by the social conditions in which the intellectual finds himself. Rejecting with passion or cynicism a socialist perspective, he fails to answer its challenge, refusing both an ideological apology for imperialism and any attempt to find a new perspective for capitalism" (69). Humanity's impotence and helplessness are all that such an author can affirm. Gordimer rejects the transformation of the world by style of the modernists as an option for South Africa (*Essential* 296–97).

4. Brief biographies are available in *World Authors 1975–80* and *Current Biography Yearbook 1987*. Also see Penner 1–4.

5. Watson 376. For such complaints from the left, see Vaughan and Knox-Shaw.

6. The most comprehensive introduction to the New Historicism is found in Veeser, who has collected essays from many of the leading New Historical critics, including Stephen Greenblatt, Louis A. Montrose, Catherine Gallagher, and Brook Thomas. An earlier attempt to define the New Historicism is found in Lindenberger. The movement was first begun, many scholars believe, with Greenblatt's study, *Renaissance Self-Fashioning*. Brook Thomas is the most prolific New Historicist in American literature; he also is concerned that this critical approach be applied in the classroom. See his *Cross-Examinations of Law and Literature* and "Historical Necessity." Other diverse critics who have been termed New Historicists include Jonathan Goldberg and Jerome McGann. A perceptive critique of some of the limitations of New Historicism as practiced by Renaissance scholars is provided by Pechter.

7. The text of Coetzee's speech has not appeared in English. It was published in a French translation by Sophie Mayoux in *Le Nouvel Observateur* in May 1987. My

citations are to this version; the English translations have been provided by Irene Konyndyk. See Coetzee, "Apartheid: La Littérature Mutilée" 58.

8. In 1979, Coetzee wrote a promotional account of a new literary journal, *Staffrider,* which was attempting to survive financial and political pressure and to publish new young black writers. "The group who launched the magazine did so in the hope of fostering the growth of relevant, contemporary, mainly black writing, and of building up a readership for it" ("Staffrider" 235). Further evidence of Coetzee's support for black writers is his inclusion of many such writers in the anthology of contemporary South African literature, *A Land Apart,* which he edited with André Brink.

2. Naming the Other

1. Said conducts a Foucauldian analysis of the creation of Others in discourse about the Orient in *Orientalism.* The concept of the Other also arises in existential phenomenology, and is discussed and applied to male/female relations by Simone de Beauvoir in *The Second Sex.* She argues that the Self-Other dichotomy is both political and psychological: the socially dominant group is established as the Self, the norm; the subordinate groups are Other, seen as deviant, inessential, objects (xviii–xxiii). As many feminist critics note, both women and people of color have been systematically categorized and marginalized in this fashion.

2. Carbon dating has established the existence of settlements in South Africa dating from the early Iron Age. Elphick's work has concentrated on the history of the various peoples living on the Cape when Europeans first arrived. He demonstrates that both the "Bushmen" and "Hottentot" were members of the same basic genetic group and that their ancestors had lived in South Africa for many millennia before the whites landed at the Cape. Other revisionist histories appear in Wilson and Thompson, Cohen, and Harms. A thorough history of how historical myths develop and change in South Africa appears in Thompson.

3. Raven-Hart, *Before Van Riebeeck* 57–58. This book, along with Raven-Hart's *Cape Good Hope,* provides a useful compilation of early writing about South Africa.

4. Thompson 62. Also see Dean, Hartmann, and Katzen. Thompson provides an excellent summary of this study, as well as other research establishing that South African textbooks are invariably used for "indoctrination in negrophobia" (59).

5. Van Jaarsveld notes many of these oppositions (6). A popular early nineteenth-century history of the Afrikaners by J. H. Malan was called *Boer and Barbarian* (Thompson 181). JanMohamed terms this opposition "the Manichean allegory," and believes that in colonialist literature, such a dichotomy can, in effect, never be overcome: "Genuine and thorough comprehension of Otherness is possible only if the self can somehow negate or at least severely bracket the values,

assumptions, and ideology of his culture. . . . however, this entails in practice the virtually impossible task of negating one's very being, precisely because one's culture is what formed that being" (83–84). Such a view appears to negate the possibility of meaningful interaction between the self and Others, a possibility that I am not ready to give up. However, it does highlight some of the difficulties a writer such as Coetzee faces.

6. This is only one of hundreds of examples of typological rhetoric given by the preeminent South African historian F. A. van Jaarsveld in *The Afrikaner's Interpretation of South African History* (11).

7. Templin notes: "In orthodox Reformed thought, the Old Testament is of Christian significance because Christ is prefigured there. This tends to infuse the Old Testament narratives with a certain Christian tolerance and compassion. In South Africa, however, this assumption that Christ is prefigured in all Old Testament narratives disappeared. The Afrikaner theological nationalism did not have a Christological dimension, but rather, the Old Testament narrative was taken literally. This may account for the fact that the Europeans' oppression of the indigenous peoples of South Africa is much more severe and merciless than in most other examples of European colonialism" (279–80).

8. Van Jaarsveld claimed in 1961 during a lecture at the Afrikaans Cultural Council of Pretoria, "At the present time one is frequently confronted with the assertion that the Afrikaner people has been assigned a place in the southern corner of Africa for 'a purpose' and to fulfill 'a mission'" (1). He believes that this understanding of history first developed in the eighteenth century as an outgrowth of the early trekkers' Calvinism and reading of the Old Testament. Other studies, such as those by De Klerk, Patterson, and Moodie, similarly claim that the early nineteenth-century Boers saw themselves as a Chosen People. The more recent work of Du Toit and Hexham argues that this particular mythology did not develop until the second half of the nineteenth century. Given the numerous instances of typological rhetoric employed in the early part of the nineteenth century, Templin sensibly suggests, "The roots of the idea of a . . . particular destiny were deeply imbedded in the cultural development of the nation even before the ideas were enunciated, certainly before any attempt was made to systematize them" (8). What began in the popular piety of the settlers became articulated more formally in the years following the Great Trek.

9. For accounts of the practice of banning, see Dugard (88) and Benson (52, 119).

10. A good account of the proliferation of performance art during this period is that of Kelwyn Sole. Attributing the growth in oral poetry and drama to the influence of the Black Consciousness movement and a renewed interest in African culture, Sole argues that "oral performance and musical accompaniment have widened the scope and aspirations of black South African literature considerably in the last twenty years" (266). He also sees a renewed politicizing of black literature:

"At funerals and political meetings, a combination of poetry, dance and freedom songs renders palpable the determination felt by people for political liberation" (267). Also see Alvarez-Pereyre, *The Poetry of Commitment in South Africa*.

11. "*Staffrider* does not in the first place set itself up to be an arbiter of the best. Rather, it aims to provide an outlet for the writer's groups that have been springing up all over in the townships. . . . The group who launched the magazine did so in the hope of fostering the growth of relevant, contemporary, mainly black writing, and of building up a readership for it" (Coetzee, "Staffrider" 235).

12. Details of the crackdown can be found in Hachten and Giffard, and Lodge. I discuss the particular events of 1977 and 1978 in more detail in Chapter 5.

13. Gordimer explains the new mode of silencing: "What is clear is that the Censorship Committee regards it as necessary to prevent black readers from reading their own prejudices, their own frustration, given expression in the work of a black writer; outside the considerations assiduously to be taken into account by a new and enlightened censorship there is an additional one, operative for black writers only, that nullifies most of the concessions so far as black writers are concerned—they may not say what white writers say because they are calculated to have a wider black readership, and to speak to blacks from the centre of the experience of being black, to articulate and therefore confirm, encourage what the black masses themselves feel and understand about their lives but most cannot express" (*Essential* 255–56). Also see Brink's essay "Censorship and Literature" in *Writing in a State of Siege* (231–56).

14. See Aikenhead and C. Smith. A preliminary analysis of news reports through February 1986 concluded that neither coverage nor public opinion had been affected by the increased censorship (Singer and Ludwig). However, that conclusion might have been premature, as is suggested by the data presented by Alex Jones. Many of the restrictions on the press were lifted on February 2, 1990, by President de Klerk, and the international news media descended on South Africa to record and chronicle the historic moment when Nelson Mandela walked out of Victor Verster Prison to freedom on February 11. In a demonstration of the new freedom of the press, Mandela's release and his subsequent public address in Cape Town were broadcast not only internationally but also within South Africa by the government-owned South African Broadcasting Corporation.

15. My history of the development of Afrikaans is taken from Cope (19–27) and Hexham (*Irony* 123–46). Also see Giliomee's "The Development of the Afrikaner's Self-Concept."

16. The government has frequently used language and education as one of its means of control. With the institution of Bantu Education in 1953, the National government attempted to make all black education take place in a tribal language

rather than a common language. In transferring the control of education from the provincial education department to the national Department of Native Affairs, the government began its program to divide the indigenous people into tribal units. Previously most black education had been conducted in mission schools in the medium of English. But with the Bantu Education Act, schools became segregated by means of various tribal languages. Even "tribal colleges" were established. However, until the decree in 1976 that was met with such resistance, English was also taught in secondary schools. For more on education in South Africa, see Malherbe.

17. In her list of ten myths of South African history, Cornevin identifies Myths 9 and 10 as "that the homelands correspond to the areas historically occupied by each black 'nation' and that their fragmentation was the result of tribal wars and succession disputes" (121–26). Also see Laurence 86–90, and Wilson and Thompson xi.

18. Quoted and translated by Hexham, *Irony* 37.

19. Parker notes these two routes in his survey of the South African novel in English. His Marxist analysis results in scorn for the liberalism of authors such as Alan Paton and Peter Abrahams, a scorn which I do not share. Parker argues that such authors do not "recognise that what is of overriding importance is the power relationship: how those in power can continue to maintain their position; how those without power can evolve strategies for the acquisition of power" (21). While I would agree that power relationships are important, I also think individual relationships and questions of responsibility are issues pertinent to an ethical response to the South African situation. As we might expect, Parker views Coetzee as an irresponsible escapist; he fails to note that Coetzee's concern with language and authority is, in itself, a consideration of power as well as responsibility.

20. In *Southern African Literature: An Introduction,* Stephen Gray identifies a major vein of South African fiction to be the liberal realism stemming from Olive Schreiner's *The Story of an African Farm* (133–59). Gordimer provides an interesting example of a contemporary author who has moved from novels focusing on personal responsibility to novels dealing more with social and political responsibility. Michael Vaughan suggests that the modernism of Coetzee and the populist realism of Matshoba are the two current trends in South African fiction that have replaced the liberal aesthetic.

21. In an interview with Stephen Watson in 1978, "Speaking: J. M. Coetzee." Although in some interviews, Coetzee has brushed off questions about the influence of Kafka, when he spoke with Jean Sévry in 1985, he admitted, "Kafka is such an enormous presence in modern literature that for one to deny totally that he has been affected by Kafka would be extremely foolish. I have not only read Kafka—and in fact have been reading Kafka since I was an adolescent—but

I have worked very closely with some of Kafka's texts in German, so it would be even more foolish for me to deny that Kafka has left his traces on me" (Coetzee, "Interview" 5).

22. Vaughan argues that Coetzee "casts himself in the role of a diagnostician of the malady of Western culture who is unable to propose any cure for this malady. He sees the historical fate of this culture as annihilation at the hands of alien racial-historical forces, or as the achievement of world-destruction effected by its own ineluctible imperatives" (134). Since Coetzee indicts all of Western civilization and negates any possibility of transcendence for his protagonists, Vaughan says, his works are not a protest, for there is no point in protesting.

23. See Coetzee, "Two" 456, 459. Coetzee states about his publishing strategy: "Ravan Press still publishes me in South Africa. It is entirely a commercial decision that Viking Penguin publishes me in the U.S. and Britain. I try not to address a specifically South African or specifically international audience" (letter to the author, July 24, 1989).

3. The Master Myth of History: Dusklands

1. The long tradition of travel writing in western Europe reached its peak of production, according to Percy Adams, in the seventeenth and eighteenth centuries (57). Charles L. Batten, Jr., writes, "Although Englishmen had been describing their voyages and journeys for many years, the eighteenth century . . . witnessed a new era in which non-fiction travel literature achieved an unparalleled popularity" (1). The wealth of eighteenth-century travel literature included numerous books about the southern part of Africa.

2. Coetzee explored this kind of writing in detail in his critical study *White Writing: On the Culture of Letters in South Africa* (1988).

3. According to Coetzee, "If memory serves me right, the whole of *Dusklands* was drafted in the US" (letter to the author, July 24, 1989). He told Folke Rhedin, "I wrote most of that in the USA" (Coetzee, Interview 9). However, in an interview with Stephen Watson, Coetzee refers to coming back to South Africa in 1971 "with half of what later turned into *Dusklands*" (Coetzee, "Speaking" 23).

4. Most analyses of *Dusklands* have examined the common way in which both novellas depict the mind of the oppressor, the dark psychology of colonialism. Readings with variations on this theme and different degrees of approval include Crewe, R. Gray, Knox-Shaw, Penner, Vaughan, Watson, and Wood. Knox-Shaw and Vaughan are particularly disappointed with Coetzee's failure to focus on the material origins of colonialism and claim that his work falls victim to the very forces it critiques: "Awareness is no transcendence. The world-colonisation project has encountered serious reversals in the later twentieth century: this does not mean that intellectuals who recognise this (as who does not?), and are critical

of the project, can reject their ascribed racial-historical place, and inhabit a new medium—a new consciousness, a new history" (Vaughan 124). In one of the best essays on Coetzee's work, Watson explains that failure in terms of the material circumstances informing Coetzee's fiction: the author himself is a colonizer who does not want to be a colonizer. Although he shows how the two halves of *Dusklands* are bound by their "exploration of the mentality of colonialism," Penner concludes, "the two *nouvelles* do not really merge as one work, despite their shared themes" (32, 52).

5. Eugene Dawn uses the phrase "the master-myth of history" in his report to Coetzee (26).

6. Exact statistics are found in Mueller (chap. 3) and Roper. A summary of these changes is found in Hallin 168–69.

7. For details concerning these cases see *The Journals of Brink and Rhenius* xiii, and the foreword to Van Pallandt's *General Remarks on the Cape of Good Hope*.

8. On this point, see Batten 13, 39–41.

9. The proliferation of Coetzees in South Africa, descended from the historical Jacobus Coetzee, is paralleled in *Dusklands* by the author's use of his own name for several persons in the text. Such a device serves not only to indicate the mutual responsibility of Afrikaners, whether colonial explorers or contemporary writers, but also to highlight the textuality of the text, the fact that an author is constructing the text. In talking about the various Coetzees, for the sake of clarity, I will refer to the author as *Coetzee*, to Eugene Dawn's editor as *J. M. Coetzee*, to the fictional Jacobus Coetzee as *Jacobus*, to Jacobus Coetzee's translator as *J. M.*, to Jacobus Coetzee's editor as *S. J.*, and to the historical Jacobus Coetzee as *Coetse*, following the original spelling.

10. In assigning Dawn a place in the propaganda machine, Coetzee directs our attention to another important form of discourse on the Vietnam War. Psychological warfare was a key element in the United States' "pacification program" throughout the war. Leaflets, radio broadcasts, and television programs formed the primary means of convincing the people of South Vietnam that the Vietcong were their enemies and that they should support the Republic of Viet Nam and its United States ally. The consensus today is that the United States' propaganda efforts in Vietnam were woefully ill-informed, culturally ignorant, and consequently inadequate. For accounts of the propaganda debacle, see Gibson 282–89 and Chandler.

11. A detailed account of the eighteenth-century European fascination with African sexuality is found in Gilman.

12. Penner suggests, "The purpose of such counterfeiting can only be to remind the reader that the adventure he is experiencing is solely controlled by the narrator, and that behind the mind of Jacobus is another consciousness, that of J. M. Coetzee" (51). Similarly, Crewe says that the "two equally plausible accounts of Klawer's death" alert us to the fact that the two novellas "are fictions about

fictions: about the fundamentally problematic question of the 'meaning' of fictions; about the writing of fictions" (91). While I agree that *Dusklands* has much to say about the creation of fictions, I do find it significant that the contradictory historical accounts appear in Jacobus's story without any comment, rather than in Dawn's. When *Dusklands* first appeared in South Africa, Ravan Press received several phone calls from readers who thought that the proofreaders had made a mistake by including the two different versions of Klawer's death (Marquard 84).

13. Coetzee discusses other literary treatments of the possibility of an infinite regression of self-awareness and self-doubt in confession in his essay, "Confession and Double Thoughts: Tolstoy, Rousseau, Dostoevsky." What he terms "double thought," the possibility that one is always deceiving the self, makes secular confession powerless to tell the truth and so come to an end. Coetzee notes that Dostoevsky indicates that "true confession does not come from the sterile monologue of the self, or the dialogue of the self with its own self-doubt, but . . . from faith and grace. It is possible to read *Notes from Underground, The Idiot,* and Stavrogin's confession as a sequence of texts in which Dostoevsky explores the impasses of secular confession, pointing finally to the sacrament of confession as the only road to self-truth" (230). I see Eugene Dawn's own drive to analyze his "sickness" as another such exploration of the impasses of secular confession.

14. Christie, Hutchings, and Maclennan discuss Coetzee's "fiction-making imagination" in very general terms, suggesting that he "invokes myth in order to claim that there is no myth, only the phenomenon of self, and that even this is elusive" (182). This solipsism, they conclude, is ultimately unsatisfactory. Penner also discusses several instances of "fictive reflexivity" in the novel (47–52). Two essays that explore Coetzee's subversive reconstruction of myth and history are those by Gardiner and Dovey ("Coetzee and His Critics"). Gardiner examines how *Dusklands* exposes the narrative structures and themes of *Robinson Crusoe*, a key text in the colonizing process of the West. Coetzee thus takes "as his subject the representations by which South African colonialism has interpreted itself to itself" (183). Looking at a different genre of colonizing literature, Dovey argues that *Dusklands* is a critique of the historiographical project, and that Coetzee's "stance as translator of the three accounts of Jacobus Coetzee's journey is a means of drawing attention to the work of reconstruction going on" in what purports to be a purely objective account (18).

15. Besides the two sources I discuss in the text, Coetzee borrowed very heavily from Barrow, particularly for the afterword. Another significant source is Wikar's *Journal,* which appears in the same Van Riebeeck volume as Coetse's *Relaas* and Brink's *Journal.* Wikar was a Swede in the service of the Dutch East India Company who deserted his post because of debts and insults and fled to the interior, accompanied by the same Hottentot who had traveled back from Namaqualand with Coetse. In the journal he kept of his experiences, he chron-

icles his struggle for survival near the end of his journey. Travelling on foot with few supplies, he learns to live off the land, eating rock-rabbits, honey, and edible roots. "Now I am learning to live in Bushman style when the necessity arises," he writes (*Journal of Wikar* 57). Similarly, Jacobus views himself as resorting to Bushman techniques to survive on his solitary journey back to civilization: "My retrogression from well set up elephant hunter to white-skinned Bushman was insignificant. What was lost was lost, if it was irretrievably lost, for the time being" (99).

16. Knox-Shaw notes, "Of the four documents that comprise the second part of *Dusklands* only the last is authentic: the three-page deposition made by Jacobus Coetzee at the castle in 1790" (27). The only change in the deposition that Knox-Shaw points out is the editorial "sic" inserted into a passage concerning the Narrator's discovery of gold dust. Knox-Shaw argues this "sic" highlights how in the fictional narrative "nothing is made of the gold dust which Jacobus Coetzee gathered on the banks of the Great River and later displayed at the castle" (28). This examination of the *Relaas* and several other sources concludes that "the fictional narrative is distinguished throughout by a virtual effacement of economic motive" (28). It is true that the fictional narrative is not very concerned with economic motives; however, the editorical "sic" usually indicates that something is incorrect in the source one is citing. It seems more likely to me that this "sic" notes the omission of the pronoun "it." Coetzee's version of the deposition reads: "that Narrator found both banks covered with a kind of fine yellow glistening dust or sand of which, on account of its beauty, he gathered a little and brought [*sic*] back with him" (123).

17. *Dusklands* 124. My comments on the translation are based on information supplied by Martin Bakker of the Calvin College Dutch Department.

18. Ibid. Comparing the fictional account to the fictional deposition, Penner notes that the narrative contains no mention of the Damroquas, "an odd omission for such a colorful tale teller." He suggests: "The solution [to this lacuna] seems to be that Jacobus Coetzee . . . has created his own fiction of the long-haired people in order to persuade the Castle to underwrite his second journey, wherein he covertly planned to take revenge on his betrayers" (50). This interpretation does not take into account the historical source of the story of the Damroquas. However, the additions that Coetzee made to the historical deposition function, as I have suggested, to reveal Jacobus's obsession with betrayal, and so might support Penner's reading.

19. For an account of the Van Riebeeck Society, see Bradlow. Penner details more of the "narrative spoofery" of the preface (48).

20. Penner calls S. J.'s history "revisionary" (48), but it actually echoes traditional South African history. Younger South African historians are only recently beginning to issue revisionist accounts, demonstrating the vitality and viability of the indigenous cultures before the white invasion of South Africa. A useful

account of the differences in South African universities is found in Crapanzano 107–9.

21. The quotation in note 4 omits a phrase and actually extends over an additional page (Philip ix–x). In note 8, S. J. has put together two accounts; for details see Raven-Hart, *Before* (166–70). Note 9 contains the most serious mistakes, as S. J. significantly distorts Barrow's words and intentions. The afterword quotes Barrow as "justly" calling the Hottentots "the most helpless, the most wretched of the human race, whose faces are continually overspread with gloom and melancholy, whose name will be forgotten or remembered solely as that of a deceased person of little note" (117). Barrow actually attributes this state to the Dutch treatment: "These weak people, the most helpless, and in their present condition perhaps the most wretched, of the human race, duped out of their possessions, their country, and finally out of their liberty, have entailed upon their miserable offspring a state of existence to which that of slavery might bear the comparison of happiness. It is a condition, however, not likely to continue to a very remote posterity. The name of Hottentot will be forgotten or remembered only as that of a deceased person of little note." This decline will occur, predicts Barrow, because of the "continual dejection of mind, arising from the cruel treatment they receive from an inhuman and unfeeling peasantry, who having discovered themselves to be removed to too great a distance from the seat of their former government to be awed by its authority, have exercised, in the most wanton and barbarous manner, an absolute power over these poor wretches reduced to the necessity of depending on them for a morsel of bread" (144–45).

4. A Feminine Story: In the Heart of the Country

1. Of all Coetzee's novels, *In the Heart of the Country* is most often seen as referring to the South African situation, and most interpretations contain allegorical explications of Magda's isolation, paralysis, and madness as representative of the plight of white South Africa. In an early review, Paulin claims, "we have to read her action symbolically as a prophetic account of the historical destiny of South Africa. . . . In less rigid societies change is possible without violence, but in this situation only the bloodiest murder will liberate it 'into the world' and return it forcibly to history" (88). Similarly, Maes-Jelinek states, "her long monologue is an allegory of the South African situation; what she calls her own 'spinster fate'. . . can be read as a reference to the isolation of South Africa" (90). Wilhelm sees Magda as "a terminal symbol of the disease that lurks at the heart of the country: the self-defining lovelessness of father and daughter, master and slave, self and shadow" (44). Roberts identifies the farm as South Africa, the father as "the Afrikaner *baas*," and Magda as "the ineffectual, dreaming liberal" (30). Yet another reading claims that Magda represents the persecuted blacks of South

Africa: "Emblematic of blacks, she is kept barren and made sexless by white authority" (Post, "Oppression" 70). Strauss sees the novel as an allegory of white South Africa's sense of impotence; Penner argues that it represents modern South Africa's dependence on master/slave relationships.

An intriguing reading, but one which I finally must reject, is offered by Dodd, who argues that the allegorical interpretations marginalize Magda and participate in her oppression: "By naturalizing Magda's narrative as 'really' being about her father or South Africa or politics and so on, the critic disallows Magda's difference, renders her other and confirms his sense of self. Criticism of this nature must be seen for what it is: an imperialist activity" ("Naming" 160). I agree with Dodd that not enough attention has been paid to the particulars of Magda's situation and of her narrative's form, but Magda's story is about South Africa because Magda and her discourse are a particular part of South Africa. My discussion examines Magda's role as a woman in Afrikaner discourse and the feminine history she writes in refusal of her patriarchal heritage. Gillmer's reading of Magda as representative of the feminine principle provides a general account of what I attempt to locate in more historically and culturally concrete terms.

2. Crapanzano found South Africans still repeating these legends in the 1980s (52).

3. See ibid.; Spies 183; Hexham, "Afrikaner Nationalism" 397; and Harrison 40.

4. Totius was not alone in employing the figure of the Afrikaner woman in poetic discourse. Other early Afrikaner poets, such as Jan F. E. Celliers (1865–1940) and C. Louis Leipoldt (1880–1947), also concentrated on depicting the suffering of women and children during the Anglo-Boer War.

5. Translation by Hexham, in *Irony* 40.

6. Alan Paton's *Cry, the Beloved Country* (1949) appears to be drawing on this tradition in its depiction of the dangers of the city and the renewal possible with a return to the country village and farms.

7. Rich sees Magda as embodying the "cultural rootlessness" and the "inner existential dilemma confronting the inheritors of a European colonial culture that stands without roots or history" ("Tradition" 70, 72). Although this allegorical claim has merit, Magda's isolation and loneliness also arise from her *particular* colonial history, and her rootlessness includes a deliberate attempt to eradicate the weeds of her South African history. As child, as woman, as desert-dweller, Magda has experienced isolation and marginalization. As text-constructor, she explores alternatives.

8. The official governmental South African account of Afrikaans literature states, "The first developments of literary significance were apparent in the poetry after 1900. The main preoccupation of the early poets was historical and local: South Africa's Second War of Independence (the Anglo-Boer War, 1899–1902) and the South African landscape, fauna, and flora" (*South Africa 1983* 785). In *White*

Writing, Coetzee examines the tradition of landscape poetry in great detail in chap. 7, "Reading the South African Landscape" (163–177). Also see Povey's essay, "Landscape in Early South African Poetry."

9. Michael Du Plessis argues a similar point in an essay comparing *In the Heart of the Country* and Wilma Stockenström's *The Expedition to the Baobab Tree* (1981), an Afrikaans novel translated by Coetzee into English in 1983. He says that both novels "are exemplary explorations of a textual femininity that is inscribed in silences, gaps, or pure sounds, elements that are marginal to any authoritative, transparent discourse" (118).

10. The hermit crab may also be a literary joke. *In the Heart of the Country* is a literary pastiche, full of quotations from and echoes of a wide variety of texts. The hermit crab could evoke Eliot's Prufrock: "I should have been a pair of ragged claws / Scuttling across the floors of silent seas." Another modernist work that repeatedly cites the sea as a place of cosmic and social unity is Virginia Woolf's *Mrs. Dalloway.* Michael Du Plessis comments on the significance of allusions to water in French feminist thought and explores how this image is used in Stockenström's novel, but he says little about Coetzee's use of it.

5. *The Novelist and Torture:* Waiting for the Barbarians

1. A recent history of torture appears in Peters.

2. The magistrate's verdict is printed in Woods 261. A full transcript of the inquest appears in Woods 181–260. Also see Amnesty International's account in *Report 1978* 77. An interesting sidelight is the fact that two Coetzees were involved in the inquest and accused of bearing some responsibility for Biko's death—Brigadier J. Coetzee and Warrant Officer B. Coetzee. Coetzee is a common Afrikaans surname, but the coincidence does suggest the degree of cultural responsibility that the novelist Coetzee may feel.

3. Woods entitles his list "In Memoriam" (6–7). More recent figures indicate the mistreatment of detainees continued in the 1980s. The Johannesburg *Star* calculates that fifty-four people died in detention between 1968 and 1984 (Frederikse 189).

4. Coetzee gives this information in a biographical sketch that he wrote for *World Authors 1975–80* ("Coetzee, J(ohn) M." 146).

5. Castillo states, "The magistrate, despite his skepticism as to the validity of truth told in pain, still believes in truth, in the Truth, a truth which is revealed in the telling of a story" (85). However, Castillo argues that the novel reveals the inadequacy of such belief, "the powerlessness of the historical sense" (78). According to Castillo's analysis, the magistrate's sense of self and history are destroyed, and he is never able to bridge the gap between himself and the barbarian.

6. Neo-Marxist critics are particularly doubtful about the value of Coetzee's work.

In conclusions similar to Olsen's though reached through Marxist analyses, Richard G. Martin believes *Waiting for the Barbarians* ends in "suffocating despair" (20), and Rich points to Coetzee's "moral dead end" ("Apartheid" 389). Both, like Rowland Smith, critique Coetzee's work in comparison to Nadine Gordimer's novels, which they view much more favorably.

7. Jolly says, "The geography of the fiction may not correspond to an identifiable geo-political entity, but its depiction is both detailed and comprehensible" (70). Her essay examines the implications of the territorial metaphors found throughout the novel.

8. Penner explores the theme of blindness and sight with respect to Colonel Joll, the barbarian woman, and the magistrate (77–81).

9. Gilman traces this conjunction and its manifestations in literature, art, and science in *Difference and Pathology*. Gilman also notes the widespread association of the black woman, particularly the Hottentot, with concupiscence (76–108). The barbarian woman's failure to arouse the magistrate when the bird-like prostitute succeeds may suggest another undermining of a common sexual myth.

10. Penner similarly argues for the magistrate's "evolving ethical awareness, which parallels his developing sight in relation to the girl" (84). He sees compassion and a will to the truth as the heart of the magistrate's ethics.

6. *Apocalypse:* Life & Times of Michael K

1. On the cryptic and temporally inconclusive nature of biblical apocalypse, see McGinn.

2. The ANC was the first guerrilla organization to sign a protocol of the Geneva Convention legally binding them to avoid attacks on civilian targets and to "humanitarian conduct of the war." Despite a few isolated acts carried out by individuals ignoring the organization's directives, the official policy was to avoid white civilian casualties. This policy was not changed until 1985, when the ANC called upon its military arm to carry the conflict into white civilian areas (Davis 121–23).

3. During the late 1970s and early 1980s several white South Africans were imprisoned for refusing military service on the grounds of their conscience. Church leaders repeatedly called for a wider definition of conscientious objector. Five religious denominations were termed "peace churches" and their members allowed exemption from combatant service: Jehovah's Witnesses, Plymouth Brethren, Christadelphians, Suppliant Faithists, and Seventh Day Adventists (*Survey 1980* 208). In 1982, San Francisco, Oakland, Berkeley, and Santa Cruz resolved to offer refuge to those South Africans who object to military service because of "their refusal to participate in the military forces of apartheid" (*Survey 1982* 198). Gordimer depicts this crisis of conscience in *A Sport of Nature* when Sasha flees South Africa rather than perform his compulsory military service.

For American onlookers, the parallels with draft resistance during the Vietnam War are striking.

4. After years of negotiating, the United Nations finally brokered peace between South Africa and Angola, with an agreement signed in December 1988, under which Namibia gained independence from South Africa, and Cuba withdrew fifty thousand troops from Angola. Under the terms of the United Nations independence plan, all SADF forces had to leave Namibia a week after the announcement of election results. As the Namibian Constituent Assembly began drawing up a constitution in November 1989, the final SADF troops moved out of Northern Namibia to south of the Orange River.

5. *The Essential Gesture* 262. Gordimer's use of "the interregnum" comes from Gramsci: "The old is dying, and the new cannot be born; in this interregnum there arises a great diversity of morbid symptoms." The epigraph for *July's People,* this quotation provides the title of her James Lecture given at the New York Institute of the Humanities in 1982, "Living in the Interregnum," reprinted in *The Essential Gesture* 261–84.

6. Brink discusses in general terms a number of apocalyptic South African novels in his essay, "Writing Against Big Brother: Notes on Apocalyptic Fiction in South Africa." He claims that with *Life & Times of Michael K,* "the apocalyptic novel in South African fiction reaches its culmination" (193). The constant military turmoil throughout the continent of Africa has also given rise to a popular new genre in Nigerian fiction, the "war thriller." See Wylie et al.

7. *Waiting for the Barbarians* presents us with the exact opposite: the only characters who are given proper names are the torturers Joll and Mandel.

8. Coetzee's use of the letter K has prompted numerous readers to connect his hero with that of Kafka. Although Coetzee has at times shrugged off this connection ("I don't believe that Kafka has an exclusive right to the letter K" ["Two" 457]), Zamora argues, "It is untenable to dismiss the existence of any of the meanings of a literary symbol, though one may wish to dismiss their importance. There is no possibility of avoiding the reference to Kafka in this character's name, however many other names or meanings may also be contained in that single and singular letter" ("Allegories" 13). A detailed analysis of the resemblances between Michael K and several of Kafka's characters appears in Dovey, *The Novels of J. M. Coetzee* 265–302. Also see Post 72–73. Although I see parallels between the nightmarish worlds depicted by Coetzee and Kafka, it seems to me that Coetzee's Michael K is markedly different from Kafka's K in his passivity and silence. Suggestions that the phone call the medical officer makes to the Castle must refer to Kafka (Lehmann-Haupt 22) are misguided; the Castle has held the Cape's administrative offices since the time of the original Dutch settlers.

9. The Catch–22 quality of much of the bureaucratic paperwork blacks must comply with is chronicled in Mark Mathabane's memoir *Kaffir Boy,* in which he

tells of his mother's dogged attempts to obtain a birth certificate for him so he would be allowed to go to school (108–19).

10. "The Agentless Sentence as Rhetorical Device" (1980), "The Rhetoric of the Passive in English" (1980), and "Newton and the Ideal of a Transparent Scientific Language" (1982). The proximity of the publication dates of these essays with Coetzee's writing of *Life & Times of Michael K* demonstrates that passive structures were on his mind during this time.

11. In *White Writing,* Coetzee examines how Smith asserts and supports existing myths about the Afrikaners by her linguistic transfer of certain Afrikaans patterns into her English prose. He states, "In particular, Smith's practice of transfer is meant to validate the homegrown Calvinist myth in which the Afrikaner has his type in the Israelite, tender of flocks, seeker after a promised national homeland, member of an elect race *(volk)* set apart from the tribes of the idolatrous, living by simple and not-to-be-questioned commandments, afflicted by an inscrutable Godhead with trials whose purpose is to test his faith and his fitness for election" (118).

12. For accounts of the concentration camps and Hobhouse's campaign, see Spies 167–82 and Pakenham 533–49. On the origins of the ACVV, see Patterson 261.

13. Although I am concentrating on Coetzee's work in the South African context, the pastoral myth has played an important role in other national literatures, such as British, American, and German. *Life & Times of Michael K* could profitably be examined in relationship to these wider contexts as well. Coetzee himself looks at the tradition of the South African farm novel and the *plaasroman* within this wider context in *White Writing.* Penner sees *Life & Times of Michael K* as "laying the ghost" of silence about the black man's relation to the earth that exists in the traditional *plaasroman* (100–101).

14. Perhaps coincidentally, one of the families who has fled in Schoeman's novel is named Visagie. When George Neethling, the expatriate Afrikaner in *Promised Land,* finally reaches his grandparents' deserted farm, he finds that all of the buildings have been destroyed, blown up by soldiers who discovered that the farm had been used as a base of operations for the Afrikaner guerrillas. The resemblance to the fate of the Visagie farm in Coetzee's novel is striking.

15. Coetzee demonstrates a similar ecological concern in both *Dusklands* and *Waiting for the Barbarians.* In the first book, Eugene Dawn considers at great length the chemicals that the United States could employ to "show the enemy that he stands naked in a dying landscape" (29). Like Agent Orange, "PROP–12 spraying could change the face of Vietnam in a week" (29). Similarly, when the army of the Empire burns off the underbrush on the riverbank in order to keep the barbarian troops from using it as cover, the magistrate thinks, "They do not care that once the ground is cleared the wind begins to eat at the soil and the desert advances. Thus the expeditionary force against the barbarians prepares for its campaign,

ravaging the earth, wasting our patrimony" (82). Linking *Life & Times of Michael K* to the tradition of the agrarian-protest novel, Penner says, "Both Steinbeck and Coetzee stress the wastage and spoilage which inevitably results from an indifferent or destructive attitude toward the earth" (105).

16. Dodd discusses these implications in her thesis, "The Crossroads of Power and Knowledge."

17. Lasdun 70. Luc Renders defends the medical officer's section: "I believe the second part gives greater relevance to Michael's story as it makes him into a victim of the war and consequently gives the war a reality it does not have in Michael's life. Moreover, as the doctor sympathizes with Michael, he reinforces the validity of the ideal Michael is striving for" (102).

18. See Penner 89, and Zamora, "Allegories" 11.

7. Writing for the Other: Foe

1. Watt 97; Sutherland 139. Other standard commentaries on *Robinson Crusoe* include Hunter, Novak, and Starr.

2. For example, see Downie, and Zelnick. Gardiner says that Coetzee's novels "have all subversively inscribed Daniel Defoe's *Robinson Crusoe* with the deliberate aim of rejecting its canonical formulation of the colonial encounter" (174). He discusses only *Dusklands* in detail, though.

3. "It has been supposed that he showed snobbishness in prefixing 'De' to the plebian name of Foe in middle life. Defoe himself jested about the inconvenience of the name Foe for a man so often engaged in public controversy. But the obvious truth is that he never did change his name. The original spelling was something like Defawe, and that had been anglicized to Foe by his ancestors only a few generations before" (Moore 7). Numerous versions of Defoe's name appeared in documents and publications throughout his life.

4. Her citation of a story written by Foe about a woman who embraced and spent the afternoon conversing with a ghost refers to Defoe's *A True Relation of the Apparition of One Mrs. Veal*. Susan calls the woman "Mrs Barfield"; in Defoe's story, the woman is Mrs. Bargrave. All of the names in Coetzee's account are slightly different from Defoe's, which suggests the corruption that authorship entails.

5. Post's reading of *Foe* as an allegory in which Friday represents South African blacks, Cruso the Afrikaner government, and Susan the white liberal seems overly simplistic to me and takes little account of what seems to be the primary issue raised by the novel: how can the Other be given voice in fiction? His claim that *Foe* shows Coetzee's "endorsement of the writing, beliefs, and philosophy of Daniel Defoe" ("The Noise of Freedom" 143) is not supported by the novel's subversion of the eighteenth-century fiction and its depiction of the author as both Susan's and Friday's "foe." In this more recent essay, Post has dramatically

changed his critical approach from the universalist reading in "Oppression in the Fiction of J. M. Coetzee."

6. Packer 404. Williams takes a similarly negative perspective, arguing, "The text . . . has as its major concern the inability of art to copy reality and the unbridgeable gap between text and world" (34). To enter reality, Williams says, "J. M. Coetzee's characters have to stop writing, stop perceiving as Cartesian selves who separate from the world by consciousness, and join Friday's dance of ecstacy. But to do this means abandoning the very form that articulates the problem" (38).

7. Beressem points out that the four parts resemble the different narrative modes of *Robinson Crusoe* (222). Spencer and Spender both examine the forgotten history of the novel in their accounts of the "mothers" of the novel.

8. Gilbert and Gubar explore these paradigms in the life and work of nineteenth-century women writers in *The Madwoman in the Attic* 45–92.

9. Nicholson 53; ibid.; Packer 404; Auerbach 37.

8. The Unquiet Dead: Age of Iron

1. The scene in which Mrs. Curren visits Guguletu takes place in 1986, as an exchange between her and Mr. Thabane reveals (99).

2. For a more extensive discussion of the censorship crisis of 1986, see Chapter 2.

3. This translation was provided by Professor Mark Williams, Department of Classics, Calvin College.

4. D. J. Taylor is less convinced of the novel's success, claiming that its "didactic urges [are] everywhere apparent." He thinks that "Mrs. Curren ceases to be something actual and immediate and becomes symbolic, a vehicle for expressing argument" (5).

Works Cited

Ableman, Paul. "End of Empire." Rev. of *Waiting for the Barbarians. The Spectator* 13 Dec. 1980: 21.

Abrahams, Lionel. "Reflections in a Mirror." Rev. of *Dusklands. Snarl* 1.1 (1974): 2–3.

Achebe, Chinua. *Anthills of the Savannah.* New York: Anchor, 1988.

———— "An Image of Africa." *Massachusetts Review* 18 (1977): 782–94.

Adams, Percy G. *Travel Literature and the Evolution of the Novel.* Lexington: UP of Kentucky, 1983.

Aikenhead, Sherri. "Black Out in South Africa." *Macleans* 18 Nov. 1985: 55–56.

Alvarez-Pereyre, Jacques. *The Poetry of Commitment in South Africa.* Trans. Clive Wake. London: Heinemann, 1984.

Amnesty for Terrorism. Pretoria: South African Dept. of Information, 1978.

Amnesty International. *Report on Torture.* New York: Farrar, Straus and Giroux, 1975.

Amnesty International Report 1978. London: Amnesty International Publications, 1979.

Auerbach, Nina. "A Novel of Her Own." Rev. of *Foe. New Republic* 9 March 1987: 36–38.

Bakhtin, M. M., and P. M. Medvedev. *The Formal Method in Literary Scholarship: A Critical Introduction to Sociological Poetics.* Trans. Albert J. Wehrle. Cambridge: Harvard UP, 1985.

Barnett, Ursula A. "South Africa: 'Dusklands.'" *Books Abroad* 50 (1976): 459–60.

———— *A Vision of Order: A Study of Black South African Literature in English (1914–1980).* Amherst: U of Massachusetts P, 1983.

Barrow, Sir John. *An Account of Travels into the Interior of Southern Africa in the Years 1797 and 1798.* 2 vols. London: T. Cadell and W. Davies, 1801.

Batten, Charles L., Jr. *Pleasurable Instruction: Form and Convention in Eighteenth-Century Travel Literature.* Berkeley: U of Calif. P, 1978.

Beauvoir, Simone de. *The Second Sex.* Trans. H. M. Parshley. New York: Vintage, 1952.

Benson, Mary. *Nelson Mandela: The Man and the Movement.* New York: Norton, 1986.

Beressem, Hanjo. "Foe: The Corruption of Words." *Matatu: Zeitschrift fur Afrikanische Kultur und Gesellschaft* 2 (1988): 222–35.

Biko, Stephen. "Black Consciousness and the Quest for a True Humanity." In *Black Theology: The South African Voice.* Ed. Basil Moore. London: C. Hurst, 1973.

Bledsoe, J. O. Letter. *Focus on South Africa* Dec. 1989: 16.

Booth, Wayne C. *The Company We Keep: An Ethics of Fiction.* Berkeley: U of Calif. P, 1988.

"Brink, André." *Contemporary Authors.* Vol. 104. 1982.

Brink, André. *A Dry White Season.* New York: Penguin, 1984.

——— "Writing against Big Brother: Notes on Apocalyptic Fiction in South Africa." *World Literature Today* 58.2 (1984): 189–94.

——— *Writing in a State of Siege: Essays on Politics and Literature.* New York: Summit, 1983.

——— and J. M. Coetzee, eds. *A Land Apart: A Contemporary South African Reader.* New York: Penguin, 1986.

Buell, Lawrence. "American Pastoral Ideology Reappraised." *American Literary History* 1 (1989): 1–29.

Bunting, Brian. Foreword to *And A Threefold Cord,* by Alex La Guma. Berlin: Seven Seas, 1964. 9–16.

Burns, John F. "At Least 8 Killed in South Africa as Police and Demonstrators Clash." *New York Times* 18 June 1980: A1.

——— "South African Saboteurs: An Evolution to Violence." *New York Times* 4 June 1980: A14.

Castillo, Debra A. "The Composition of the Self in Coetzee's *Waiting for the Barbarians.*" *Critique: Studies in Modern Fiction* 27 (1986): 78–90.

Cavafy, Constantine P. "Waiting for the Barbarians." *Voices of Modern Greece: Selected Poems by Cavafy, Sikelianos, Seferis, Elytis, Gatsos.* Ed. and trans. Edmund Keeley and Philip Sherrard. Princeton: Princeton UP, 1981. 7–8.

Chandler, Robert W. *War of Ideas: The US Propaganda Campaign in Vietnam.* Boulder, Colo.: Westview, 1981.

Christie, Sarah, Geoffrey Hutchings, and Don Maclennan. *Perspectives on South African Fiction.* Johannesburg: Ad. Donker, 1980.

Cixous, Hélène. "The Laugh of the Medusa." *Signs* 1 (1976): 875–93.

Clingman, Stephen. *The Novels of Nadine Gordimer: History from the Inside.* London: Allen and Unwin, 1986.

Coetzee, J. M. "The Agentless Sentence as Rhetorical Device." *Language and Style: An International Journal* 13 (1980): 26–34.

——— *Age of Iron.* New York: Random House, 1990.

——— "Alex La Guma and the Responsibilities of the South African Writer." *Journal of the New African Literature and the Arts* 9–10 (1971): 5–11.

——— "Apartheid: La Littérature Mutilée." *Le Nouvel Observateur* 8–14 May 1987: 57–58.

——— "Art and Apartheid." Rev. of *Notebooks 1960–1977,* by Athol Fugard. *New Republic* 9 April 1984: 25–28.

——— "Confessions and Double Thoughts: Tolstoy, Rousseau, Dostoevsky." *Comparative Literature* 37 (1985): 193–232.

——— *Dusklands.* New York: Penguin, 1985.

——— *Foe.* New York: Viking, 1987.

———— "The Great South African Novel." *Leadership SA* 2 (1983): 74–79.

———— "How I Learned about America—and Africa—in Texas." *New York Times Book Review* 9 April 1984: 9.

———— *In the Heart of the Country.* New York: Penguin, 1982.

———— Interview. *Kunapipi* 6.1 (1984): 6–11.

———— "An Interview with J. M. Coetzee." By Jean Sévry. *Commonwealth Essays and Studies* 9.1 (1986): 1–7.

———— "Into the Dark Chamber: The Novelist and South Africa." *New York Times Book Review* 12 Jan. 1986: 13, 35.

———— *Life & Times of Michael K.* New York: Penguin, 1985.

———— "Listening to the Afrikaners." Rev. of *Waiting: The Whites of South Africa,* by Vincent Crapanzano. *New York Times Book Review* 14 April 1985: 3, 28.

———— "Man's Fate in the Novels of Alex La Guma." *Studies in Black Literature* 5 (1974): 16–23.

———— "Newton and the Ideal of a Transparent Scientific Language." *Journal of Literary Semantics* 11.2 (1982): 3–13.

———— "The Novel Today." *Upstream* 6.1 (Summer 1988): 2–5.

———— "A Note on Writing." *Momentum,* 11–13.

———— "The Rhetoric of the Passive in English." *Linguistics* 18 (1980): 199–21.

———— "Satyagraha in Durban." Rev. of *A Revolutionary Woman,* by Sheila Fugard. *The New York Review of Books* 24 Oct. 1985: 12–13.

———— "Speaking: J. M. Coetzee." Interview with Stephen Watson. *Speak* May/June 1978: 21–24.

———— "Staffrider." *African Book Publishing Record* 5 (1979): 235–36.

———— "Tales of Afrikaners." *New York Times Magazine* 9 Mar. 1986: 19, 21–22, 74–75.

———— "Tales out of School." Rev. of *Fools and Other Stories,* by Njabulo Ndebele. *New Republic* 22 Dec. 1986: 36–38.

———— "Too Late the Liberal." Rev. of *Save the Beloved Country,* by Alan Paton. *The New Republic* 8–15 Jan. 1990: 39–41.

———— "Two Interviews with J. M. Coetzee, 1983 and 1987." By Tony Morphet. *Triquarterly* 62 (1987): 454–64.

———— *Waiting for the Barbarians.* New York: Penguin, 1982.

———— "The White Tribe." *Vogue* March 1986: 490–91, 543–44.

———— *White Writing: On the Culture of Letters in South Africa.* New Haven: Yale UP, 1988.

"Coetzee, J(ohn) M." *Current Biography Yearbook.* 1987.

"Coetzee, J(ohn) M." *World Authors 1975–1980.* 1985.

Cohen, David William. *Womunafa's Bunafu: A Study of Authority in a Nineteenth-Century African Community.* Princeton: Princeton UP, 1977.

Cope, Jack. *The Adversary Within: Dissident Writers in Afrikaans.* Cape Town: David Philip, 1982.

Cornevin, Marianne. *Apartheid: Power and Historical Falsification.* Paris: UNESCO, 1980.

Cowell, Alan. "Pretoria Admits Detaining Children." *New York Times* 9 Dec. 1986: A3.

——— "South African Schools Boycotted; U.S. Weighs Naming Black Envoy." *New York Times* 15 July 1986: A1.

——— "South Africans Close 40 Black Schools." *New York Times* 6 Nov. 1986: A3.

Crapanzano, Vincent. *Waiting: The Whites of South Africa.* New York: Random House, 1985.

Crewe, Jonathan. Rev. of *Dusklands. Contrast* 9.2 (1974): 90–95.

Davenport, T. R. H. *South Africa: A Modern History.* 2nd ed. Toronto: U of Toronto P, 1978.

Davis, Stephen M. *Apartheid's Rebels: Inside South Africa's Hidden War.* New Haven: Yale UP, 1987.

Dean, Elizabeth, Paul Hartmann, and Mary Katzen. *History in Black and White: An Analysis of Southern African School History Textbooks. A Report to UNESCO.* Leicester: Centre for Mass Communication Research, 1981.

Defoe, Daniel. *The Fortunes and Misfortunes of the Famous Moll Flanders.* New York: Penguin, 1978.

——— *Robinson Crusoe.* New York: Norton, 1975.

De Haas, Mary. "Is Millenarianism Alive and Well in White South Africa?" *Religion in Southern Africa* 7.1 (1986): 37–45.

De Klerk, W. A. *The Puritans in Africa: A Story of Afrikanerdom.* London: Rex Collings, 1975.

Derrida, Jacques. "Racism's Last Word." *Critical Inquiry* 12 (1985): 290–99.

——— "White Mythology: Metaphor in the Text of Philosophy." *New Literary History* 6 (1974): 5–74.

Dodd, Josephine. "The Crossroad of Power and Knowledge: Discursive Policy and the Fiction of J. M. Coetzee." Thesis. U of Alberta, 1987.

——— "Naming and Framing: Naturalization and Colonization in J. M. Coetzee's *In the Heart of the Country.*" *World Literature Written in English* 27 (1987): 153–61.

Donoghue, Denis. "Her Man Friday." Rev. of *Foe. New York Times Book Review* 22 Feb. 1987: 1, 26–27.

Dovey, Teresa. "Coetzee and His Critics: The Case of *Dusklands.*" *English in Africa* 14 (1987): 15–30.

——— *The Novels of J. M. Coetzee: Lacanian Allegories.* Human Sciences Research Council Publication Series, no. 86. Johannesburg: Ad. Donker, 1988.

Downie, J. A. "Defoe, Imperialism, and the Travel Books Reconsidered." *Yearbook of English Studies* 13 (1983): 66–83.

Dugard, John. "Racial Legislation and Civil Rights." *Race Relations in South Africa 1929–1979,* 79–96.

Du Plessis, Menàn. "Towards a True Materialism." *Contrast: South African Literary Journal* 13.4 (1983): 77–87.

Du Plessis, Michael. "Bodies and Signs: Inscriptions of Femininity in John Coetzee and Wilma Stockenström." *Journal of Literary Studies / Tydskrif Vir Literaturwetenskap* 4.1 (1988): 118–28.

Du Toit, André. "No Chosen People: The Myth of the Calvinist Origins of Afrikaner Nationalism and Racial Ideology." *American Historical Review* 88 (1983): 920–52.

Dyer, Geoff. "White Spaces." Rev. of *Foe. Listener* 2 Oct. 1986: 25.

Eckstein, Barbara. "The Body, the Word, and the State: J. M. Coetzee's *Waiting for the Barbarians.*" *Novel* 22 (1989): 175–98.

Elphick, Richard. *Khoikhoi and the Founding of White South Africa.* 2nd ed. Johannesburg: Ravan, 1985.

Faulkner, William. *The Sound and the Fury.* New York: Modern Library, 1929.

Finch, Anne. "The Introduction." *Norton Anthology of Literature by Women,* 100–102.

Forbes, Vernon S., and John Rourke. *Paterson's Cape Travels 1777 to 1779.* Johannesburg: Brenthurst, 1980.

Frederikse, Julie. *South Africa: A Different Kind of War.* Boston: Beacon, 1986.

Gardam, June. "The Only Story." *Sunday Times Review* 7 Sept. 1986: 49.

Gardiner, Allan. "J. M. Coetzee's *Dusklands:* Colonial Encounters of the Robinsonian Kind." *World Literature Written in English* 27.2 (1987): 174–84.

Gargan, Edward A. "U.S. Group Charges Wide Beating of Children by South Africa Police." *New York Times* 18 April 1986: A4.

Gates, Henry Louis, Jr. "Writing 'Race' and the Difference It Makes." *"Race," Writing and Difference,* 1–20.

Géniès, Bernard. "Lifting Coetzee's Veil." *World Press Review* July 1985: 59–60.

Gerwel, Jakes. "Liberation Now, Education Later?" *Africa Reports* March-April 1986: 8–9.

Gibson, James William. *The Perfect War: Technowar in Vietnam.* Boston: Atlantic Monthly Press, 1986.

Gilbert, Sandra M., and Susan Gubar. *The Madwoman in the Attic: The Woman Writer and the Nineteenth-Century Literary Imagination.* New Haven: Yale UP, 1979.

Giliomee, Hermann. "The Development of the Afrikaner's Self-Concept." *Looking at the Afrikaner Today.* Comp. by Hendrik W. van der Merwe. Cape Town: Tafelberg, 1975. 1–39.

Gillmer, Joan. "The Motif of the Damaged Child in the Work of J. M. Coetzee." *Momentum,* 107–119.

Gilman, Sander L. *Difference and Pathology: Stereotypes of Sexuality, Race and Madness.* Ithaca: Cornell UP, 1985.

Goldberg, Jonathan. *James I and the Politics of Literature.* Baltimore: Johns Hopkins UP, 1983.

Goodheart, Eugene. *Culture and the Radical Conscience.* Cambridge: Harvard UP, 1973.

Gordimer, Nadine. *Burger's Daughter.* New York: Viking, 1979.

———— "Censorship of 'The Word.'" *Africa Reports* July-August 1987: 50–52.

———— "English-Language Literature and Politics in South Africa." Heywood 99–120.

———— *The Essential Gesture: Writing, Politics and Places.* Ed. Stephen Clingman. New York: Knopf, 1988.

———— "The Idea of Gardening." *New York Review of Books* 2 Feb. 1984: 3, 6.

———— "Interview." By Pat Schwartz. *New South African Writing.* Hillbrow, S. Africa: Lorton Publications, 1977. 74–81.

———— *July's People.* New York: Viking, 1981.

———— "The Novel and the Nation in South Africa." Killam 33–52.

———— *Something Out There.* New York: Viking, 1984.

———— *A Sport of Nature.* New York: Knopf, 1987.

———— John Dugard, and Richard Smith. *What Happened to "Burger's Daughter", or How South African Censorship Works.* Johannesburg: Taurus, 1980.

Gray, Rosemary. "J. M. Coetzee's *Dusklands:* Of War and War's Alarms." *Commonwealth Essays and Studies* 9.1 (1986): 32–43.

Gray, Stephen. *Southern African Literature: An Introduction.* Cape Town: David Philip, 1979.

Green, Robert J. "Politics and Literature in Africa: The Drama of Athol Fugard." Heywood 163–73.

Greenblatt, Stephen. *Renaissance Self-Fashioning: From More to Shakespeare.* Chicago: U of Chicago P, 1980.

Gwala, Mafika. "Writing as a Cultural Weapon." *Momentum,* 36–53.

Hachten, William A., and C. Anthony Giffard. *The Press and Apartheid: Repression and Propaganda in South Africa.* Madison: U of Wisconsin P, 1984.

Hallin, Daniel C. *The "Uncensored War": The Media and Vietnam.* New York: Oxford UP, 1986.

Harms, Robert W. *River of Wealth, River of Sorrow: The Central Zaire Basin in the Era of the Slave and Ivory Trade 1500–1891.* New Haven: Yale UP, 1981.

Harrison, David. *The White Tribe of Africa: South Africa in Perspective.* Berkeley: U of Calif. P, 1981.

Hart, Francis R. "Notes for an Anatomy of Modern Autobiography." *New Directions in Literary History.* Ed. Ralph Cohen. Baltimore: Johns Hopkins UP, 1974. 221–47.

Hewson, Kelly. "Making the 'Revolutionary Gesture': Nadine Gordimer, J. M. Coetzee and Some Variations on the Writer's Responsibility." *Ariel* 19 (1988): 55–72.

Hexham, Irving. "Afrikaner Nationalism 1902–14." Warwick 386–403.

———— *The Irony of Apartheid: The Struggle for National Independence of Afrikaner Calvinism against British Imperialism.* New York: Edwin Mellen P, 1981.

Heywood, Christopher, ed. *Aspects of South African Literature*. London: Heinemann, 1976.

Hjalmar, Thesen. *A Deadly Presence*. Cape Town: David Philip, 1982.

Hondius, Jodocus. *A Clear Description of the Cape of Good Hope*. 1652. Trans. L. C. van Oordt. Cape Town: Van Riebeeck Festival Book Exhibition Committee, 1952.

Hope, Christopher. *Kruger's Alp*. New York: Viking, 1984.

Howe, Irving. "A Stark Political Fable of South Africa." Rev. of *Waiting for the Barbarians*. *New York Times Book Review* 18 Apr. 1982: 1, 36.

Hunter, J. Paul. *The Reluctant Pilgrim: Defoe's Emblematic Method and Quest for Form in Robinson Crusoe*. Baltimore: Johns Hopkins UP, 1966.

Irigaray, Luce. "This Sex Which Is Not One." *New French Feminisms*, 99–106.

JanMohamed, Abdul R. "The Economy of Manichean Allegory: The Function of Racial Difference in Colonialist Literature." *"Race," Writing, and Difference*, 78–106.

Jardine, Alice A. *Gynesis: Configurations of Woman and Modernity*. Ithaca: Cornell UP, 1985.

Jolly, Rosemary Jane. "Territorial Metaphor in Coetzee's *Waiting for the Barbarians*." *Ariel* 20 (1989): 69–79.

Jones, Alex S. "Pretoria's Press Curbs Limiting Coverage of Strife." *New York Times* 1 Mar. 1987: A20.

Jones, Ann Rosalind. "Inscribing Femininity: French Theories of the Feminine." *Making a Difference: Feminist Literary Criticism*. Ed. Gayle Greene and Coppélia Kahn. London: Methuen, 1985. 80–112.

Joubert, Elsa. *Die Laaste Sondag*. Cape Town: Tafelberg, 1983.

The Journal of Wikar, Coetsé and Van Reenen. Ed. E. E. Mossop. Cape Town: Van Riebeeck Society, 1935.

The Journals of Brink and Rhenius. Trans and ed. E. E. Mossop. Cape Town: Van Riebeeck Society, 1947.

The Kairos Document: Challenge to the Church. Grand Rapids, Mich.: Eerdmans, 1986.

Killam, G. D., ed. *African Writers on African Writing*. Evanston: Northwestern UP, 1973.

King, Francis. "Telling Stories, Telling Tales, Telling Fiction." Rev. of *Foe*. *Spectator* 20 Sept. 1986: 33.

Knox-Shaw, Peter. "*Dusklands*: A Metaphysics of Violence." *Contrast* 4.1 (1982): 26–38. Rpt. in *Commonwealth Novel in English* 2.1 (1983): 65–81.

Koenig, Rhoda. "Taking Liberties." Rev. of *Foe*. *New York* 9 Feb. 1987: 91–92.

Kolb, Peter. *The Present State of the Cape of Good Hope*. 1719. 2 vols. London, 1731.

Kristeva, Julia. "Oscillation between Power and Denial." *New French Feminisms*, 165–67.

Lasdun, James. "Life's Victims." Rev. of *Life & Times of Michael K*. *Encounter* 62.1 (1984): 69–73.

Laurence, John C. *Race, Propaganda and South Africa*. London: Victor Gollancz, 1979.

Lehmann-Haupt, Christopher. "Books of the Times." Rev. of *Life & Times of Michael K. New York Times* 6 Dec. 1983: C22.

Lelyveld, Joseph. "Black Challenge to Pretoria: Rebellion, Still Puny, Is Showing More Muscle." *New York Times* 12 Oct. 1983: A8.

Lentricchia, Frank. *After the New Criticism*. Chicago: U of Chicago P, 1980.

Lewis, Neil A. "In Washington, South Africa Recedes as an Issue." *New York Times* 1 Mar. 1987: A21.

Lewis, Peter. "Types of Tyranny." Rev. of *Waiting for the Barbarians. Times Literary Supplement* 7 Nov. 1980: 1270.

Lichtenstein, Henry. *Travels in Southern Africa: In the Years 1803, 1804, 1805 and 1806*. Trans. Anne Plumptre. 1812. Cape Town: Van Riebeeck Society, 1928.

Lindenberger, Herbert. "Toward a New History in Literary Study." *Profession: Selected Articles from the Bulletins of the Association of Departments of English and the Association of Departments of Foreign Languages*. New York: MLA, 1984. 16–23.

Lodge, Tom. *Black Politics in South Africa since 1945*. London: Longman, 1983.

Lukács, Georg. *The Meaning of Contemporary Realism*. Trans. John and Necke Mander. London: Merlin, 1963.

McDowell, Edwin. "Publishing: Focus on South Africans." *New York Times* 4 Dec. 1981: C26.

McGann, Jerome. *The Beauty of Inflections: Literary Investigations in Historical Method and Theory*. Oxford: Clarendon, 1985.

McGinn, Bernard. "Revelation." *The Literary Guide to the Bible*. Ed. Robert Alter and Frank Kermode. New York: Harvard UP, 1987. 523–41.

MacIntyre, Alasdair. *After Virtue: A Study in Moral Theory*. 2nd ed. Notre Dame: U of Notre Dame P, 1984.

Maes-Jelinek, Hena. "Ambivalent Clio: J. M. Coetzee's *In the Heart of the Country* and Wilson Harris's *Carnival*." *Journal of Commonwealth Literature* 22.1 (1987): 87–98.

Malherbe, E. G. "Conflict and Progress in Education." *Race Relations in South Africa 1929–1979*, 155–86.

Marder, Murrey. "Our Longest War's Tortuous History." *A Short History of the Vietnam War*, 13–43.

Marquard, Jean. "Novel as a Critical Tool." *Contrast* 12.1 (1978): 83–86.

Martin, Richard G. "Narrative, History, Ideology: A Study of *Waiting for the Barbarians* and *Burger's Daughter*." *Ariel* 17.3 (1986): 3–21.

Martin, Wendy. "From Patriarchy to the Female Principle: A Chronological Reading of Adrienne Rich's Poems." *Adrienne Rich's Poetry*. Ed. Barbara Charlesworth Gelpi and Albert Gelpi. New York: Norton, 1975. 175–89.

Mathabane, Mark. *Kaffir Boy: The True Story of a Black's Coming of Age in Apartheid South Africa*. New York: NAL, 1986.

Mentzel, O. F. *A Geographical and Topographical Description of the Cape of Good Hope*.

1785. Trans. H. J. Mandelbrote. Part 1 and Part 2. Cape Town: Van Riebeeck Society, 1921, 1925.

Miller, J. Hillis. "Presidential Address 1986." *PMLA* 102 (1987): 281–91.

Mitgang, Herbert. "Coetzee Wins Writing Prize." *New York Times* 16 Dec. 1986: C24.

Moi, Toril. *Sexual/Textual Politics: Feminist Literary Theory.* London: Methuen, 1985.

Momentum: On Recent South African Writing. Ed. M. J. Daymond, J. U. Jacobs, and Margaret Lonta. Pietermaritzburg, S. Africa: U of Natal P, 1984.

"The Month in Focus." *Focus on South Africa* Dec. 1989: 6.

Montrose, Louis. "Renaissance Literary Studies and the Subject of History." *English Literary Renaissance* 16 (1986): 5–12.

Moodie, T. Dunbar. *The Rise of Afrikanerdom: Power, Apartheid, and the Afrikaner Civil Religion.* Berkeley: U of Calif. P, 1975.

Moore, John Robert. *Daniel Defoe: Citizen of the Modern World.* Chicago: U of Chicago P, 1958.

Moyana, T. T. "Problems of a Creative Writer in South Africa." Heywood 85–98.

Mueller, John E. *War, Presidents and Public Opinion.* New York: Wiley, 1973.

Neuhaus, Richard John. *Dispensations: The Future of South Africa as South Africans See It.* Grand Rapids, Mich.: Eerdmans, 1986.

New French Feminisms: An Anthology. Ed. Elaine Marks and Isabelle de Courtivron. Amherst: U of Mass. P, 1980.

Nicholson, Maureen. "'If I Make the Air around Him Thick with Words': J. M. Coetzee's *Foe.*" *West Coast Review* 21.4 (1987): 52–58.

Nkosi, Lewis. *Home and Exile and Other Selections.* New York: Longman, 1983.

———— *Tasks and Masks: Themes and Styles of African Literature.* New York: Longman, 1981.

Nortje, Arthur. "Native's Letter." *Dead Roots: Poems.* London: Heinemann, 1971.

The Norton Anthology of Literature by Women: The Tradition in English. Ed. Sandra M. Gilbert and Susan Gubar. New York: Norton, 1985.

Novak, Maximillan E. *Defoe and the Nature of Man.* Oxford: Oxford UP, 1963.

Olive Schreiner and After: Essays on Southern African Literature in Honour of Guy Butler. Ed. Malvern van Wyk Smith and Don Maclennan. Cape Town: David Philip, 1983.

Olsen, Lance. "The Presence of Absence: Coetzee's *Waiting for the Barbarians.*" *Ariel* 16.2 (1985): 47–60.

Ozick, Cynthia. "A Tale of Heroic Anonymity." Rev. of *Life & Times of Michael K. New York Times Book Review* 11 Dec. 1983: 1, 26.

Packer, George. "Blind Alleys." Rev. of *Foe. Nation* 28 Mar. 1987: 402.

Pakenham, Thomas. *The Boer War.* New York: Random House, 1979.

Parker, Kenneth. "The South African Novel in English." *The South African Novel in English: Essays in Criticism and Society.* Ed. Kenneth Parker. New York: Africana, 1978. 1–26.

"Paton, Alan." *Contemporary Authors—Permanent Series.* Vol. 1. 1975.

Paton, Alan. *Cry, the Beloved Country.* New York: Scribner's, 1948.

———— *Journey Continued.* New York: Scribner's, 1988.

Patterson, Sheila. *The Last Trek: A Study of the Boer People and the Afrikaner Nation.* London: Routledge & Kegan Paul, 1957.

Paulin, Tom. "Incorrigibly Plural." Rev. of *In the Heart of the Country. Encounter* Oct. 1977: 82–89.

Pechter, Edward. "The New Historicism and Its Discontents." *PMLA* 102 (1987): 292–303.

Penner, Dick. *Countries of the Mind: The Fiction of J. M. Coetzee.* Westport, Conn.: Greenwood, 1989.

Peters, Edward. *Torture.* New York: Basil Blackwell, 1985.

Philip, John. *Researches in South Africa; Illustrating the Civil, Moral, and Religious Condition of the Native Tribes.* 2 vols. London: James Duncan, 1828.

Plott, David. "A Deathbed Letter from Cape Town." Rev. of *Age of Iron. Wall Street Journal* 26 Sept. 1990: A13.

Political Imprisonment in South Africa: An Amnesty International Report. London: Amnesty International Publications, 1978.

Post, Robert M. "The Noise of Freedom: J. M. Coetzee's *Foe.*" *Critique: Studies in Modern Fiction* 30 (1989): 143–54.

———— "Oppression in the Fiction of J. M. Coetzee." *Critique: Studies in Modern Fiction* 27 (1986): 67–77.

Povey, John. "Landscape in Early South African Poetry." *Olive Schreiner and After,* 116–128.

Pratt, Mary Louise. "Scratches on the Face of the Country; or, What Mr. Barrow Saw in the Land of the Bushmen." *"Race," Writing and Difference,* 138–62.

"Pretoria Says Its Police Killed 716 Last Year." *New York Times* 7 March 1987: A4.

Price, Robert M. "Pretoria's Southern African Strategy." *African Affairs* 83 (1984): 11–32.

Race Relations in South Africa 1929–1979. Ed. Ellen Hellmann and Henry Lever. New York: St. Martin's, 1980.

"Race," Writing and Difference. Ed. Henry Louis Gates, Jr. Chicago: U of Chicago P, 1986.

"Raid by Blacks at Pretoria Bank Leaves Whites Worried but Firm." *New York Times* 28 Jan. 1980: A2.

Raven-Hart, R. *Before Van Riebeeck: Callers at South Africa from 1488 to 1652.* Cape Town: Struik, 1967.

———— *Cape Good Hope 1652–1702: The First Fifty Years of Dutch Colonisation as Seen by Callers.* 2 vols. Cape Town: Balkema, 1971.

Renders, Luc. "J. M. Coetzee's Michael K: Starving in a Land of Plenty." *Literary Gastronomy.* Ed. David Bevan. Amsterdam: Rodopi, 1988. 95–102.

Rich, Adrienne. *The Fact of a Doorframe: Poems Selected and New, 1950–1984.* New York: Norton, 1984.

———— "When We Dead Awaken: Writing as Re-Vision." *College English* 34 (1972): 18–25.

Rich, Paul. "Apartheid and the Decline of the Civilization Idea: An Essay on Nadine Gordimer's *July's People* and J. M. Coetzee's *Waiting for the Barbarians.*" *Research in African Literatures* 15 (1984): 365–93.

———— "Tradition and Revolt in South African Fiction: The Novels of André Brink, Nadine Gordimer, and J. M. Coetzee." *Journal of Southern African Studies* 9 (1982): 54–73.

Richardson, Samuel. *Pamela: or, Virtue Rewarded.* New York: Penguin, 1980.

Rive, Richard. "The Black Writer in South Africa." *Momentum,* 92–95.

———— "Storming Pretoria's Castle—To Write or Fight?" *New York Times Book Review* 17 Jan. 1988: 1, 32–33.

Roberts, Sheila. "Character and Meaning in Four Contemporary South African Novels." *World Literature Written in English* 19 (1980): 19–36.

Roper, Burns W. "What Public Opinion Polls Said." *Big Story: How the American Press and Television Reported and Interpreted the Crisis of Tet 1968 in Vietnam and Washington.* Ed. Peter Braestrup. Boulder, Colo.: Westview, 1977. 674–704.

Said, Edward W. *Beginnings: Intention and Method.* New York: Basic Books, 1975.

———— *Orientalism.* New York: Pantheon, 1978.

———— *The World, the Text, and the Critic.* Harvard UP, 1983.

Schoeman, Karel. *Promised Land.* Trans. Marion V. Friedmann. New York: Summit, 1978.

Schott, Webster. "At the Farthest Outpost of Civilization." Rev. of *Waiting for the Barbarians. Book World—The Washington Post* 2 May 1982: 1–2, 12.

Sepamla, Sipho. *A Ride on the Whirlwind.* London: Heinemann, 1984.

Serote, Mongane. *To Every Birth Its Blood.* London: Heinemann, 1986.

Shakespeare, William. *The Tempest. The Complete Works.* Ed. Alfred Harbage. New York: Viking, 1969.

A Short History of the Vietnam War. Ed. Allan R. Millett. Bloomington: Indiana UP, 1978.

Siebers, Tobin. *The Ethics of Criticism.* Ithaca: Cornell UP, 1988.

Singer, Eleanor, and Jacob Ludwig. "South Africa's Press Restrictions: Effects on Press Coverage and Public Opinion toward South Africa." *Public Opinion Quarterly* 51 (1987): 315–34.

Small, Adam. "In the Crucible: A Situation of Change for South African Literature." *Race Relations in South Africa 1929–1979,* 249–72.

Smith, Charlene. "The Death Rattle of Freedom." *World Press Review* Sept. 1986: 62.

Smith, Pauline. "The Pain." *South African Stories.* Ed. David Wright. London: Faber and Faber, 1960. 212–24.

Smith, Rowland. "The Seventies and After: The Inner View in White, English-Language Fiction." *Olive Schreiner and After,* 196–204.

Sole, Kelwyn. "Oral Performance and Social Struggle in Contemporary Black South African Literature." *Triquarterly* 69 (1987): 254–71.

"South Africa Acknowledges Detention of Blacks under 12." *New York Times* 13 Feb. 1987: A10.

South Africa 1983: Official Yearbook of the Republic of South Africa. 9th ed. Johannesburg: Dept. of Foreign Affairs and Information, 1983.

Sparks, Allister. "The Universal Themes of a Private Person." *Washington Post* 29 Oct. 1983: C1, C8.

Sparrman, Anders. *A Voyage to the Cape of Good Hope . . . 1772–76.* Ed. V. S. Forbes. Trans. and rev. by J. and I. Rudner. Cape Town: Van Riebeeck Society, 1975.

Spencer, Jane. *The Rise of the Woman Novelist: From Aphra Behn to Jane Austen.* New York: Basil Blackwell, 1986.

Spender, Dale. *Mothers of the Novel: 100 Good Women Writers before Jane Austen.* London: Pandora, 1986.

Spies, S. B. "Women and the War." Warwick 161–85.

Starr, George A. *Defoe and Spiritual Autobiography.* Princeton: Princeton UP, 1965.

Steiner, George. *Language and Silence: Essays 1958–1966.* London: Faber and Faber, 1967.

Stern, Laurence. "America in Anguish, 1965 to 1973." *A Short History of the Vietnam War,* 3–12.

Strauss, Peter. "Coetzee's Idylls: The Ending of *In the Heart of the Country.*" *Momentum,* 121–28.

Study Commission on U.S. Policy toward Southern Africa. *South Africa: Time Running Out.* Berkeley: U of Calif. P, 1981.

Survey of Race Relations in South Africa 1979. Ed. Loraine Gordon. Johannesburg: South African Institute of Race Relations, 1980.

Survey of Race Relations in South Africa 1980. Ed. Loraine Gordon. Johannesburg: South African Institute of Race Relations, 1981.

Survey of Race Relations in South Africa 1981. Ed. Muriel Horrell. Johannesburg: South African Institute of Race Relations, 1982.

Survey of Race Relations in South Africa 1982. Ed. Peter Randall. Johannesburg: South African Institute of Race Relations, 1983.

Survey of Race Relations in South Africa 1983. Johannesburg: South African Institute of Race Relations, 1984.

Sutherland, James. *Daniel Defoe: A Critical Study.* Boston: Houghton Mifflin, 1971.

Taylor, D. J. "Death of a Nation." Rev. of *Age of Iron. The Sunday Times* 16 Sept. 1990, sec. 8:5.

Temple, Peter. "The Private World of a Major New SA Talent." *The Star* 14 June 1974: 3.

Templin, J. Alton. *Ideology on a Frontier: The Theological Foundations of Afrikaner*

Nationalism, 1652–1910. Contributions in Intercultural and Comparative Studies, No. 11. Westport, Conn.: Greenwood, 1984.

Thomas, Brook. *Cross-Examinations of Law and Literature: Cooper, Hawthorne, Stowe, and Melville*. New York: Cambridge UP, 1987.

———— "The Historical Necessity for—and Difficulties with—New Historical Analysis in Introductory Literature Courses." *College English* 49 (1987): 509–22.

Thompson, Leonard. *The Political Mythology of Apartheid*. New Haven: Yale UP, 1985.

Thornton, Lawrence. "Apartheid's Last Vicious Gasps." Rev. of *Age of Iron*. *New York Times Book Review* 23 Sept. 1990: 7.

Thunberg, Carl Peter. *Travels at the Cape of Good Hope 1772–1775*. 1793–95. Ed. V. S. Forbes. Trans. J. and I. Rudner. Cape Town: Van Riebeeck Society, 1986.

Tolstoy, Leo N. *The Long Exile and Other Stories*. Vol. 15 of *The Works of Lyof N. Tolstoï*. New York: Scribner's, 1929.

Tucker, Martin. *Africa in Modern Literature: A Survey of Contemporary Writing in English*. New York: Frederick Ungar, 1967.

Tudor, Henry. *Political Myth*. New York: Praeger, 1972.

Vaillant, M. *Travels from the Cape of Good Hope*. Trans. Elizabeth Helme. 2 vols. London: William Lane, 1790.

Valentijn, François. *Description of the Cape of Good Hope with the Matters Concerning It*. 1726. 2 vols. Ed. E. H. Raidt. Trans. R. Raven-Hart. Cape Town: Van Riebeeck Society, 1971, 1975.

Van Jaarsveld, F. A. *The Afrikaner's Interpretation of South African History*. Cape Town: Simondium, 1964.

Van Pallandt, Baron A. *General Remarks on the Cape of Good Hope*. 1803. Cape Town: South African Public Library, 1917.

Vaughan, Michael. "Literature and Politics: Currents in South African Writing in the Seventies." *Journal of Southern African Studies* 9.1 (1982): 118–38.

Veeser, Aram, ed. *The New Historicism*. Boston: Routledge and Kegan Paul, 1989.

Vigne, Randolph. "The Literature of South Africa." *The Commonwealth Pen: An Introduction to the Literature of the British Commonwealth*. Ed. A. L. McLeod. Ithaca: Cornell UP, 1961. 78–99.

Villet, Barbara. *Blood River: The Passionate Saga of South Africa's Afrikaners and of Life in Their Embattled Land*. New York: Everest, 1982.

Warwick, Peter, ed. *The South African War: The Anglo-Boer War 1899–1902*. Harlow, Great Britain: Longman, 1980.

Watson, Stephen. "Colonialism and the Novels of J. M. Coetzee." *Research in African Literature* 17 (1986): 370–92.

Watt, Ian. "*Robinson Crusoe* as a Myth." *Essays in Criticism* 1.2 (1951): 95–119.

Wauthier, Claude. "Jean-Marie Coetzee contre la répression." *Le Nouvel Observateur* 4 July 1985: 61.

Wilhelm, Cherry. "South African Writing in English, 1977." *Standpunte* 32.3 (1979): 37–49.

Williams, Paul. "*Foe:* the Story of Silence." *English Studies in Africa: A Journal of the Humanities* 31 (1988): 33–39.

Wilson, Francis, and Mamphela Ramphele. *Uprooting Poverty: The South African Challenge.* Report for the Second Carnegie Inquiry into Poverty and Development in Southern Africa. New York: Norton, 1989.

Wilson, Monica, and Leonard Thompson, eds. *The Oxford History of South Africa.* 2 vols. London: Oxford UP, 1971.

Wood, W. J. B. "*Dusklands* and 'the impregnable stronghold of the intellect.'" *Theoria* (1980): 13–23.

Woods, Donald. *Biko.* New York: Paddington, 1978.

The World of Nat Nakasa. Ed. Essop Patel. Rev. ed. Johannesburg: Ravan, 1985.

Wylie, Hal, et al., eds. *Contemporary African Literature.* Washington, D.C.: Three Continents, 1983.

Zamora, Lois Parkinson. "Allegories of Power in the Fiction of J. M. Coetzee." *Journal of Literary Studies / Tydskrif Vir Literaturwetenskap* 2.1 (1986): 1–14.

——— Introduction. *The Apocalyptic Vision in America: Interdisciplinary Essays on Myth and Culture.* Ed. Lois Parkinson Zamora. Bowling Green: Bowling Green U Popular P, 1982. 1–10.

Zelnick, Stephen. "Ideology as Narrative: Critical Approaches to *Robinson Crusoe.*" *Bucknell Review* 26 (1982): 79–101.

"Zulu Asserts Botha Uses 'Boer War Diplomacy.'" *New York Times* 9 Aug. 1986: A3.

Acknowledgments

I am grateful for the support of Calvin College in granting me release time to write the majority of this book. In addition, a grant from the Calvin Alumni Association made possible the research for Chapter 3.

My thanks go to Clarence Walhout, James Vanden Bosch, and Margaret Masson for their perceptive reading and criticism of early drafts of this work. Also, I wish to thank the members of the Summer Study Group, particularly Mark Walhout, for challenging and stimulating me to evolve as a critic. Alma Walhout provided expert and gracious secretarial support, and my student assistant, Tess Terpstra, spent many long hours in the library.

My thoughts on Coetzee's fiction have benefited from the many other readers in book clubs, Sunday school classes, and college courses who have shared their insights and dilemmas with me. Thomas D'Evelyn, of Harvard University Press, has provided steadfast support for this project and for the direction of my criticism; I will never forget the first telephone call I received from him. The final thanks must go to my husband, John, whose love and encouragement is expressed daily. Chapter 8 owes its existence to John's expert care of our newborn Joseph while I retreated to the office.

Some parts of Chapter 4 appeared first as "Torture and the Novel: J. M. Coetzee's *Waiting for the Barbarians*" in *Contemporary Literature* Vol. 29, No. 2 (© 1988 by the Board of Regents of the University of Wisconsin System), pp. 277–85.

I also wish to acknowledge the following publishers who have granted permission to reprint material:

From J. M. Coetzee, *Age of Iron* (New York: Random House, 1990). Reprinted by permission of Random House.

From J. M. Coetzee, *Dusklands.* Copyright © 1974, 1982 by J. M. Coetzee. Reprinted by permission of Viking Penguin, a division of Penguin Books USA Inc.

From J. M. Coetzee, *Foe.* Copyright © 1986 by J. M. Coetzee. Reprinted by permission of Viking Penguin, a division of Penguin Books USA Inc.

From J. M. Coetzee, *In the Heart of the Country*. Copyright © 1976, 1977 by J. M. Coetzee. Reprinted by permission of Viking Penguin, a division of Penguin Books USA Inc.

From J. M. Coetzee, *Life and Times of Michael K.* Copyright © 1983 by J. M. Coetzee. Reprinted by permission of Viking Penguin, a division of Penguin Books USA Inc.

From J. M. Coetzee, *Waiting for the Barbarians*. Copyright © 1980 by J. M. Coetzee. Reprinted by permission of Viking Penguin, a division of Penguin Books USA Inc.

From J. M. Coetzee, *Age of Iron* (London: Secker and Warburg, 1990). Reprinted by permission of Martin Secker and Warburg Limited.

From J. M. Coetzee, *Dusklands* (London: Secker and Warburg, 1982). Reprinted by permission of Martin Secker and Warburg Limited.

From J. M. Coetzee, *Foe* (London: Secker and Warburg, 1986). Reprinted by permission of Martin Secker and Warburg Limited.

From J. M. Coetzee, *In the Heart of the Country* (London: Secker and Warburg, 1977). Reprinted by permission of Martin Secker and Warburg Limited.

From J. M. Coetzee, *Life and Times of Michael K* (London: Secker and Warburg, 1983). Reprinted by permission of Martin Secker and Warburg Limited.

From J. M. Coetzee, *Waiting for the Barbarians* (London: Secker and Warburg, 1980). Reprinted by permission of Martin Secker and Warburg Limited.

From Irving Hexham, *The Irony of Apartheid: The Struggle for National Independence of Afrikaner Calvinism against British Imperialism*. (Lewiston, N.Y.: The Edwin Mellen Press, 1981).

From Edmund Keeley and Philip Sherrard, ed. and trans. "Waiting for the Barbarians" by Constantine P. Cavafy. In *Voices of Modern Greece: Selected Poems by Cavafy, Sikelianos, Seferis, Elytis, Gatsos*. (Princeton, N.J.: Princeton UP, 1981.

From Lewis Nkosi, *Home and Exile and Other Selections* (London: Longman, 1983).

From Dick Penner, *Countries of the Mind: The Fiction of J. M. Coetzee*. (New York: Greenwood, 1989). Reprinted by permission of Greenwood Publishing Group, Inc., Westport, Conn. Copyright © 1989 by Allen Richard Penner.

From Adrienne Rich, "Diving into the Wreck," reprinted from *The Fact of a Doorframe, Poems Selected and New, 1950–1984,* by permission of the author and W. W. Norton & Company, Inc. Copyright © 1984 by Adrienne Rich. Copyright © 1975, 1978 by W. W. Norton & Company, Inc. Copyright © 1981 by Adrienne Rich.

From Jean Sévry, "An Interview with J. M. Coetzee," in *Commonwealth Essays and Studies* 9.1 (1986): 1–7.

Index